Institute for
Information
Studies

This book provided with the compliments of the Institute for Information Studies.

A program of
Northern Telecom
in association with
the Aspen Institute

THE GREAT EUROPEAN ILLUSION

Developmental Management
General Editor: Ronnie Lessem

Charting the Corporate Mind
*Charles Hampden-Turner**

Managing in the Information Society
Yoneji Masuda

Developmental Management
Ronnie Lessem

Foundations of Business
Ivan Alexander

Greening Business
John Davis

Ford on Management
*Henry Ford**

Managing Your Self
Jagdish Parikh

Managing the Developing Organization
Bernard Lievegoed

Conceptual Toolmaking
Jerry Rhodes

Integrative Management
Pauline Graham

Total Quality Learning
Ronnie Lessem

Executive Leadership
Elliott Jaques and Stephen D. Clement

Transcultural Management
Albert Koopman

The Great European Illusion
Alain Minc

The Rise of NEC
Koji Kobayashi

Developmental
MANAGEMENT

The Great European Illusion

BUSINESS IN THE WIDER COMMUNITY

ALAIN MINC

WITH A FOREWORD BY
RONNIE LESSEM

Translated by Lindsey Jones

First published in France as *La grande illusion*,
Copyright © Éditions Grasset & Fasquelle, 1989
This translation copyright © Blackwell Publishers, 1992.

The right of Alain Minc to be identified as author of this work has been asserted in
accordance with the Copyright, Designs and Patents Act 1988.

First published 1992

Blackwell Publishers
108 Cowley Road
Oxford   OX4 1JF,
UK

Three Cambridge Center
Cambridge, Massachusetts 02142
USA

British Library Cataloguing in Publication Data
A CIP catalogue record for this book is available from the British Library.

Library of Congress Cataloging in Publication Data
Minc, Alain.
The great European illusion / Alain Minc; with a foreword by
Ronnie Lessem.
p.   cm. — (Developmental management)
Includes bibliographical references and index.
1. Europe—Economic integration.   2. European federation.
3. Europe 1992.   I. Title.   II. Series.
HC241.M53   1992   337.1'4—dc20   91–23290
ISBN 0–631–17695–0

Typeset in 11 on 13pt Ehrhardt
by Hope Services (Abingdon) Ltd.
Printed in Great Britain by
T. J. Press Ltd, Padstow, Cornwall

This book is printed on acid-free paper

Contents

Foreword:
The Great European Illusion

by Ronnie Lessem

Introduction

Management over Time

Alain Minc is one of a distinct breed of contemporary French intellectuals who have combined their business insights with an acute appreciation of the socio-political environments in which companies are operating today. Minc, who has been a close business associate of Carlo de Benedetti, has managed, in recent years, to be both a powerful member and a severe critic of the European business establishment.

In *The Great European Illusion*, Minc argues that the 1992 phenomenon needs to be seen as part of a much wider evolutionary process. In his uniquely broad sweep, Minc assesses the military, the economic and the social and cultural options facing the European continent, both East and West. Insofar as his perspective is much wider, and deeper, than that of most of his business contemporaries, he offers a panoramic view for the global manager of our day. In essence, Minc argues, as I do,[1] that Europe as a whole is entering a new stage in its development.

Countries, like businesses, develop in stages. From their parochial origins (stage one) they have the potential to grow into nation states (stage two), before assuming a transnational identity (stage three), and finally even a global one (stage four). However, in any individual, organization or society – as for de Benedetti, for Volvo or for Germany – there will be aspects of each stage present at any particular time. Development is a cumulative process.

Management across Space

There are acknowledged centres of management theory, and geographically emergent ones. Europe, then, has a western, a northern, an eastern and a southern outlook. Whereas the UK is closely identified with its cross-Atlantic partner the USA, and the Soviet Union is the bridge between Europe and Asia, Scandinavia, is northerly in outlook while Spain and Greece point towards the south.

Each part of Europe has something distinctive – potentially if not actually – to contribute to management thought and activity. However, if business in Bulgaria or Portugal, to take two diverse examples, remains instinctive (primal) that contribution will be inhibited. Moreover, imports of rational approaches, if not fully embedded in the primal ground, will remain rootless and vulnerable to corruption or extinction. Japan is the one clear example of a country which has successfully imported management techniques from the West, because they have been firmly embedded in the country's own primal ground, that is, in Japan's underlying social structures.

Global Business Development

Structure Building and Structure Changing

Both individual businesses like Lafarge or Unilever, then, and whole economies – be they French, German, British or Belgian – develop in stages. As this development takes place there is a change in the nature and extent of differentiation (division) and integration (unity) within the business and without. As a result, the institutions' nature is progressively transformed. In fact, as can be illustrated in the European case, the same applies to whole societies as to individual institutions.

This progressive transformation takes place through alternating processes of transition, or structure changing and of progression, or structure building. It arises at the level of the whole economy or society and of the individual firm.

Stage 1: Primal – Economic

Structure building

On the global economic scene international trade first began to take place in the nineteenth century, as economic and political motives began to merge. Economic trade and political ambition intermingled as merchant adventurers like Clive of India and Cecil Rhodes in Africa advanced their imperial ambitions.

This primal outlook in fact existed, indeed flourished, within Thatcherite Britain, and was carried over into the free market philosophy that pervades the European Community. Thus the initial breaking down of trade barriers between EC countries in the sixties served to differentiate and integrate European economic activity in a newly and primally invigorated way. Enterprise and community began to reinforce one another, as in the United States of America.

Structure changing

Transition periods between one stage and another, whether for individuals or collective units, are always difficult and therefore very often avoided. For they involve a kind of death of the old in order to give birth to the new. Inevitably there will need to be a period of anger and despair before the person, the organization or the nation can let go of the dearly departed and face up to the shock of the new. Having been down in the emotional or economic dumps, if they let go, they will then be able to begin to see new meaning, and even a new vision of the future.

Within the EC the recent wave of 'defensive mergers', whereby companies have banded together to protect themselves against rampant American and Japanese invaders, is a manifestation of such a transition between primal (economic) and rational (organizational) motives. However, in moving from a primal to a newly rational orientation these companies will have to create new forms of merged identity. Inevitably people and institutions have to regress, and rejuvenate, before they can progress, and become more mature.

Stage 2: Rational – Organizational

Structure building

Once we enter into the second stage of business and economic
development free trade, involving a multiplicity of small entrepreneurial
units, is transformed. The economic stage is now dominated by
rationally coordinated multinational organizations.

Therefore, in the EC context, physical, technical and fiscal
barriers, hitherto institutionally imposed and controlled, come to
occupy pride of place. The evolution from the sixties and seventies,
when trade liberalization took pride of place, to the eighties and
nineties, when standardization of regulations becomes the order of
the European day, marks an advance from the primal stage to the
rational stage.

In a sense, therefore, Margaret Thatcher was swimming against
the tide. However, in another sense, as we shall soon see, her
individualistic stance has some prophetic overtones.

Structure changing

Between the second and third stages, as we advance from individual
and institutional adulthood to mid-life, there is another major
change. With individuals, this is called a mid-life crisis. Nations,
having outgrown their previous parochial identities and become fully
fledged nation states, now begin to shed their wholly national
identities. This loss of personal, institutional or societal ego is very
difficult to sustain. Yet it is a vital part of on-going development.

In fact it is the proliferation of joint ventures, on the one hand, and
of individual learning and self-development, on the other, which is
helping the evolutionary process along. Both within the EC, and
between Europe and America or Japan, the development of co-
partnership arrangements in the past five years has been dramatic.

Stage 3: Social – Developmental

In the third, developmental stage of being, international organizations
and multinational business are replaced by a transnational architecture
of economic, social and political organizations. Wholly owned

subsidiaries and colonial dependencies recede into the background and joint ventures become the norm. In the respect of such organizational interdependence, at least in a business context, Japan is a long way ahead of Europe and America.

As I have indicated, then, in this transnational stage of interdependent development, cooperation replaces competition as the overriding business ethic. In that sense, both Jacques Delors and Margaret Thatcher glimpsed parts of the truth but not the whole of it.

For it is the juxtaposition of individual – as diversity and interdependence – and unity that marks stage three. Social differentiation and integration replace their economic and organizational equivalents. Recognizing and relating individual human beings becomes the greatest priority.

In the European context, therefore, it is the sharing of nations' individual and institutional identities – as authentically economic, political and social partners – that really counts. In other words, if I am to realize my truly individual identity as an Englishman, I have to accommodate the Frenchman (Norman), the German (Saxon) and the Dane (Viking) in me, not to mention the Celt whose origins are spread throughout Europe. Similarly, in IBM (Europe) if I am to succeed, I shall have to absorb the historically based vision of the ancient Greeks, the powerful logic of the modern French, the artistic intuition of the Italians and the practical method of the Germans – just for starters.

Structure changing

In between the third and fourth stages there is a final transition, through which individual, institutions or societies begin to interfuse to such a point that their personal identity is totally subsumed within a global whole. Attention therefore shifts from individual development to the transformation of relationships between people, organizations and nations.

Stage 4: Cultural – Metaphysical

The fourth and most rarely attained stage of development for the individual or the collective is that of the truly wise human being or of the genuinely universal institution or civilization.

In a European context, at stage four, we must move beyond the bounds of the EC to accommodate Eastern Europe and the other non-EC nations of Europe. We also have to take into account the rest of the world with which Europe is intimately engaged. Finally, we need to return to Europe's origins, in ancient Crete, to uncover its original and ultimate vision.

Among the ancient Greeks, in fact, we shall discover *arete*, excellence or human virtue in a shape and form that is very different from that of conventional and current business wisdom.[2] However, before we do that, and by way of a conclusion, I want to return to the four stages – primal, rational, developmental and metaphysical – and review their impact on business and on Europe.

Perspectives on 1992

Stage 1: The Age of Enterprise

Enterprise and community in 1992

Through encouraging heroic personalities, from the different European countries – inclusive of employees, suppliers and customers – to come forward and be recognized for their achievements, and by celebrating their accomplishments in social settings that enable employees to merge different languages and customs, food and drink, songs and stories, primal differentiation and integration will be achieved.

A primally oriented company, then, looking youthfully towards Europe 1992, would be seeking to inculcate a spirit of healthy competition between its national constituencies, while also bringing about physical and social contact, through continuous sharing of language and custom and by rapid physical and international exchange of personnel. Thus the break-down of trade barriers within the EC as a whole would be replicated within the company. An appropriate management checklist for this domain is one that addresses 1992 concretely and directly.

Transaction checklist for the big time

- Which new customers should we get close to?
- What makes the French, German, Italian and Spanish – not to

mention the people of the Benelux nations, Danes, Greeks and Portuguese – tick?
- How would going European fuel our entrepreneurial fire?
- Which of our European competitors is most likely to give us a hard time, and how can we fight back?
- Who in Europe is ripe for take-over?
- How can we inject a family feeling throughout our European-wide business?
- How do you deal with a Frenchman, a German, an Italian, a Spaniard, a Benelux national, a Dane, a Greek, a Portuguese?
- How can the boss be turned into a born-again European?

Stage 2: The Age of Reason

Freedom and order towards 1992

Running a business, like the administration of the Common Market, requires knowledge, skills and attitudes which are different from the start-up phase. In this second and rational case, professional freedom replaces business enterprise as the differentiating factor, and organizational order displaces familiar community as an integrating force.

Professionally based specialization and formally estabished coordination, both within the EC's governmental institutions and in its constituent business organizations, serve to reinforce these attributes. Standardization, centralization and regulation as well as professionalization, decentralization and self-control become necessary parts of an evolving organizational whole. Institutional hierarchies are complemented by professional and information networks. Rationally based questions supplant primal ones.

Action checklist for a single market[3]

- How has the market changed for our business?
- Should we develop a European market strategy, looking at Europe as our primary market rather than just the UK?
- How would becoming a European business alter the scale of our targets and plans?
- In what way will we be vulnerable to more competition in our present markets?

- Should we form links with, merge with or acquire businesses to strengthen our market presence?
- Is our management and structure appropriate to exploit new opportunities or defend our position?
- What training, in languages and other skills, do we need to be ready for the single market?
- Who in our firm is going to take responsibility for deciding how to make the most of a single market?

Through encouraging its knowledge workers and major clients to participate in EC-based professional networks and training programmes, while, on the other hand, providing action learning programmes for them, whereby internationally based product and service groups would begin to think and act as a European team, rationally based differentiation and integration would be achieved.

An established European company looking towards 1992 would therefore be building up, on the one hand, a spirit of nationally based professional and commercial competencies, and, on the other, a team spirit through which such specialized competencies were standardized and integrated within a European whole. Thus the break-down of externally based technical and fiscal (non-trade) barriers would be replicated within the company's component, national parts.

Stage 3: The Age of Development

Evolution and harmony towards 1992

Renewing a company or a whole society, which has become too inwardly focused and resistant to change or which has begun to lose momentum and direction, requires yet a third set of qualities.

In that context Margaret Thatcher was right to remind us that the realization of each nation's inner potential must be sought, rather than repressed, within the EC. However, the path leading to such individual adaptivity is a cooperative rather than a competitive one, both commercially and nationally, which cuts across the primal grain.

Cooperative strategies, moreover, necessitate the formation of an interdependent organizational architecture, along Japanese lines, rather than an independently based, formal organization. This whole approach involves the manager in an intuitively and aesthetically planned evolution rather than in orthodox corporate planning. Finally, rather than sticking with technologically based innovation, he or she is inevitably concerned with a much more broadly based process of corporate, even inter-corporate, renewal. This leads us into the developmental domain, via an interactive checklist.

Interactive checklist for a diverse market

- What is unique about each European, national environment?
- How can we recognize and develop the full potential underlying each such marketplace?
- How would the development of a truly European business alter the content and context of our future activities?
- What opportunities will emerge for cooperation between ourselves and our former European competitors?
- What varied forms of co-partnership should we enter into, where and with which types of company?
- How do we develop an interdependent company, accommodating – synergistically – European individuality?
- How do we develop real insight into the underlying business and social attitudes of each nation, and subsequently apply it?
- How can we renew our business – taking due account of the breadth and depth of European diversity – in products and markets, and in individuals and organizations?

Through encouraging all its stakeholders, both organizationally and nationally, to participate in self-development programmes – as both individuals and societies – stage three management stimulates individual adaptivity. Moreover, this developmental approach, whereby evolution from youth through to maturity is facilitated, needs to be applied to product and market as well as to individual and societal adaptation.

As individuals, organizations and whole societies begin to differentiate themselves in this profound way, so awareness of interdependence will be heightened – individually, commercially and nationally. For I can only become myself, as a person or as a nation, through my manifold relationships with others. The same applies to each member state in relation to the EC, and to the EC in relation to both the rest of Europe and to the entire globe.

A truly developmental company, therefore, facing 1992, would be inviting each of its national representatives to express their respective individualities through their unique products and services, while also adapting them and themselves to emerging technological, economic and social trends. At the same time it would be pursuing to the ultimate the benefits of such synergy that might arise out of the intimate meeting of such differences. Such meeting could only arise out of intense interactivity.

Stage 4: The Age of Transformation

The consciousness revolution towards 1992

Corporate culture has become a prevailing management concern. This represents a fundamental shift in business and human consciousness. This reorientation forms part of our global economic development.

The entrepreneurial revolution in the nineteenth century followed a leap forward in humanity's acquisitive impulses. As economic historian Robert Heilbronner puts it, in *The Worldly Philosophers*, it is only in the last 200 years that the desire for systematic material gain has entered mankind's immediate horizons.

The managerial revolution, in its turn, heralded an era of not only material expansion and growth, but also of the advancement of 'human capital'. A subsequent design revolution reflects a shift in orientation towards quality as opposed to mere quantity.

Now that culture, and its associated myth and ritual, has entered into the corporate mainstream, we are witnessing a further evolutionary step. For it is the great myths throughout the ages – whether in the east, west, north or south – that have stirred people's inner spirit.

Ultimately it is a business's or a nation's spirit which controls its destiny. Thanks to people like Peters and Waterman, this is now becoming recognized within the corridors of corporate power. Corporate culture, myth and ritual therefore marks the end of the journey from physical matter towards human spirit via mind and heart. This form of corporate being is still the least manifest of all stages of business development.

A transcendent checklist for a unified Europe

- How do we tap the spirit of Europe?
- How can we transform an insular national orientation into a cosmopolitan European one, encompassing Europe East and West?
- How would becoming a European company transform the essential nature of our business, including our core product or service?
- How can we turn our entire industry, across Europe, into the centre of global production and distribution?
- How can we develop a community spirit amongst all our stakeholders, transcending parochial and national boundaries?
- How do we transform a nationally based institution into a quintessentially European one?
- How do we transform our business image so that our pan-European identity dissolves any national sub-identities?
- How can we recognize and tap that universal energy which is serving to transform national organizations into global ones?

Conclusion

Europe today, as Alain Minc shows, stands at the threshold. For the first time in human history an entire continent is facing up to the prospect of conscious self-renewal. As the era of powerful nation states passes into the economic history books, notwithstanding the rise of modern Japan (which is physically and environmentally unable to contain its expansion), so the prospect of a truly trans-national economy and indeed polity emerges.

Whichever global corporation rises to the trans-national challenge, most particularly in the European context, it will pave the way for its own enduring development. Such a business entity, be it called SAS or Europa itself, would assume the molecular form that I have identitifed in *Developmental Management*. Through such an organizational form, and developmental strategy, the accommodation of professional freedom would ensue, within a networked organizational order, that would befit the role of Europe in the global economy and society.

January, 1992

Notes

1 R. Lessem, *Developmental Management*, Blackwell, 1990.
2 R. Lessem, *Total Quality Learning*, Blackwell, 1991.
3 Drawn from the DTI's *Action Checklist* for 1992.

Preface

Let's stop fooling ourselves. The mythical aspect of 1992, in all its pomp and ceremony, is preventing us from noticing the gradual establishment of a new Europe. The entire continent is being buffeted by the combined effect of certain very powerful forces: the isolationist thrust in America, the recentring of Germany and the insistent pressure of the Soviet Union. This new Europe will in no way correspond to the present European Community, not as regards its priorities, nor its frontiers, nor its very identity. Perhaps, relieved of its former trappings, it will constitute no more nor less than an immense free zone.

Let's stop fooling ourselves. The question we are addressing is not one of Europe, but of Germany. Germany is regaining its place at the centre of Europe, neither Western nor Eastern, a development that is both natural and valid, and puts neither the democratic values nor the market economy of the former Federal Republic at risk. On the other hand, it disposes once and for all of the old European dream. A few years ago, the movement was scarcely noticeable:[1] now it is self-evident. The post-war period is over, we are currently in the final stages of an era in which we were ready to believe in the reality of Western Europe.

Let's stop fooling ourselves. Time is running out; the future is unfolding under our very eyes. If the evolution of Germany is allowed to run its course, Europe will stretch from the Atlantic to the Urals. In other words, Europe, as we know it, will no longer exist: in the twenty-first century, it will be what was known in the nineteenth century as the Balkans. Judging from the distance covered in fifteen years, we are now on the home straight: is it still possible to influence the course of events? France certainly still has some cards up its sleeve. Until now, they were simply jokers; at the moment they are trumps, but will soon be completely worthless.

Let's stop fooling ourselves. Even if, on 1 January 1993, Europe were to resemble the rosy picture that is being painted of it, it would not be possible to halt the change in the shape of the continent. The reality of the situation is far removed from the myth: the market is not in itself enough to bring about a real economic identity, nor can an economic identity alone produce a future community. Natural selection in business and competition cannot take the place of historical forceps.

Let's stop fooling ourselves. It is tempting to adopt a policy of *laissez faire*: détente in Europe is very pleasant and alienation appears to be so far removed as to be nonexistent. Revolutions are no longer full of sound and fury, but peaceful, gentle, 'civilized', reflecting our society. Because less crude, they are less visible; but, being less visible, they are no less decisive. History, whether Raymond Aron likes it or not, is not always 'tragic'; it can take less dramatic forms which are, perhaps, in themselves more productive.

Let's stop fooling ourselves. Our passion for Europe displays all the symptoms of a psychoanalytical projection. We expect the European miracle to release us from obligations within our own national framework. The nirvana of 1992 displaces our own reality; our vision of Europe displaces real achievements, as if in shifting the pitch one changes the rules of the game. But this dream will suffer the same fate as all such psychoanalytical projections: it is a great illusion which offers a transitory sense of well-being.

If we were to stop fooling ourselves we would not necessarily become prophets of doom. The concept of European unity, naive rhetoric and transient enthusiasm, all skirt around a question of vital importance: what kind of Europe do we actually want? Is Western Europe a transitory state or a viable entity in itself? Is the economy the only real motive force? To the idealist, Europe appears to be advancing; in reality it is hovering between two different geographical situations: a communal Europe, which occupies an indeterminate space in our minds, and a continental Europe which is being imposed surreptitiously. One picture is very attractive; the other rather unsettling, but in thinking only of the first, we choose the second by default. The battle is not yet over; there is still some room for manoeuvre, but in three or four years it will have disappeared. The situation is still wide open; nothing is irrevocably lost, but the alarm raised is an indication of the urgency of the remaining courses of action. We must respond to it.

Notes

1 Alain Minc, *Le Syndrome finlandais*, le Seuil, 1986.

PART I

From a Western to a Continental Europe

From an Atlantic to a Continental System

Western Europe does not go back into the mists of time. Brought into being by the Iron Curtain, the likelihood, strategically speaking, is that it will disappear with it. The time now surely belongs to Europe pure and simple, neither Western nor Eastern, an evolution which has been caused by the substitution of one system of security for another. Might we soon be witnessing the demise of the present Atlantic system, and, due to some strange historical resurgence, the reappearance of a continental security system?

In the fifties and sixties, everything seemed to be simple and clear cut. The superiority of US military power gave Europe the assurance of complete protection. Kennedy's '*Ich bin ein Berliner*' established a straightforward strategic equation: Berlin = Chicago; London = New York; Paris = San Francisco. For Europeans, this meant absolute and automatic security. This system functioned all the more efficiently because the 'frontier post of the empire', that is to say the Federal Republic, was at the time the brightest pupil of the Atlantic class. Contrary to all the old ways of thinking, which viewed border zones as the least solid and most unstable, Germany represented the strongest link in the occidental chain, rather than, as might have been expected, the weakest. With Britain as an honorary state of the Union, and a deeply rooted stability in Federal Germany, the US, confident in its nuclear superiority, was to have no problem guaranteeing peace within the Western Alliance. During such a period of security (in strategic terms), the caprices of the French carried little weight: although gratifying for France and irritating for the US, they were a matter of indifference to everyone else. Nuclear independence, an absolute system of defence and ideological anti-Americanism were all national demonstrations, but it is easy to forget that they took place under the protection of the American nuclear umbrella. And, as General de Gaulle proved himself the strongest of allies when things really got hot in Berlin in 1961, or during the Cuban missile crisis of the following year, the vague impulses of the French hardly disturbed the strategic balance of the Western world.

This situation obviously represented an optimum for the West from which things could only deteriorate. The disappearance of American nuclear omnipotence was to attack the idea of absolute security at its very roots. A policy of total retaliation – destruction of the USSR in response to any attack on Germany – lost all credibility as soon as the Soviets had at their disposal inter-continental nuclear missiles capable of striking US territory. From then on, security had a price which appeared to the US to be largely one-sided. At that point, their whole defence doctrine was changed, with the adoption of the theory of 'limited retaliation'. The substitution, for all or nothing, of a more subtle approach might seem to have been a step forward; in fact, its only aim was to allow the US to escape automatic engagement in a thermo-nuclear conflict. The Europeans, trapped by the words and rhetoric of solidarity, took ten years to comprehend that the disassociation of the US and Europe had its roots in the limited retaliation; that is, the refusal of the former to risk nuclear annihilation in order automatically to safeguard the latter.

The centre of the system, then, was beginning to weaken, along with its periphery. The first steps of *Ostpolitik* brought Germany to the end of its political hibernation. Links and relations with the East, that had never really been severed, gradually began to be re-established. Like a hemiplegic who progressively recovers sensory mobility, the Federal Republic slowly emerged from its torpor *vis-à-vis* the East: firstly with the GDR, then with the popular democracies of old Germany, and lastly with its traditional sphere of influence. Oriented exclusively Westward for twenty years, Germany almost imperceptibly repositioned itself at the centre of Europe. In this way, the old idea of *Mittel Europa*, a Europe based on the principle of nationalities, was to emerge.

The change was a slow one, but gradually an exclusive relationship with the US was replaced by a complex diplomatic network in which the American alliance constituted a dominant force, rather than an entire framework. The deployment of Pershing represented the final manifestation of this Atlantic system, but it showed all the signs of a

Pyrrhic victory. Anyone at the time could see that a less obtuse policy on the part of the Soviets could scupper it entirely. A little skill and tactical sense on their part, and the heady nature of Western pacifism would have its way. Indeed the effort of reaffirming the association served only to expose its fragility. There was not long to go.

Sudden accelerations in the pace of change are well known in history, even to the point of being clichés. And yet these key moments do exist: the past three years have been one. The weakening of American power and the shift on the part of Germany were, until then, covert. All it took to bring them into the open was for Soviet pressure to assume a more attractive aspect. The time had to be ripe for the sun to shine on history. The deployment of Pershing will be seen to have been the last manifestation of the Atlantic security system; its dismantling constitutes the beginnings of the continental security system which will succeed it. We are tumbling into a different universe, even though strategic thinking cannot yet light our path. The fact that such strategists view reality through an apothecary's list of missiles and nuclear warheads, means that they are unaware of the movements in society, the weight of history, the strength of the desire to reclaim one's country. Strategic thought in the modern age has become a by-product of war games, rather than of history. Von Neumann now rules over Clausewitz and every day the price must be paid.

The process of disassociation from the US has become a reality, the repositioning of Germany in the centre of Europe, a fact, and the uncertainty of French nuclear thinking, self-evident. Americans are less determined to die for Hamburg than our fathers were for Danzig; Germans are rediscovering that, for them, national identity and state unity are not indivisible; the French still dream of a Europe with two nuclear powers at its extremities, France and the Soviet Union, as if the old concepts of the 'accord of nations' retained the slightest meaning. This is how the new continental system is being drawn up. But history does not retrace its steps: the previous system presupposed a balance of strength between the European superpowers; the present one postulates the crushing superiority of one of the protagonists. It is no longer a system of security; rather an instrument of latent domination.

When the Soviets talked, with a catch in their voices, of 'Europe, our common home', they were taking for granted this dissociation: a US out of the action and becoming more isolationist as strategic disarmament progressed; a central Europe with increasing access through the Iron Curtain; two Germanies that were more interested in relations than in confrontations once they recognized the intangible nature of their political and economic differences; a France that oscillated between acting as a link with the US and the temptation of strategic isolation under the protection of its nuclear Maginot line; peripheral countries, Spain and Italy, convinced that, in the course of time, the US would evacuate the bases it occupied on their territory, since they would cease to be of any use; a Great Britain that, in order to preserve its solidarity with the US, would insist on picking and choosing from Europe, accepting such and such an aspect, while rejecting another and so on. These are not nightmare visions, simply a projection of the strategic area which was taking shape under our very eyes. The path we now have to follow is fainter than the one left behind, but if a mediator were needed, it could be the double zero option. The symbolic nature of this agreement carries even more weight than its military reality. It demonstrates the pressure of public opinion and speeds up the action far more than the removal from either side of some hundreds of missiles.

The old continental system did at least have one virtue: that of stability. Will the new system have the same result? In the past, when one power moved its frontier too far, a rapid conflict would soon bring it back into line. Nowadays, the extreme strength of one superpower produces only docility in the others. Is this continental drift destined to end in a 'Finlandization'?[1] How can one apply to the whole of Europe a concept which happens to work for a small country at the edge of Atlantic Europe? With its back to the wall and the US far away, Europe would be infinitely more Finlandized than Finland itself. It would retain its market economy and its democratic system, but would live in a state of osmosis with the East, at an ever-increasing strategic distance from the US, despite the latter's cultural and economic proximity. In effect, neither democracy nor the market would be at stake, since for decades the Soviets have abandoned the idea of occupation, which would lead to a renewed state of conflict with the US. Nowadays, they take a respect for democratic principles completely for granted, not as a price they have to pay for the withdrawal of the US, but rather as a guarantee that they will have efficient partners at their disposal who, thanks to capitalism, will be capable of compensating for the irremediable deficiencies of socialism.

Obviously this Europe has some very attractive aspects. Movement from East to West will be much freer; shared cultural values will be rediscovered; links long buried will come to the surface. Prague is no longer light years away from Vienna in social terms, nor is Budapest from Munich. The Soviet Union will have to pay a price for the resurgence of continental Europe, in terms of freedom for the popular democracies. And there lies the appeal as far as the public is concerned. It answers a natural desire to rediscover our kith and kin in the East and to put an end to an intolerable hemiplegia: in our hearts Europe has always remained one. What can one set against such a spontaneous movement? Long-term risk, strategic isolation, insidious dependence? How can one persuade democratic governments, with their eyes fixed on the short term, to forego immediate satisfactions in favour of a remote and uncertain future? It is not the experts who determine strategy, it is the rhythm and mood of civilian societies. Disarmament has struck home; peace is tantalising; détente reassuring. And why not? The concessions seem minimal, a mere matter of honour. Why should we worry? Democracy and the market economy appear to be safe in Finland at the moment, displaying the more attractive face of Finlandization; an example of its less pleasant side is the immediate expulsion back to the Soviet Union of refugees captured in Finland before they can cross over to Sweden. But such moral concerns are so easily forgotten.

Distanced in this way from the US, continental Europe will also have a clear conscience, persuading itself that, along with this process of osmosis between societies, will go a liberalization in the East, as Europe will necessarily have more influence on the USSR than vice versa. The contagiousness of the democratic system, the inevitable effects of the free circulation of people and capital, commercial and cultural exchanges, the odd migration here and there: the malleability of the Soviet system is well known. At that point, the scope of the vision will have changed. Instead of a few symbols of détente there will be some real links, both solid and reciprocal.

The asymmetrical nature of this revolution means that it is absolutely irreversible. Once continental, we can never return to an Atlantic Europe, but a liberalized Soviet Union could once more harden its attitude. The ratchet that operates alongside a democracy prevents any backsliding. As far as the US goes, it will not be in a position to take up any of its previous commitments: raising the level of the military budget becomes more difficult day by day; continued tension involves paying a price, in terms of public support, that is becoming more and more intolerable, and civilian society is increasingly refusing to put up with any policy of confrontation. In the East a tightening of policy would certainly no longer be painless. We only need to look at the forced retreat from Afghanistan to realize that, even in the most closeted systems, public opinion counts for a great deal.

A new age is beginning and is rapidly becoming established. Although for the moment it is still hidden, it will gradually become both evident and unavoidable. With our eyes glued on 1992, we are blind to the real issue which, like all long-term movements, demands the coincidence and interaction of several vital phenomena: in this case, the resurgence of US isolationism; the repositioning of Germany; the subtle pressure of the Soviets, and to a lesser degree, the inhibited nature of French strategic thinking.

Notes

1 Finlandization: that is, the attitude of the Finns who, after 1945, traded a diplomatic policy favourable to the Soviet Union for freedom and a market economy. See Minc, *Le Syndrome finlandais*, le Seuil, 1986.

2

The US in Retreat

The Americans are continuing to play a historic role that goes against their very nature. Monroe's doctrine, which consisted of leaving the rest of the world to its own devices, as long as America was allowed to make its own decisions, is still very much alive. Do we really have to remind ourselves of the accumulation of events needed to provoke America into entering World War I? The Germans were so convinced of American isolationist policy as to think that they could act freely. As for the Second World War, it involved such features as a truly Manichaean conflict in Europe, susceptible to a simplistic analysis of the kind generally able to incite the American people towards a conflict between good and evil; a country turned totally towards its East Coast; an elite steeped in European culture and reference and a president ostensibly on the side of democracy: all to no avail. Nothing could counter the tyranny of public opinion. This isolationism is further revealed in the hypothesis that Roosevelt knew about the attack on Pearl Harbour in advance, and did nothing to prevent it, so that from then on, his hands would not be tied. This has never been proved, but even the fact that the suggestion was made is significant.

The anti-imperialist militants of the fifties and sixties never understood the US, believing it to be expansionist by nature and imperialist by vocation, while in fact any imperialism was arrived at totally by accident. The libertarian and capitalist nature of America may be contagious but is not in itself imperialist. In this process imitation plays more of a role than the armed forces, the dynamism of capitalism more than naval armadas, a cultural omnipresence more than defence agreements. That is why it will be possible one day for Europe to sever its military links, but to retain all cultural relations with America. Nevertheless, the absolute power of America since the Second World War has obscured the reality of the situation. The

Americans, cast in an imperialist role, have played it to the hilt, but it is not a state of affairs that is natural to them. They can live without the need for total domination, unlike the Soviet Union, whose whole strategy grows out of and is dependent on that very requirement. The aims of the Soviet Union, to cut Europe loose from the US, and to contain the power of China, are both clear objectives, scarcely altered since the days of Imperial Russia, and they cannot be abandoned, either wholly or partially. Could the strategic designs of the US be defined so clearly? The defence of the free world: simply an ideological rehashing of their policy of containment, in other words a resistance to Soviet expansionism, and as such an empty strategy based not on action but on reaction; the domination of energy supplies: the aim of any major oil producer; the multiplication of military bases: now more a matter of keeping the existing ones than of adding others. Is this being naive? What about the CIA in Chile? And Panama, Santa Dominica and the banana republics? And the bolstering up of such and such a dictator in Latin America . . . ? All these actions are incontestable, but they do not add up to any sort of a coherent vision. What was their aim? Apart from the desire to safeguard all things American, which in itself is a throw back to Monroe's doctrine, there was no concrete strategy. Brought to a position of superpower by the vagaries of history, the US is now preparing to quit this position and return to its old isolationism, whether we like it or not. Everything is conspiring to push them in that direction.

The End of Military Domination

The Atlantic community has never been more integrated than during the period of American superiority. In the fifties, Europe benefited from the same protection as Michigan: an attack on Berlin meant an attack on Chicago. As long as the Soviet Union was considerably less advanced than the US, security was assured: when the Soviets began to master the atom bomb, the Americans had developed the hydrogen bomb; by the time the former had acquired the hydrogen bomb, the latter had reached a position of total domination over missile launchers. This led to the formulation of a very simple doctrine based on brute force and involving massive reprisals. Any attack on

Hamburg, and the Soviet Union would literally be completely annihilated.

This initial concept was obviously based on the assumption that American territory was safe, i.e. that no Soviet long-range missiles could reach it. An inevitable consequence of this was a total imbalance; the Soviets risked everything, and the Americans nothing.

Once the USSR had mastered strategic missiles, the policy of massive reprisals became rather more hazardous: from the point at which the US itself was threatened, the security of Europe became less certain. On balance, the greater the threat to the US, the less guarantee afforded to Europe. For some years American strategy had juggled with reality, under the misapprehension that this theory, built as it was on the idea of an invulnerable US, could still survive. When eventually this became untenable, massive reprisals were replaced by 'limited retaliation'.

Behind these anodyne words, the world underwent a transformation, and Europe lost its hitherto total security. What was it that the theoreticians were actually saying? Quite simply, that the response had to be proportional to the attack and the intervention of American strategic arms a last resort. As a result, Europe was turned once more into a potential battlefield. Previously, a raid on Berlin would have elicited the same response from the US as an all-out attack on the Federal Republic. Henceforth, the classic strategy of matching response to attack would reassert itself. This gave no indication of the point at which the Americans would mount a full-scale defence, or indeed if they would ever do so. The policy of limited retaliation contained the seed of the dissociation of Europe and America, even though it took several years to take root. The USA's advantage at the time was such that the credibility of the strategic threat was not brought into question: the Americans risked so much less than the Soviets in a nuclear conflict that this imbalance alone seemed to testify to the USA's preparedness to act. However, when the Soviets began to reach an equilibrium with the US, measured retaliation began to slide towards this dissociation. As early as 1979, Henry Kissinger was admitting that the Europeans could not take for granted that America would employ its strategic nuclear arsenal in the event of conflict in Europe. The debate over Pershing demonstrated only too clearly this ambiguity. Some people thought that its installation equipped Europe with a deterrent powerful enough to protect its own territory: others, that any use of it in Europe would oblige America to employ its strategic arms as a back-up. The former opinion allowed for the prospect of disassociation, while the latter demonstrated a belief in enforced association. Given such a degree of ambivalence, the strategy lost all credibility: instead of being flexible, it had become contradictory.

Whether this was a final effort from a position of association between Europe and America, or the first operation outside it, the debate did not stay open for long. Agreement on Euromissiles did away with the ambiguities involved when it was decided that there would henceforth be no Pershing and no SS 20s. First the zero option, then the double zero option (relating to missiles with a range of between 700 and 3,000 miles) were to alter the strategic equilibrium. If we imagine a progressive and extreme escalation, the United States would be obliged to go straight from tactical warfare to strategic missiles, i.e. from a limited confrontation to an apocalypse, something they will never do. The Soviets, on the other hand, still allow for the possibility of limiting the conflict to Europe, and not attacking American territory at all. It is this imbalance that is inevitably leading towards American nuclear isolationist policy.

Moreover, the Americans have never misled the world with regard to their true feelings on the matter. From the beginning of the Pershing debate they declared themselves open to the zero option. And, if one disregards all the myths surrounding Star Wars, surely the aim of the system is nothing other than to provide a protection against nuclear attack on American territory? Reagan's gaffes at Helsinki, and also the alacrity with which Soviet overtures were accepted, seem to bear that out. The unconscious desire of all Americans was for the disappearance of missiles capable of leading them, against their will, towards a nuclear apocalypse: such was apparent through all the diplomatic rigmarole.

The adoption of Star Wars had very little impact on the balance of military strength; its importance lay rather in the fact that it symbolized an evolution in American thinking. This space shield is nowhere near to being a reality and, in the final analysis, represents little more than an improved anti-missile system. The hermetic nature of this system will never make for the sort of bucolic pacifism evoked by President Reagan. This technological vision is a reincarnation, in our thermo-nuclear age, of good old isolationism. The US has but one wish: to be protected by this shield in the twenty-first century, just as they were by their oceans in Monroe's time. What contortions they must have put themselves to in order to support the claim that the same beneficent security would be extended to Europe: an easy promise but one which would not stand up to technological reality. Taking into account the derisory amount of time necessary for Soviet missiles to reach Europe, a European shield would require as much progress, vis-à-vis the American shield, as the latter vis-à-vis its present anti-missile capability. Coming so late in the day, is this half-hearted assurance even worth the paper on which it is written?

The situation from now on, then, is clear, albeit unofficially: the US will try to retain the wherewithal to protect its own territory from a Soviet attack; it is ready to contribute to the defence of Europe; it is not, however, prepared to let itself be dragged into a nuclear apocalypse for the sake of our well-being. Given this reading of the situation, American strategy and its objectives become clear: to maintain the credibility of their strategic forces by a combination of increased budgetary responsibility and certain disarmament measures; to eliminate every type of weapon and every situation which could lead them unwillingly into a thermo-nuclear conflict, and to maintain modular defence systems with their European or Japanese allies, which would allow them the maximum amount of security for the minimum risk. The first objective justifies military action in the eighties, the launching of the Star Wars programme and the search for new agreements on disarmament. The second leads to the double zero option and soon, perhaps, to the third, which is the elimination of short-range weapons, at a time when the complete denuclearization of central Europe is no longer seen as a desertion. The third aim demands the rediscovery, as in 1988, of a diplomatic rhetoric aimed at producing a balance between the pursuit of a duopoly with the Soviet Union on the one hand and the ritual reaffirmation of Atlantic solidarity on the other.

However, in these matters, progress is uneven and cumulative. Each apparently peaceful initiative on the part of the Soviets brings an overwhelming response from the US. The Soviets whistle and the Americans come running with an ever-greater alacrity. The Atlantic security system no longer exists: it is incompatible with the new isolationism of America. This impetus is not purely military, but stems from the more general weakening of the US: from its turning westwards, along the hidden axis of Seattle–Dallas and from movements within its own society.

Moving Westwards

The US which flew to the aid of democracy in 1941 was still an offshoot of Europe. Aspects such as culture, mentality, economic relations, first-generation immigration, snobbery and even social relations all show that the attraction of our 'lofty spires' was as strong as ever. But now the currents have changed.

In the past, Italians and Poles formed the minority groups; now these consist of the blacks, Hispanics and Jamaicans. It is no longer Naples and Warsaw that provoke nostalgia, but Mexico, Caracas and Santa Dominica. In the south, the US is becoming Hispanicized just as fast as the Hispanics are becoming Americanized. This situation is gradually uniting Mexico and North America, in that the influx of legal and illegal immigrants is creating a strange no-man's land, which is neither wholly US nor truly Mexican. The Hispanics there are not concerned with Madrid; it is Madrid that concerns itself with them. A land of immigrants is far more affected by the last generation to arrive than one might think. Established Americans no longer have the group solidarity of new Americans. What does Europe mean to a recently naturalized Mexican, a black from Atlanta busy settling in, a Chinaman prosperously established in San Francisco? A vague area on a map: a destination on a tour operator's guide; a few yellowing postcards? Why should they want to die for Berlin?

America's elite is also having to come to terms with this situation. The 'Wasps' (White Anglo-Saxon Protestants) have lost their monopoly of power. President Carter's Georgians and President Reagan's Californians would have seemed very exotic to Morgenthau and Hopkins in the forties! And along with this exoticism, they brought with them another vision of the world. Perhaps Kissinger will prove to have been the last of Europe's heirs in charge of US politics.

Where, in the most influential circles, are those Harvard and MIT professors who are still steeped in European culture? What residual position are the last Wasps going to manage to occupy? Did not George Bush, a bourgeois liberal from the East Coast, decide to make a big thing out of his having been a Texan for a part of his life, in order to reap the greatest electoral returns? A transformation in the US has created a new elite, and with it new horizons in terms of an alternative diplomatic and strategic system.

Whether one likes it or not, the US has made an about turn. Its centre of gravity is no longer in the East Coast: even if this coast were to regain some ground, it can never retrieve its previous dominant position. The heart of the economy, from now on, will clearly be in Chicago, Atlanta, Dallas and Houston, and, above all, in California. Its pulse will be one of growth and technology; of a new flow in society, both inventive and dynamic. Gone are the days when New York was able to regard the Middle East in the same way as Paris regards the Limousin. What is more, these changes are not just happening in the interior, but also on the periphery of America. In the next few years, we can expect to see a growing overlap with Canada and Mexico. If this were to result in a kind of union, the commercial deficit of the entire area taken together would be a half of the current American deficit. This clearly demonstrates the nature of the relevant contributions: Mexico would provide petrol, immigrants and cheap labour comparable with Taiwan, while the US would bring with it its balance of payments. Canada already constitutes the fifty-first state of America: rich in raw material and offering the possibility of 'new frontiers'. With this process of interlinking, we will see North America's centre of gravity shifting southwards, due to its growing relationship with Mexico, and westwards, due to its already well-established contacts with the most dynamic region of Canada. Such an America would not be attracted by exterior forces such as Europe, or for that matter, Japan. In fact, it is very difficult to believe that the biological links existing between Europe and America could possibly be replaced by the same sort of relationship with Japan. It is true that trade in the Pacific world is currently overtaking Atlantic commerce; true also that there is a growing economic collaboration between the two Pacific coasts; that complex links involving both competition and cooperation are forming between American and Japanese enterprises; that the relation between the yen and the dollar has become the keystone of the international monetary system; that the US represents an expansion tank for Japanese industry; that nowadays Americans are fearful, jealous and respectful of Japan; that the vaguest impulse towards diplomatic autonomy on the part of the Japanese brings Washington out in a cold sweat, and that Japan, in the long term, is undoubtedly a more important strategic pawn than Europe. However, it will not be possible for the two Pacific coasts to establish a relationship as intimate and profound as that existing between Europe and the US in the sixties. One cannot imagine the same nostalgia-based immigration, the same sense of cultural community, the same human links between two worlds which remain profoundly foreign to each other. As such, the 'Pacific universe' of the year 2000 will bear no resemblance to the 'Atlantic family' of 1950.

Faced with an economic and strategic shift towards the West, a North America turning inwards, this time incorporating Mexico and Canada, and a relative indifference to the Pacific world, Europe will be left completely out in the cold.

The Price of Economic Decline

The isolationism evident in the US has been accelerated by the downward spiral of its economy. Having benefited for several years from an income derived from the War – the US having been the only winner to emerge unscathed – it has nevertheless spent the last fifteen years slipping down the economic ladder. The first external deficits in 1965, the unconvertibility of the dollar in 1971, the monetary breakdown of 1978, and the consequently humiliating situation of being the world's largest debtor, were all steps on the road to decline.

Expansionist policy in the eighties represented a final mad fling. A Keynesian reflation of unprecedented proportions was disguised by the 'supply-side economy'; the currency was kept under sedation by prohibitive interest rates, an external deficit and a budget deficit financed by foreign investment. Such aberrations demanded that the one-sided privileges of the dollar be absolutely solid. Disillusionment set in when the US, by continuing to borrow, became a net debtor, i.e. when it began to have debts greater than its credits, a state of affairs which led to the sudden fall of the dollar.

Meanwhile, the Americans have managed to postpone the day of reckoning. The crash of October 1987 seemed at first to be evidence of a new reality. However, instead of the expected recession due to a reduction in available capital, an expansionist policy was still pursued. As a result of a massive injection of money, there was a return to inflation. Deprived of the necessary course of treatment, there is now, in the US, a new threat of thrombosis; and this time it is critical.

The commercial deficit, more than ten billion dollars per month, will not be absorbed by a fall in the value of the dollar. The dollar has already lost 50 per cent of its value. This plummeting has had the obvious effect of bringing down imports and increasing exports. However, this in no way has led the US to face up to the problem: at the present rate, it would require ten or twelve years to redress the balance. For the US, such a timescale is not viable. So it is now their turn to accept the recession to which all countries must submit, when faced with an external imbalance and without being able to fall back on a reserve money supply. America is going to discover a basic truth that has remained hidden because of its privileges since the War: that only recession can lower imports and raise exports to the point of regaining an economic balance. There has been too much consumerism in the States: Americans have lived beyond their means, while producing too little. Undoubtedly a large percentage of the population will soon have to suffer a severe reduction in their standard of living.

Nevertheless this drastic treatment will not be enough to set to rights the second imbalance, namely the budget deficit. For 50 per cent of it has been financed up to now by foreign investment, and is therefore vulnerable to the slightest crisis of confidence. According to a process characteristic of the market economy, higher and higher rates of interest are needed in order to attract more and more reluctant capital, an escalation which in itself serves to accelerate the recession. The Americans are losing out, whether they increase their debt or sell off their assets, a situation which is precarious to say the least.

Although inevitable, no date has yet been fixed for this recession and the details involved are still unclear. Just as the free distribution of credit managed to limit the influence of the crash, it will also succeed in postponing sanctions for as long as possible. They will either have to be imposed by the market, or demanded by senate. In the first case, the chain of events is clear: a new crisis, an uncontrolled rise in the rate of exchange, and the collapse of the stock market, with a consequent drastic fall in consumption. The authorities will at least be lucky enough to be faced with a *fait accompli*. According to the second scenario, the American president will have to take responsibility for the purge in an appeal to common-sense. This is always difficult to sell to an electorate to whom a gradual easing up is far preferable to a sudden and therefore severe depression. A rise in the level of income tax would have the double virtue, from that point of view, of reducing the budget deficit while at the same time lowering consumption and consequently imports. In a country of low taxation, with no VAT and no tax on petrol, the introduction of such levies, even in small doses, would be enough to put things back in order, although such reasoning rather ignores the price to be paid politically.

At any rate, whether the recession is spontaneous or not, whether or not there is a rise in income tax, the US will have to limit its spending, leading to the old choice between 'bread and bombs': the welfare state and the military budget. This time, though, the economic crisis will be of a rather different nature. It will no longer be a question of a period of expansion being followed by one of contraction in order to reduce inflation and create order generally; it will be necessary to settle the accounts accumulated during fifteen years of illusion and of an ever-present desire to dodge any constraints.

An economy in long-term recession limits the power of the state and a diminishing budget reduces the amount spent on the military. While totalitarian systems manage to avoid these constraints, by making the people carry the brunt of any new effort, democracies cannot evade the issue in such a way, thank goodness. This set of circumstances will be a body blow to America. In a country based on consumerism, any crisis has a collective cost greater than the sum of its component parts: in this case, extreme pessimism, a drop in collective energy, a freezing of action, and a refusal to see the world outside. As for the defence budget, it will be presented, as always, as a treasure trove to be plundered, especially if an atmosphere of détente provides the slightest alibi. Faced with a list of commitments which cannot be kept and the need for a reduction in general running costs, continued American presence in Europe will be seen to be unrealistic. GIs are not going to become involved in a great national debate on relations between the US and Europe; they will return in dribs and drabs in response to bureaucratic restrictions on the budget. When the first regiment is recalled, the US Government, in an attempt to reduce the impact of the decision, will organize a great media bonanza along the lines of: less men but more sophisticated weaponry, in order to produce a more efficient American presence. With the symbolism obscured, and emotional reaction held in check by sheer bluster, an irreversible process will be under way. Each budgetary year will bring its share of repatriations.

The American military presence in Europe will decline each year, with the additional help of *perestroika*, until such time as the dynamic of disarmament does away with it entirely. The principal agent of this détente will clearly be the pressure of the deficit. On the one hand, we have a highly prosperous nation, the United States, that, in order to avoid a marginal reduction in spending power, will economize on its defence budget; on the other, we have a poor country, the Soviet Union, tired of financing its military operation by imposing drastic restrictions on its populace. These two countries will disarm together – what could be better! But we must be aware of the cost for Europe: the more the Americans reduce their central system of protection, the less disposed they will be to use it to defend a third party, Japanese or European. Disarmament both confirms and spurs on the disassociation between Europe and America. The path of least resistance for North America is now a minimal protection of its own domestic space.

The Irresistible Rise of Pacifism

President Reagan's first term of office was the only one in which there was an actual growth in military spending. It took both the ideological power carried by the man himself and the illusion given by supply-side economics to change the current of events. The 'evil empire', together with imaginary budgetary gains, provided the necessary conditions for this financial effort, however short-lived. In the event, today everything is conspiring to push the US towards pacifism. National strategy is a by-product of society as a whole, not of economic infrastructures: maybe the last remaining Marxists will come to comprehend this truism. Today Americans have a rational choice between two policies: the one involving increased military effort in order to drain the energy of the Soviets and increase their own international influence; the other, a policy of détente and withdrawal. In theory, they have the option of pursuing both, since the Soviet Union is not itself able to step up the pace. But this possibility is illusory: it was the belief that growth would finance the defence effort that allowed the military development of the eighties. However, such a growth in military spending led to an even greater reduction in consumption. Such a policy went against the natural aspirations of a democracy.

In the US, now more than ever before, the public, faced with the choice between bread and bombs, is proving obstinate. Consumption has increased, to the point where peope are living on credit; they will not allow themselves to be plunged still deeper into a recession they will find difficult to bear, merely to increase the strategic bargaining power of the government. The naivety of American public opinion, its natural feeling of power, its conviction that it is being protected from all menace, are all reasons which make a strategic commitment more difficult. How can one expect a peaceable, individualist society to give up the pleasures of détente? How can one ask it to integrate into its system of defence a Europe from which it is becoming ever more distant? How can one imagine that the US will resist the temptation of disarmament? How can one, in a word, hold their pacifism against them?

3

Germany at the Centre

Myths are fast disappearing: the Federal Republic, closest ally of the United States; West Germany, the pride of the Atlantic class; Germans and Americans as blood brothers. We have lived so many years with these rosy images that we will find it difficult to give them up. Germany is on the move, and is carrying Europe in its wake. As always, any question of Europe's future unfailingly comes down to a question of Germany's. With the advent of *Ostpolitik* in the seventies, history took up its old course, imperceptibly at first, but gradually more and more overtly until the Soviet Union brought things out into the open by playing its German card: substituting charm for menace and *glasnost* for ideological aggression. Such an evolution is not the result of a kind of armchair strategy, nor is it a question of fate inevitably bringing Germany back to its proper course. It is the product of countless different factors: the evolution of civil society; the progress of the economy; the dynamic of political forces; a natural *rapprochement* with the GDR; the re-emergence in both the East and the West of *Mittel Europa*; and, last but not least, the ambiguities surrounding Western alliances, with a United States on the retreat and a France ready to share everything except security. The equation from now on is simple: Germany will return to the centre; Western Europe will be replaced by the whole of Europe; Atlantic solidarity will disappear in favour of a continental system of security.

For a long time the taboo surrounding Germany has blinded us to the true state of affairs. To recognize the movement of Germany was to give in to all the old myths, to give rein to base Germanophobia, to refuse to believe in the European miracle. In fact Germany has begun its move without abandoning any of its democratic values or economic principles. Democracy and the market economy, from now on, are more integral to Germany than to any other country, including

France. How can one but admire the moderation shown by the Germans for the past forty years in accepting their enforced separation, their national hemiplegia? And if one is looking for chastening comparisons, we need only ask ourselves how the French would have reacted if the dividing line of war-time had carried on for almost a half a century. One can not help paying homage to the reasoned approach which has always characterized the Germans in choosing between their moderate left and right wings. Before Le Pen France had to be careful, but now the French must have increased regard for those who, in historically difficult situations, have avoided feverish impulses, extremes and demagogy.

But the respect we owe to the democratic vitality of Germany must not be synonymous with blindness and false illusions. Germany has started to move, and nothing will stop her; she is taking up her place again at the heart of Europe, in the name of Europe itself. It is not a matter of chance that the myth of 1992 finds no echo across the Rhine: the Germans have much to gain from an open market, but not as much as from a resurrection of trading with the East. With the continued growth of the EC, Germany will end up thinking that there is a better strategic use for its budgetary generosity than forever subsidizing the other eleven countries. The great dream of 1992 is not going to run aground on the backward nature of southern countries, nor on the residual nationalism of France, nor even on the indifference of the UK, but on the impossibility of Germany's becoming a part of the West at the expense of the East.

The Pressure Exerted by Society

Reality begins to counter received ideas: on the one hand, we have Germany astute, productive and stable; on the other, an agitated, inefficient and volatile France. However, such clichés no longer bear any resemblance to our modern society. Behind the gentle bourgeois façade of German cities is a seething cauldron; French society by comparison is '*luxe, calme et volupté*'. The Greens, now rooted in the culture; the strength of the alternative movement; ecological pressure; a hatred of nuclear power changing slowly into a rejection of nuclear weapons, and a rising anti-Americanism are just some examples of this ferment.

German society is no longer contested by a minority, as it was in

1968, nor attacked by a handful of terrorists, as in the time of the Red Army Faction. Coiled in its breast there exists a counter-society, whose values are those of nature, ecology and peace. Its culture is a strange melting pot of anarchy, left-wing ideals, myths of nature, and pacifist reflexes, but with the conspicuous absence of Marxism. Its politics have, in the course of time, found expression through the Greens who are now embedded in the parliamentary mire. These members of parliament have directed themselves through the classic procedures of interpolation, question and answer, to the extent that their manner of speech jars less than the clothes which have become their only distinguishing feature. This counter-society, more importantly, has its own zones, its own districts. Anyone who has left the centre of Berlin, or the business area of Düsseldorf, to plunge into the 'alternative' districts, will never have any problem understanding German schizophrenia. What picture would Paris present if its fifth and sixth *arrondissements* encompassed a self-contained village, inhabited not by society's rejects, but by the real fringe, with their alternative schools, health centres, associations, taxes, even their alternative systems of law and order. A city within a city, sharing neither customs, values, rituals, life style, graphic art nor advertising. The dominant culture has given up even trying to win back these enclaves, hoping simply that this extra-terrestrial invasion will not spill over into a break-down of beliefs, into delinquency and terrorism However, at this stage of development, the counter-culture is starting to rub off onto the main culture. Magazines, advertising, clothes, way of life have been influenced in such a way that an impact is being felt, beyond the alternative world in its strict sense, which is poles apart from the classical German model.

This brings us to ecology, a movement which goes much further in terms of commercial fundamentals than either the Green or alternative factions. Is it a resurgence of the old Germanic cult of nature, perhaps the result of an industrial society having been confined within a limited space, an ideological substitute in a country without ideology, a throwback to the idea of the German soul, a consequence of the great debate from which Germany, diminished by war, felt excluded? The reasons are numerous, but still do not fully explain the phenomenon. Behind the arguments in defence of the environment it is society itself which is under question. With nature as a yardstick, nothing is sacred. Growth, investment, the nature of the market, the direction of social forces, the policies of employers and of the government, all are open to criticism. As a means of protest it becomes outdated much more slowly than the old class analyses which had nothing to do with reality. Nature does not leave us in the lurch in the same way as the labour force. It leads to a strange sort of society where the most violent clashes with the police occur during demonstrations against the extension of Frankfurt airport. Only Japan has known the same type of movement, resulting from the expansion of the airport at Narita: what a bizarre parallel! The progression here is clear, from ecology to a rejection of anything nuclear and then to pacifism. Look at the number of demonstrations there have been against the construction of atomic centres. The number of marches against the reprocessing of nuclear fuel. The number of meetings to protest against the atom. An evangelical zeal, a touch of ecology, a few Lutheran principles and we have all the ingredients that turn 'better red than dead'[1] into a collective ethic.

What reservations and wild imaginings lay behind the outcry against the installation of Pershing and Cruise: anyone would have thought that the Americans were in the process of occupying Germany. A love of nature leads to a hatred of all things nuclear, from there to pacifism and finally to the disassociation of Europe from America. All of this serves to explain how a civil, democratic society, by dint of its very vitality, can become the strongest ally of the Soviet Union, the only country with no true civil society.

Ecology has gone hand in hand with a profound and unexpected anti-Americanism. When Brezhnev arrived on an official visit to Bonn, he was welcomed by an anti-Reagan demonstration. And that in a country with no Communist party to organize such a 'spontaneous' mass movement. In twenty years, the feelings of the Germans *vis-à-vis* the Americans have passed from devotion, to a certain circumspection and then to downright hostility.

Surveys in Germany showed that Brezhnev, even Chernenko, emerged as men of peace, to say nothing of Gorbachev, in contrast with a bellicose Reagan. Innumerable demonstrations outside American bases; a progressive rejection of American icons; the return of reference to *Mittel Europa*; the disappearance of gestures of collective solidarity with regard to the US and militant action on behalf of Nicaragua are all indications of a surge of opinion which from now on will underpin the strategic position of the German government.

Such a society could not care less about Atlantic solidarity. Germans refuse to allow their territory to become a 'nuclear dustbin';

their only dream, apart from the double zero option, is of a process of complete denuclearization. They would feel even safer without American bases, seeing in the American presence an obstacle to peace rather than a source of protection. They wish for a Europe without frontiers, enhanced by German unification, and freed of the Iron Curtain, where freedom of movement alone will take the place of all other freedoms: they are ready, in a word, for Finlandization. But the Germans are not alone in this.

The Central Economic Empire

The people responsible for the German economy are the only ones in Europe not to be preoccupied with 1992: either as the promised land, or as a substitute for hell. Their priorities lie elsewhere. The possibility of an open market would certainly favour the most powerful country, in this case Germany; it would serve to expand its areas of strength, especially in sectors such as banking and insurance, where national frontiers have the most inhibiting effect. Consequently, the Deutsche Bank and l'Allianz are impatient to be allowed full rein, in the same way as Siemens or Bayer in the past. But economic ambition goes far beyond the limited horizon of 1992. With an economy of world-wide dimensions, Germany is thinking, above all, in terms of an international market: that alone would match up to the strength of its enterprises. The United States, South America and the Far East are all potential areas of expansion, both for Germany and for its main competitors. But in addition to this business map of the world, Germany is in the process of creating a monopoly for itself in Eastern Europe and the Soviet Union.

The German economy relies more heavily on export capability than any other country. This is not because of the contribution that foreign trade makes to its gross national product, but because of the long-term importance of such trade to a country without growth and with a diminishing population (hence the importance of the former East Germany).

Before unification, West Germany was in the position of seeing its internal market collapse: demand had reached saturation point, the population having consumed all it could in the way of cars, electrical gadgets, hi-fi. Add to that a growth in savings at the expense of consumerism on the part of an ageing population. In fact they were putting something by for their retirement, through a justified fear of pinning their faith on their allotted pension. It is against this background that the ravaging effects of an increasingly childless society made their mark.

Since the mid-sixties, everyone knew that one day, the population of Federal Germany would decrease, but no one really believed it. At the end of the eighties, that point was reached. Its birth rate of 1.3, the lowest in Europe, was far from the sacred figure of 2.1 children per woman needed to keep the number of inhabitants at the same level: with the time lag inherent in such demographic cycles, long and inexorable as they are, the decline was already under way. All things being equal, i.e. without massive immigration or a sudden rectifying of the birth rate, the population of what was West Germany will fall to the level of thirty-eight million by the year 2030. Thirty-eight million! This means that as many people will be lost to her through not being born, as were killed during the Second World War. Germany, that great nation, would waste away to nothing with the dwindling and ageing of its population. As a phenomenon, it is devastating, overshadowing all others, whether economic, political, cultural or psychological. If an infrastructure, in the Marxist sense, still exists, it is to be found in the demographic process. Its shock waves rock everything, especially questions of macro-economics, in which exports assume a vital importance as a means of compensating for an inevitable contraction in internal demand. For Germany, with its decreasing internal market, there will be no life-line from Europe, since the Community is ultimately condemned, albeit to a lesser degree, to the same population decline. Any life-line has to come from the wider world: in this frantic race for new outlets, the East again becomes a major objective.

Culturally, Germany is better placed than anyone: *vis-à-vis* what was its twin in the GDR; *vis-à-vis* the popular democracies which, before the advent of the Iron Curtain, all came under Germany's economic sphere of influence, and also *vis-à-vis* the Soviet Union, which has steadfastly maintained certain privileged commercial relations with Germany, following in the footsteps of old Russia. In a world market with so many competitors, how could one expect Germany not to take advantage of this? Germany will not rest until the East is solvent, well provided for, and ultimately transformed into a low paid subcontractor.

Since the only obstacle to imports within the popular democracies is their financial paucity, the new Germany is quietly developing a plan worthy of Marshall. No bureaucratic procedures here for the granting of subsidies, no socio-political rumpus; instead a redoubtable efficiency. Financial aid to the East has adopted many forms. Some are not at all obvious: take, for instance, the case of the relative value of the mark in West and East Germany. According to a principle that remained inviolate for decades, the two marks exchanged at the rate of one for one. This meant that a flimsy currency had artificially the same spending power as one of the strongest currencies in the world. Also not evident was the acceptance of financial responsibility for pensioners of the East, who were authorized to emigrate to the West and who were covered by an equivalent system of social security; likewise the increased spending power bestowed on the East in the shape of vast numbers of personal gifts, donations from associations, the charitable works of the Church and the thousand and one organizations which gravitate around it. And along with these links went other, more classic, relations: in the first place, loans from the old Federal Republic which were financed by budgetary resources benefiting the GDR, Poland and Hungary. Also there was aid with exports, so as to allow enterprises to sell to their clients, to the very limits of solvency. And lastly, massive credit capabilities, raised by the banks of the former Federal Republic to the profit of the largest debtors of the East, i.e. the USSR and the former GDR. There is a continual development of such financial transfers. The strategy of German banks could be defined as: taking control of the deposit banks of Western Europe, and thus raising the wherewithal to increase their credit in Eastern Europe. They, of course, would reject such an interpretation, explaining that these deposits do not lose their value and that such loans are differentiated. But what else is the Deutsche Bank doing when it increases its assets in Italy by taking over the Banca d'America e d'Italia, at the same time as reducing its global loans, with the exception of Eastern bloc countries? In this way, a financial manoeuvre has been surreptitiously undertaken to draw on the resources of the West, in order to finance consumption in the East. German financial institutions are unrivalled at this game. Moreover, they link the granting of loans to the purchase of German products, thus creating openings for their industries.

German enterprises are just as well established in the East as their banking colleagues. They have no rival in France, the UK or America. This is due to a number of obvious factors: the quality of their products both at home and abroad; the effect of old relationships; a cultural proximity and the capacity of German technostructures to adapt to the meanderings, the slowness, and the malfunctioning of bureaucracies in the East. Is anyone more successful in the Soviet Union than Bayer, Siemens, AEG or Mannesmann? German company directors enjoy relationships with their Eastern-bloc colleagues of an intimacy which is rarely understood. Many of them spend more time in Moscow than in New York. Many fraternize with Soviet chancellors or vice-chancellors in winter hunts in Karelia. Many others have access to the Kremlin – such as Mr Cristiaens, the old director of the Deutsche Bank and the first foreigner to be received by Gorbachev after his appointment as president.

'*Drang nach Osten*'[2] is not merely a strategic concept: it is an economic fact and a sociological reality. Industries in Germany are not content simply with offloading their products in the East. They have discovered the existence there of local suppliers, who operate at Korean rates. Such had long been the case with the former GDR, which, one forgets, was considered a member state of the EEC. Free circulation between the former two Germanies had been possible since the origin of the Treaty of Rome. Products from the old GDR could enter Europe without paying customs duty. This was a major concession for an economy whose costs were lower than the European average, and whose productivity, although low, was nowhere near the appalling level of other Eastern-bloc countries. This explained the constant temptation for West German businesses to subcontract out to the East. A cultural similarity facilitated relations, the prices were competitive, the quality acceptable, and there was no tax to counteract these advantages. Nowadays, subcontracting is beginning to develop in Czechoslovakia, in Hungary and even in the Soviet Union. As soon as *perestroika* provides satisfactory conditions for foreign investment, with the possibility of creating subsidiary companies on a one-to-one basis, of controlling any financial flux and allowing any returns back into the original country, the phenomenon of subcontracting will really take off. How tempting and how simple it would be to shift production to Kiev rather than Singapore, Bratislava rather than Taiwan!

Germany is setting up a 'central economic empire': acting as a link between the two sides of Europe. The East will soon be as indispensable to Western economies as the West is vital to the East.

Western Europe is a kind of gigantic Hong Kong to the East: a door to the world markets, a supplier of consumer goods, a producer of technological hardware, a financial and commercial partner. The East, for its part, is the 'Hinterland' for the saturated economies of the West: it provides both outlets and subcontractors. This economic half-way house between the West and the East is being set up at the instigation of Germany and with the blessing of President Gorbachev. Strategy is not ruled by the economy alone, as marxists would have us believe, but the construction of such a half-way house does act as a further spur to the change from an Atlantic to a continental system. There is no doubt that everything is moving in this direction.

The Rise of Neutrality

The time is long passed when socio-political forces in the Federal Republic were oriented towards the United States, to the extent of rejecting the construction of a Gaullist Europe because its priorities were not sufficiently geared to the Atlantic Alliance.

The divide between left and right, SPD and Christian Democrats, has not taken into account this evolution of ideas. The dynamic at work, in this case, is galvanizing all the political parties, although principally, of course, the SPD: by initiating *Ostpolitik* in the seventies, they opened up a real Pandora's box. The Federal Republic became once more a responsible country, taking control of its strategic interests, at last escaping from the infantile and debilitating state to which it was consigned by the West, and which notably required the absence of any links with the East. Denuclearization of central Europe; the simultaneous recalling of Soviet and American forces, and the priority given to the *rapprochement* between the two Germanies within a European context, were the themes already lurking in the corridors of the SPD, a decade before the unification actually materialized. In fact, Social-Democratic thinking continues to move from a position of extreme Atlanticism to a latent neutrality. The administration of Helmut Schmidt was merely a minor setback with regard to this ideological current of events; he slowed, but could not stop, this drift.

In accordance with the old socialist convention that new ideas come from the left, the progressive wing of the SPD has been dominant now for ten years. Given certain key factors: a leader, in

Oskar Lafontaine, who used to call for withdrawal from NATO, but who has since been converted to a less provocative viewpoint; the wish, on the part of certain people, for some sort of alliance with the Greens, and on the part of others, the desire to seize the ecological initiative from them; a tendency to cling to the memory of *Ostpolitik* and a willingness to see it resuscitated; a nostalgia for the neutrality of the fifties; outbursts of anti-American feeling, occasionally fuelled by Helmut Schmidt, whose utter scepticism regarding the alliance with the US dates from the day when Jimmy Carter renounced the neutron bomb; the desire to retain the advantage it enjoys over all other German parties – that of its close relationship with the East; given all these things, we are certainly talking here of an SPD ready to play its part in the strategic reorganization of Europe.

Even the Liberals find it difficult to resist the charms of *Ostpolitik*. It was they, together with the Social Democrats, who started it all off, and who, since the reversal of political alliances in 1982, have worked away faithfully at it from within their new coalition with the Christian Democrats. Not merely worked, but acted. Is there anyone left in Bonn who does not realize that Herr Genscher's policies are not in fact the same as those of Chancellor Kohl? More eager to grasp any window of opportunity in the East, more willing to pass from the double to the triple zero option, i.e. to the complete denuclearization of central Europe; all the more open to the idea of Europe, because he envisages it as being independent of America, he is always one step ahead of Kohl, in terms of this strategic reorientation. It was he who pushed through the decision on the double zero option; he who has taken on the role of champion of détente; he who handles the alliance with France from the viewpoint of a continental balance of power; he, in effect, who provided the impetus for the *rapprochement* and ultimate unification of the two Germanies. Since 1970, the Liberals dominated German politics, and, between one coalition government and another, assured strategic continuity on the part of the Federal Republic: always, they retained the centre ground. However, this centre is neither political nor sociological, but geographic and strategic: it is the heart of continental Europe. This is to say that the liberals wish to see Germany playing the same balancing role in Europe that they are so expert at playing within the German political arena.

However, the Christian Democrats are not being forced into anything by their liberal partners against their will. Having clamoured for a return to the Atlantic fold prior to their re-election, they followed exactly the same course as their predecessors. Firstly, through political calculation: public opinion demanded its share of daily improvements in relations with the old GDR; it was ready to pay a high price for very little in return. Secondly through a growing difficulty in their relationship with the US, they had the distinct impression, after the Reykjavik encounter, that the United States had come within an ace of ditching them; lastly, through a reluctance to grant their Bavarian cousins in the CSU the monopoly of a national identity formed through contact with the East. Paradoxically, Franz Joseph Strauss played more than anyone on this Eastern aspect. At the end of his political life, he became the major advocate of an increased credit allocation to the former GDR, and the prophet of a new *Drang nach Osten*, even before the collapse of the Berlin Wall. What could be more natural in fact? Nationalism leads Germany eastwards and not towards integration into an Atlantic Alliance in which Germany is condemned, in strategic terms, to second-class citizenship. Strauss wished to be a 'German Gaullist' but, from the point of view of Germany, 'détente, entente and cooperation' went together with the restoration of *Mittel Europa*. In this context, the firmness of the German Government's decision, in 1983, to accept the deployment of Pershing and Cruise, represented the swan song of the Atlantic Alliance. Witness the ease with which they accepted the double zero option in 1987; witness the temptation on the part of the Christian Democrats to accept the triple zero option, so that Germany would no longer be Europe's atomic dustbin; witness, in 1990, how the ideological debate shifted towards reunification, transcending European unity.

The evolution of political forces, in the former Federal Republic just as anywhere else, tended to follow shifts in society, rather than precede them. Trade unions, whose reservations regarding the Atlantic Alliance outstrip those of the SPD, have woven a web of relations with the East based on the concept of worker solidarity, which is now being put into practice. Bosses of industry unceasingly wooed the East, without any of the reticence of the Christian Democrats. Churches refused obstinately to recognize the old division of Germany, because morally it should never have happened. Pastoral relations, charitable links, communal demonstrations, all stemmed from the same vision of the world. Now the Evangelical Church is reunited. It has outstripped the *rapprochement* of the civil societies to an often unrecognized extent. Along with all this, in a country which adores all cultural display, goes a rich common heritage, including the commemoration of Frederick the Great, Luther and the inauguration of the Dresden Opera House by the respective politicians of the two former states. Honeker and von Weizsäcker would stand side by side in the front row. Last but not least, the two former Germanies met up during the television news, since television, which was received throughout the East, played a fundamentally unifying role. The people always succeeded in imposing their rule, even over the former communist government. In this case, the government could not stem the tide of collective and individual aerials, and even had to provide cable television for regions such as Dresden where reception was weak, since public pressure in favour of Western television was so overwhelming.

German institutions had therefore been regrouping themselves around the old dividing line, with a feeling, among the more cultivated, of history repeating itself. Was a courtier of the king of Bavaria any closer to a Prussian bureaucrat than a worker at Siemens is to a civil servant in Pankow? German society has, for centuries, been one of plurality, diversity and contradiction: is it really any more so today?

Towards a Nation without a State?

Germans were justifiably exasperated at the French, when they brought up their old worries regarding reunification, surrendering to gut reactions, whether they be Cartesian, monolithic or nationalistic. The French feared that a reunified Germany would mean a new Reich. They refused to understand that national identity could be exhibited outside of the two separate states. A specifically French failing if there ever was one. Germany was one nation before ever being divided; it was by chance that it became two states and the process is now being reversed. Population, sociology and culture all pushed in that direction. Nature has once again asserted her rights and institutions are following this movement. From this point of view, the fall of the Berlin Wall simply accelerated the progress of history.

The GDR managed to avoid the demographic drama which was unfolding in the Federal Republic. Through a combination of incentive and coercion, it attained a fecundity equal to that of France, namely between 1.8 and 1.9 children per couple. Still no miracle: the population is destined to become old and the total number of inhabitants will decline slightly from the year 2000 on, but there will be no implosion like that in the former Federal Republic. The German nation will consist of sixty million people, forty million in the West and twenty million in the East. A deep-rooted instinct for survival will bring the former two Germanies ever closer together. A country does not willingly allow its population to plummet, without desperately seeking some solution, that much is clear. History works in mysterious ways: preoccupation with the concept of the *Herrenvolk* had driven Germany insane and she paid the price for it in the form of partition; ironically, it is demographic exigencies (amongst others) which have now allowed her to regain her identity.

Pre-empting this natural pressure, the overlap between the societies of Eastern and Western Europe is such that each day they bear a closer resemblance to each other. By 1990, West Germans were seeing their families in the East as often as Parisians see their cousins in the Loire. Ten million visits per year from the West to the East meant a frontier that was totally permeable, from that direction at least. Even from the other direction, it was somewhat porous: there was an almost unrestricted exchange of letters and telephone calls; authorized immigration from the East to the West; tens of thousands of pensioners who decided to spend their last years in the West. We have been prisoners of outdated images, such as the first visits twenty years ago, the martyrs of the Wall, the division of Berlin. A wall of silence concealed to some extent the disappearance of the Berlin Wall. Its destruction, and the consequent unification of Germany, put the finishing touches to a process that had been going on for a long time. What an amazing development: young people of West and East Germany have come to resemble each other again; their fashions, music, way of life, values and pacifism are all closely linked. Having been consistently wrong regarding the convergence of industrial societies, might Raymond Aron not at least have the right idea about Germans? In this case, would any unification have been due to their integrated industrial network, or quite simply to Germany?

The common nation which has re-emerged had long been creating for itself identical points of reference. We have talked already about television. Western channels were received throughout the East and Germany was reunified each night during the 8 o'clock news. The seeds of real schizophrenia existed in the East: a classic communist society with unlimited access to Western media, and a system of information which completely contradicted the rules of the regime. The *International Herald Tribune* was not available from news stands, but the telephone was always accessible: a totalitarian bureaucracy can always preserve its customs and its censorship, but it can no longer impose on its citizens a total exile with regard to the outside world.

The same kind of thing could be seen in the cultural field. The simultaneous commemoration of Luther, in the East and West, according to the exigencies of the calendar, had a political, rather than a cultural symbolism, but behind such displays, real channels of communication were being set up, of which Berlin was the hub. Previously a symbol of divided Germany, Berlin had become, in effect, the life blood of inter-German relations, with colloquiums, seminars, meetings, exchanges of books and of manuscripts as well as a more general intellectual osmosis. What was openly available from bookshops in one area, circulated only clandestinely in others. Western intellectuals held artificial dialogues with Eastern officials, while talking freely with underground movements. But, given the extent of the overlap between the two, the distinction, if not insignificant, was no longer essential.

The whole was reinforced by symbolism: anyone who had not seen the German press adding the sum total of the Olympic medals of the two states would never understand Germany. Anyone who had never seen the television weather reports had no idea of true German topography. Anyone who had not witnessed the meeting of West and East Germans in reunions would never recognise the reflexes that existed between local areas. We must not forget the principal factor in the creation of communities – that of language. Even the presence of another, supposedly dominant, language, in the old German provinces of Poland and Czechoslovakia, had not succeeded in destroying the original language. How much more so, then, when two countries with the same language at first refused any contact, then, as they rediscovered themselves, began to make new overtures?

Hopes for unity in fact went through an evolution. From the setting up of its 'fundamental law', to ritual discussion in international organizations, the former Federal Republic never stopped proclaiming its dream of state reunification. For fear of allowing this ambition to grow, the former GDR, for its part, refused to accept any suggestion of there being even an embryonic German national identity. For fifteen years, West Germany kept its dream of unity on ice, for the sake of more national gains, and the East was carried along the same path, ideologically less destructive perhaps, but ultimately more destabilizing. Now, the two states are back together.

Although relegated to a secondary position, institutional ambition has not totally disappeared. Western politicians will never completely give up their dreams simply to leave things in society's hands. For such people, nothing could possibly be more unbearable than to imagine something that is utterly essential as being out of one's reach. As soon as circumstances permit, therefore, their desire to engrave this evolution into their institutions will re-emerge. These will not be state institutions: that idea has disappeared; there are no wars now to create states in the way they have been created in the past – by force – and no phantom Bismarck on the horizon. Nor will these institutions be federal or even confederal: for *rapprochement* to come in that way would be an unthinkable upheaval for a Europe stretching from the Atlantic to the Urals and which at the moment is embedded in the most extreme diplomatic status quo. But perhaps the unity of the two societies will one day give birth to institutions *sui generis*: partly state, partly non-state institutions; reversible by nature, they will provide incentive rather than constraint. Initially, they will apply to specific areas: economy, culture, sport. This institutional transformation remains aleatory and of secondary importance: aleatory, because it assumes that such changes will produce an equivalent evolution in the field of politics; secondary, because the united German nation has been created by civil societies, not by hypothetical technocratic bodies.

The Return of *Mittel Europa*

Europe was disabled on three fronts: the West *vis-à-vis* the East; the Federal Republic *vis-à-vis* the GDR, and Germany as a whole *vis-à-vis* Central Europe. *Mittel Europa* is therefore making a comeback, gaining strength as Germany rediscovers its old position. In the nineteenth century, *Mittel Europa* was made up of areas under German influence strategically, militarily, politically, economically, culturally, linguistically and socially. Today, the situation is different: the former East Germany no longer exerts any influence over Poland, Czechoslovakia or Hungary, nor the former West Germany over Austria. The first because, like old East Germany itself, these small central states come under Soviet power; and the second because Austria, since becoming neutral in 1955, is no longer in a position of treating the old Federal Republic as an overlord. Other links, however, still remain.

These are, firstly, relations with the former German provinces of pre-1914 and pre-1945: these socialist states have never succeeded in eradicating German in favour of their own national languages, a situation that has led to a kind of cultural attraction. There exists, albeit to a lesser extent, the same interchange of ideas as there was between East and West Germany. In the absence of television, there exists a permanent flow of information through books, meetings and a vast amount of aid available for the restoration of castles, churches and other remaining symbols of a bygone Germany. The Federal Republic had no problem administering subsidies in this way: rather than coming directly from the state, and therefore entailing a certain amount of diplomatic friction, they were distributed through churches, charities, cultural associations and other similar institutions. Rudolf von Thadden, that great intellectual, recently talked about the inauguration of a newly restored church in a village in Western Prussia, where his family had been feudal lords: listen to him describe how he went to visit the castle, arm in arm with local officials; observe the strength of his attachment to this land and also the nature of his reception there, and you will understand the permanent nature of the fabric of society which forty years of official socialism was not able to destroy. In addition to such specifically cultural activity, there is also economic aid, especially in the old German regions of Poland. There, too, the work is done unobtrusively by churches and charities, rather than by state organizations: in this area, discretion is the key to efficiency.

Central Europe can be defined as a series of concentric circles. The first circle consists of the new Germany; the second adds the borderlands of old Germany; a third covers the central states; a fourth, the furthest away and least defined, encompasses the western regions of the Soviet Union.

The second and third circles become stronger each day, as new relations spring up between Germany and the popular democracies of Poland, Czechoslovakia, Hungary, and also Bulgaria and Romania. Everyday life, as always, reflects this better than any diplomatic initiatives: one only has to cast an eye over flight destinations from Munich airport to see that Bucharest crops up as often as Madrid;

Warsaw as often as Milan; Budapest as often as Brussels. One can do the round trip in a single day, as any French executive would between Paris and Amsterdam. Behind this profusion of new relationships, economic exchanges are becoming more and more important. Germans provide financial and commercial advantages, development and aid: in this way they are building, on their own doorstep, what the Japanese used to call a 'sphere of co-prosperity'. They have understood, better than anyone, the attraction of a real, but clandestine, Marshall plan: subsidy and influence demonstrate the reality of the plan, while its clandestine nature is an attempt to keep the monopoly of this unique position. This macro-economic equation involves a multiplicity of micro-economic relationships which are beginning to assert themselves: between a great German enterprise, born out of the ashes of the IG Farben, and a Czech state cooperative which was a former partner of the latter; between German producers of all types of equipment and socialist clients who cannot conceive of anything not being 'made in Germany'; between former West Germany's exporters and former East Germany's purchasers; between Western bankers and their Hungarian counterparts who dream only of following in their footsteps.

Germany also breathes cultural life into these countries in various ways: through its own television and radio channels; through Radio Free Europe, for a long time the only source of news of the East, until the wheel of history turned and listeners in the popular democracies, accustomed to listening to Western radios, became the first to criticize the archaic and simplistic nature of this particular institution; through a network of semi-official, semi-alternative publishing houses, busy trying to keep pace with the demand for underground publications; through telephone contact that has become so routine that every great German intellectual gives the impression of having been talking only yesterday with Geremek; through colloquiums and seminars organized with a great deal of effort, in order to give an excuse for intellectuals from the East to come and breathe in the fresh air of the West; through networks, encounters and exchanges which, little by little, reconstitute that cultural universe whose supposed disappearance had been prematurely announced by Kundera. Europe is gradually recovering its memory, emerging from its cultural amnesia. Germany is largely responsible, although it would never claim as much; France, on the other hand, is full of its usual bluster and inefficiency.

But *Mittel Europa* also encroaches on the borders of the Russian Empire; the fourth circle. Are we forgetting that there are two million people of German origin and culture in the Soviet Union, and that, despite Stalin's dissolution of the autonomous German republic of the Volga, its schools, newspapers and radios are all in German? Are we ignoring Latvia and the other Baltic states, for so long under the dynamic influence of Western Prussia? Have we overlooked the complex links between the Ukraine and Central Europe, their ambiguous pro-German impulses and habit of turning towards Germany for help in resisting Russia? It is not a matter of chance that, every week, 6,000 Soviets of German origin take advantage of *perestroika* and emigrate to the Friedland relay camp in Lower Saxony, the centre of immigration to the West. In fact, similar links to those that Hungary and, of course, the old GDR maintained with the Federal Republic are beginning to be re-established, albeit to a much lesser degree, in these border regions of the Soviet Union. This *Mittel Europa* is of course far from resembling its old pre-1914 self, but it does offer Germany a considerable degree of influence.

Drang nach Osten

Relations with the Soviet Union clearly constitute the key to this repositioning of Germany. They affect the *rapprochement* with the new democracies of the East, and exert a contrary effect on links with the United States; they even conspire to put the combined German view of Europe into action. It was in Moscow that *Ostpolitik* began, in 1970; in Moscow that the former Democratic Republic was given the go-ahead regarding its overtures to the former Federal Republic; in Moscow that Soviet/American negotiation has redefined Germany in strategic terms. All of this has led to the peculiarly German predilection for a renewed *Drang nach Osten*. In 1970, a process was set under way, which may have had periods of stasis, but has never turned back on itself, even at the time of the deployment of Pershing, by far the most tense period in the last fifteen years. In the past, the Soviets were able to exert absolute control over inter-German relations, simply by making any displeasure known. Nowadays, they have not such an easy command of the situation. At first, the former GDR wanted to go further in its relations with the West than its guardian was willing to accept, but, transfixed by the prospect of *perestroika*, it ended up having more reservations than the Soviet Union itself. With such a system of tutelage, however, the changeover was not an easy one, and we are currently in the strange situation whereby Germano-Soviet relations are beginning to find their own rhythm, while at the same time continuing to determine the atmosphere of *Mittel Europa*.

When Willy Brandt embarked on *Ostpolitik*, he was addressing a Soviet Union perceived by the majority of Germans to be the 'evil empire', to use a phrase coined by Reagan in his first term of office. The blockade of Berlin, East–West tensions, the Berlin Wall, and the repression of the popular democracies were all laid at the feet of the Soviet Union, while the United States seemed to embody democracy, the Marshall plan, abundance and freedom, all values miraculous to German eyes in the post-war period. Nowadays, things are not so clearly defined. The Green and alternative movements and the left wing of the SPD are not the only ones to have conflicting views of the Soviet Union. Look how many opinion polls in the past few years have depicted the Soviet Union as more peaceable, more friendly and more approachable than the US.

An incredible crossover occurred between French and German public opinion: the latter discovered the virtues of the USSR at the same time as the former lost all its previous faith. The old Federal Republic thus became the only country in Europe in which the Soviet Union was viewed in a favourable light, even though, paradoxically, it was still at its mercy. Anti-American demonstrations were rife; anti-American acts became more and more frequent; anti-Americanism, in general, took the form of a desire for a separation from its culture and television. Conversely, when was the last anti-Soviet demonstration, sabotage, diatribe? The USSR is *persona grata*, much more so than the United States. Against this background, the Federal Republic found it more and more difficult to resist the Sirens singing in the East. The appalling lack of skill on the part of Brezhnev and Gromyko was only just enough to tip the balance, for Kohl's Government, in favour of Pershing and Cruise. Theoretically opposed to the double zero option, they did not manage to resist the pressure of public opinion for long, impressed as it was by the gestures of peace from this seemingly pacifist superpower. Even the triple zero option, that is, the complete removal of any nuclear weapons from Germany, responds to the wishes of a population who detest all nuclear power and adore the Soviets: the Government of Germany is going to need all the help it can get from its allies, particularly France, if it hopes to stand up to this onslaught indefinitely. The feeble protest raised in the Federal Republic by Chernobyl took no one by surprise. The most fervently anti-nuclear country in Europe was the least worried by the first real atomic catastrophe. It must have taken a superhuman dose of affection for the Ukrainians and the Soviets. What would have been the reaction if the Three Mile Island catastrophe had occurred 1,000 miles from Frankfurt?

This love for the Soviets is not just the prerogative of young left-wingers. It affects everyone: politicians, who see in it a potential *rapprochement* with the East; bankers, who view the USSR as a sure bet, and are preparing long-term loans on gold reserves and raw materials; businessmen, who appreciate this particular client's seriousness, habits and ways of working; intellectuals, who have always been more interested in the old Russia than in the exoticism of America; journalists, artists and writers; political refugees, their bitterness dissipated, who now look towards the East more readily than towards the West.

This strange affection even dates back to the time of Brezhnev, Andropov and Chernenko, a time when the Soviet Union was governed by living corpses. Hardly surprising, then, that the charm of the Gorbachevs wins over so many people. With an East in which communism has toppled, anything is possible. How far will Germany go, under the influence of this spell? What price is it willing to pay? What Germano-Russian accord is looming on the horizon?

The Berlin Wall did not protect the East from the West, but the West from the East. With its demise, the scenario was obvious: some tens of thousands of additional refugees rushed headlong into the Federal Republic, but not the millions that did so in the sixties when Khrushchev was deciding on its construction. How many of them, unable to keep up with the demands of Western productivity, will prefer, in the long run, to return to the East? At this moment in time, the German horse has bolted; unity has been achieved; fantasies are let loose and Germany has quietly succumbed to Finlandization: no fanfare of trumpets, no drama and no trauma.

Faced with this trend in history, it is obvious that the West has long been protected by Soviet diplomatic paralysis. A fluid diplomacy changes the game completely, alters the rules, and shifts the goal posts. In spite of all the economic and political setbacks the Soviet

Union has experienced, it still has a strong hand to play, thanks to *perestroika*.

Notes

1 *Mehr rot als tot*: traditional slogan of German minorities.
2 '*Drang nach Osten*': 'March to the East', the key principle of Prussian policy in the nineteenth century.

4

A Second Maginot Line

In this game, France paradoxically plays a major part, much more so, in fact, than is warranted by its economic power and political influence. Thanks to the miracle of its independent striking force, it is once again a great military power, and therefore a real participant. However, lacking a sufficient economic base, this trump card is becoming less important every day. Not because it is technically obsolete, but because it is strategically absurd. The Maginot complex has struck again. Through one of history's classic tricks, the Maginot line's chief adversary, General de Gaulle, serves as guarantor and point of reference for this new Maginot line, which could be defined as a national sanctuary, protected by France's nuclear defence force. It exhibits the same perverse effects as it did between the wars: the illusion of security gives rise to a doctrine of conformism, and that, in its turn, to a refusal to face up to any changes taking place. Past advantages lead to present complacency and future risk. Under the illusory protection of this Maginot line, France is happy to permit this drift of Germany: there is no attempt to halt it by announcing that Hamburg equals Strasbourg and that therefore this sanctuary begins at the eastern border of West Germany. Twenty years ago, Germany would have laughed at this derisory protection, so sure was it of the strength of the US nuclear umbrella; it would have desired it ten years ago, at the time of the first indications of the disassociation with the US. But does it really want it now, or would it be afraid of compromising its return to the centre, to the position of equidistance which it finds so profitable? Even with an equally crucial revision of strategy, France cannot be sure of halting the course of German history; but without such a revision, it will never be able to prevent it. France has four or five years to play this final card; after that the game is over.

Nuclear Blackmail of the Strong by the Weak: An Idea Doomed to Failure

The independent striking force is supposed to deter an adversary from attacking France, just as the Maginot line was supposed to dissuade Germany from the very idea of an invasion. Army chiefs love such peaceful weapons. It is to be hoped that this second Maginot line will at least be more efficient than the first, but if France is over protected, it risks being isolated from a fluid, changing Europe. Have we not already heard certain strategists explaining that France could avoid participation in a European conflict, like some sort of democratic Albania?

This doctrine has not changed in twenty years: it still advocates dissuasion of the strong by the weak. It is based on a very simple concept: by attacking a weak country, a strong country risks such enormous damage that it will decide that victory is not worth the price. For example, the weighing up of the destruction of Leningrad and Moscow as against the total annihilation of France. In this black comedy, there can be no real winners, and therefore no one can afford to run the risk of conflict. This theory flourished at a time when nuclear arms were fairly crude. Witness the anti-city bombs: these were very imprecise and were designed for civilian targets. Such was the nuclear arsenal: a heritage of the great bombardments of the last war, and intended to terrify the populace rather than to destroy any military bases. However, the background has changed and the theory, as ever, refuses to accept the fact.

When the striking force was first initiated, no one envisaged anything other than a nuclear conflict and, bearing in mind the extent of technical progress, anything other than civilian targets. Conventional warfare consisted, hypothetically, of an exchange of fire between advanced sentinels, as in the scattered military engagements of the seventeenth century; nuclear tactics hardly existed; an extreme escalation seemed inevitable. However, all that was to disappear, overtaken by the progress in military hardware. Long-range nuclear weapons have become more precise, more accurate, more controlled. They can attack single military targets 'cleanly', according to a military jargon that is at once cynical and naive; in this way, a few Soviet missiles could completely destroy the Albion plateau, without killing the shepherds in surrounding areas. Tactical weapons have been refined and now guarantee a complete continuity between the most powerful nuclear weapons and conventional arms. 'Smart' weapons have been created, the use of which, although not as such nuclear, has something in common with tactical weapons. Finally, with the advent of the neutron bomb, there arose a system which relied on defence, whereas hitherto the atom bomb had been synonymous with attack and apocalypse. Designed to destroy people, but to leave buildings intact, this weapon provoked a moral outrage, as if it were better, all things considered, to indiscriminately annihilate soldiers, their surroundings and all the neighbouring areas.

Against such a background of technical refinement, one can imagine a whole range of conflicts, of which massive nuclear attack appears to be the least likely. Since traditional warfare has again become possible, atomic war now seems almost out of the question. And it is precisely this demise which paves the way for new military confrontations. It is an impossible paradox that nuclear arms prevented war and that their removal will open up the possibility again.

The present situation has nothing in common with that of the sixties. Doubtless, the possession of nuclear weapons discourages others from using them, just as the Maginot line convinced the Germans of the futility of a frontal attack although it did not actually prevent them from declaring war. The choice used to be one of geography: the Ardennes or Belgium; now it is technological, with the advent of new conventional weapons. But once nuclear weapons have been rendered useless, relationships between traditional forces again become important. And in that context, the weak can no longer blackmail the strong. Gone is the concept of Shakespearian mutual annihilation, as personified by General de Gaulle who, in reply to a threatening Soviet ambassador, growled: 'In that case, Mr Ambassador, we shall all die together.' Overtaken by the evolution of technology, nuclear blackmail of the strong by the weak demands an excess of Nietzscheanism on the part of the relevant head of state. He has to prove his determination to engage his nuclear arsenal in the course of traditional combat, in order to prevent conventional forces from regaining supremacy. Was not François Mitterand's message just that, when he declared, 'I *am* the deterrent'? The less effective the deterrent, the more impressive must the supporters of détente seem to be. When it is completely redundant, their determination must achieve heroic proportions. The striking force is not technologically out of date, but the theory behind its employment most definitely is. In this game, the most theoretical of all, since there can be no proof one way or the other, outdated thinking is more dangerous than outdated technology. It is possible to gauge the first, but not the second.

Does Sanctuary Actually Exist?

An all-or-nothing philosophy, such as the weak blackmailing the strong, clearly does not allow for any compromise. It must aim straight for the heart of the matter, in this case, for a national sanctuary. This is what led to a definition of the nuclear defence zone that was unbelievably restrictive right from the start: a zone consisting of national territory alone. Military technology was thus, in a strange way, to carry de Gaulle to the very limits of his nationalism: France became a purely geographic entity all over again, frontiers became a physical concept, and national interest focused exclusively on the desire to resist invasion. It was a strange alchemical mixture, blending nuclear advances with a concept of the nation that was as old as the hills. With such a culture medium, it was inevitable that some totally absurd ideas would surface. Take, for example, Ailleret's theory of 'blanket defence', in which sanctuary was such a particular notion that no special relation or alliance was held to exist, and protection against American attack was thus as necessary as against Soviet aggression. France was a strategic island and its striking force was supposed to immunize it against the outside world. Looked at that way, the presence of the Red Army at the entrance to the Bridge of Kiel must have seemed insignificant, as long as it was not permitted to cross over!

In fact, the use of this blanket defence theory was facilitated by the fact that France benefited from US nuclear protection. Sheltered by the strength of the Americans, there was a great temptation to act out the role of absolute national independence. Protected in this way, France reaped the rewards of its apparent autonomy. Nevertheless, this attitude ultimately involved solidarity with the US in the event of real danger, and General de Gaulle never let the Americans down in any serious circumstances. Surely he was the most reliable of the heads of state during the Berlin and Cuba crises of 1961 and 1962?

But if the background concerns were Atlantic, foreground concerns were most definitely nationalistic.

This ridiculous isolationism has clearly failed: it was always full of contradictions, even at the time of General de Gaulle, with his insistence on France playing a major role in world politics. How could a country which by its own admission was ready to shut itself away, like a democratic Albania, truthfully claim to be a great diplomatic power? Epigones might believe it, but not their master. And so to the replacing of the idea of sanctuary by that of 'vital interest'. France declares itself willing to engage its strategic nuclear forces as soon as a vital interest is at stake. But where do France's vital interests begin? In Hamburg? In the event of an attack on Greece? No one knows and no one must know. The imprecision of the concept is explained away by claiming that mystery is a necessary key to deterrence. The Nietzschean halo which surrounds the subject of nuclear arms has made possible this theoretical volte-face: that a kind of demigod will take a decision on the annihilation of his country, according to factors to which he alone is privy. What an amazing power the atom bomb has, that it allows a veil of secrecy to cloud the most fundamental action of the President of the Republic, while democracy demands total openness with regard to everything else, whether it be trifling or essential!

The policy of vital interest, then, has reigned supreme over French strategic thinking for twenty years. Freed from the debris of time, it is evident that it involves East–West confrontation; relieved of the burden of Ailleret's naivety, it is obviously associated with the fate of Germany, and pin-pointed on a map, it will be put into action at the slightest hint of a battle in Germany. But such common-sense is not all. The idea of indissoluble links between France and Germany is contained in remarks which move from the implicit to the explicit. The France of Valéry Giscard d'Estaing, preoccupied with the 'front-line battle'; the reopening of Franco-German military relations in François Mitterand's first term of office; Jacques Chirac's affirmation that 'Germany's battle will be France's battle': these were all milestones along this particular road – not always easily discernible. That French conventional forces will intervene in the event of an attack against Germany is obvious. That tactical nuclear forces will be used as a final warning, following official guidelines, is certain. That France will employ its striking force to defend Germany, and that the former's area of sanctuary includes the latter: nothing could be more sure. French strategists will not allow for deployment of atomic weapons on a specific boundary: they reject the idea of automatic response, in favour of protecting the President's freedom to act. But why does this go for Germany, and not for France? Why should Hamburg fall victim to such flexibility and not Strasbourg? Is it because Germany is regarded as an allied territory, whereas France's territory is sacred? What kind of strategic future does Europe have, as long as each member state believes itself to be more sacred than the others? A state cannot be satisfied with such fickle protection. Germany might feel that it was only hypothetically defended; in one scenario the defence might be genuine; in another it would not. One does not build up an alliance nor an institutional *rapprochement* in the dark. Given little assurance of safety by France, and even less by America, Germany has good reason to guarantee its own security by means of a balanced centre politics. In this great game, France holds an ace, which is the extension of its nuclear guarantee to Germany: but since the desire to show it off is matched only by reluctance to actually use it, since France has only half-heartedly explored its possibilities, she will end up losing it: the day when she finally gets around to playing it, the game might already be over.

A Window of Invulnerability

Any theoretical debate on the subject must presuppose that this defensive weapon is still in full working order. The official line certainly claims as much: everything is working, on schedule and generally hunky-dory and the striking force is gaining in credibility each year. Sceptics are more inclined to look at more negative aspects: aerial forces have no hope of penetrating enemy defences and the Albion plateau is at the mercy of preventive attacks. Nuclear submarines are alone in retaining their usefulness and even they will lose their advantage on the day that 'sniffer planes', this time for real, succeed in locating them. These sceptics are almost certainly wrong in the short term, but right in the long term. At the moment, with the build-up of Albion missiles and the proliferation of nuclear warheads on every submarine, France is enjoying a 'window of invulnerability'; for a few years nuclear arms will be at their zenith. But in technological terms this game is twenty years ahead of its time, and so is going too fast for the French. France's only option is to devote the bulk of its defence budget to nuclear weapons, thus scuppering the illusion that France is a superpower, able to retain its striking force along with both a conventional army and a capacity for overseas intervention. Such drastic measures can only come about in a European context, since it alone provides a basis for sharing out resources and responsibilities. However, even in this area there is a need for a clarification of French nuclear thinking. Europe's military capability cannot be divided into a nuclear arsenal designed exclusively for the defence of France, and the remaining conventional arsenal for the other countries. One cannot treat 'God's people' as animals. How could France possibly imagine that its partners could accept such a prioritizing of weapons, and therefore of risks?

History never retraces its steps. The drift on the part of Germany is intensifying debate but the current credibility of French nuclear capability is such that it can provide an effective answer. Tomorrow, it will be too late, and yet in the meantime, the French are being lulled by the reassuring comfort of political consensus.

The Subtle Charm of Consensus Politics

The French are so astonished by their consensus of defence, that they treat it like a precious object: they admire it, they revere it, but they never call it into question. This has led to a veritable triptych of independence – autonomy – indifference; independence as an aim and a source of pride; autonomy as a principle of action; and indifference to others an involuntary consequence of the two. For 20 years all the French political parties have rallied around nuclear arms in the fight to be the best Gaullist, not least among them the communists, strong supporters of the all-or-nothing doctrine and Ailleret's defence theory. This fact alone ought to lead us to investigate the Soviets' real feelings regarding the French nuclear capability. Why should French-style independence really worry a country which is in favour of the German drift? The communist benches exhibit the most archaic, Maurrassian fringe of Gaullism; they too wish to see the disappearance of tactical weapons and all those forms of measured retaliation that are associated with a minimum of Atlantic solidarity. Everyone else more or less endorses the official line with all its ambiguities and woolliness of thinking.

This consensus clearly has its virtues. In the first place, there is a noticeable absence of pacificism; neither civil nor military use of atomic reaction have suffered any oral objection and public opinion has allowed the authorities free rein in these areas. Secondly, the national versus international debate, which between Briand and the European Defence Community was constantly rocking the boat, has largely disappeared. And lastly it is now possible to undertake long-term projects without day-to-day political quarrels getting in the way. But conversely, this unanimity of opinion can act as a straitjacket. No one questions the validity of the theory; no one dare contest the premisses on which it is based, no one has the courage to raise a voice against it. Like hushed believers before the altar, politicians fall silent as they approach the tabernacle that consensus represents. France exhaustively discusses 1992 and its ramifications but ignores the strategic aspect of Europe out of a fear of its taboos. Germany might be shifting, but at least there is plenty of debate on the subject: strategic issues raised fill the front pages of the newspapers and the countdown of missiles is as familiar as the football results. In France, strategic thinking remains an academic matter, and an attitude of *laissez faire* allows the people in charge to leave any decision on what is good or bad, on what is sound or unsound thinking, to that god, the President of the Republic. The Maginot syndrome strikes again. To put nuclear force into question nowadays is as grave a sin as contesting the merits of the Line was previously. Moreover, there is no Colonel de Gaulle to lambast politicians, civil servants and the establishment generally, although in any case, it is probable that politicians and the army would nowadays be less inclined to accept such liberties from one of their most brilliant subjects.

Budgetary constraints have never served peaceful ends. France has a military budget comparable, as a percentage of its gross national product, to that of European countries, and therefore considerably lower than that of the US. And yet, until now, it has managed to maintain, in addition to its nuclear forces, an enormous territorial army based on conscription, a seemingly adequate conventional capability, a passable navy and a capacity for overseas engagement shown in all its glory at the time of Kolwezi's surprise attack. Never mind if the paint is peeling in the barracks, if there are not sufficient spare parts, if tanks are grinding to a halt, if aeroplanes are unable to increase their missions through want of fuel, if even an intervention in Chad is enough to weigh heavily on the budget; overall, we are presented with a picture that is impressive enough not to warrant closer inspection, under the sedative effect of national unity. But illusions do not last forever, and at some point we will be forced to tackle the subject properly through the mere weight of facts and figures. Perhaps then the area of consensus will finally crumble.

However, for the moment it will continue to act as a screen for military corporatism. Is it any coincidence that the French nuclear armoury is made up of three components which correspond to the three armed forces: land, sea and air? That their commanding officers obey the hierarchical system of each of these forces? And that there have been no technical advances which have favoured one of these forces over the others? The two superpowers must presumably have had the same problem with their military bodies, which led to this idea of three component armies, but France does not really have the means to construct a scaled-down model of the defence systems of these two countries. It takes a good helping of strategic double talk, thinly disguised by a layer of common-sense (along the lines of not putting all one's eggs in one basket), to cover up such a capitulation to military corporatism. If the armed forces were managed according to the principles of free enterprise, it would be inconceivable for a technical and strategic evolution such as the invention of nuclear weapons not to have completely overturned internal structures and organization.

Inertia knows no bounds when national consensus and military corporate logic bear each other out, provided that the books can still be balanced. Who can we expect to take the initiative, after all? Politicians have more to lose than to gain by placing themselves beyond the consensus. The military lobby just about manages to obtain its present objectives, so why should it want to rock the boat? Civil engineers do not yet have recourse to the incontrovertible argument of lack of funds. The media would hardly be interested in such an un-newsworthy subject. The public would be reluctant to sacrifice the peace of mind afforded it over the years by this consensus. Do we then have to rely on the strategic thinking of an enlightened despotism? In strategic terms, the year 2000 is over and done with; the years 2010 and 2020 are the ones currently under discussion; in other words, French defence after the striking force has disappeared. Who has the imagination and dynamism for such long-term thinking? Politicians do not think so far ahead; corporations do, sure of their own immortality. But why should they lay plans which may well be doomed to failure? The tragedy of consensus is that it makes people careless in the short term and blind to long-term consequences.

A Collective Myopia

France believes that it is making the most of the cards it holds by apeing the superpowers. It likes to think of its own armed forces as being a scaled-down version of theirs. The French army thus acquired, albeit ten or twenty years late, atomic and hydrogen bombs as well as tactical weapons, and is now thinking in terms of anti-missile rockets, even of a space shield. In a situation where imitation governs technology, where technology determines strategy, and where strategic thinking reinforces existing structures, the status quo is assured. Weapon designers have, therefore, quite naturally, produced short-range tactical weapons such as the Pluton, with an effective range of around 100 miles, and the Hades, with a range of 200 miles. The superpowers already possessed them, the technology existed and funds were available. In short there were plenty of excuses to dispense with the need for strategic thinking. As soon as these weapons were ready for use, strategists found themselves totally restricted: how could one reconcile the deployment of tactical weapons, of limited power and range, with the concept of all or nothing according to which the weak can dissuade the strong? In order to maintain the apparent coherence of the theory, it became necessary to invent the idea of the 'final warning': the tactical firing of a missile – the first nuclear strike – would demonstrate the President's determination to stop at nothing and, if necessary, engage his strategic forces.

There you have the perverse result of mimesis: for the Soviets and the Americans, tactical arms are designed for use on the battlefield, whilst for the French they have become little more than a symbol, since the nuclear blackmail theory does not allow for the idea of conflict nor, therefore, the fact of battle. Did anyone actually think this through before deciding to build them? Evidently not. Weapons designers, preoccupied with technical considerations, think no more about the possible uses for their weapons than engineers think about commercial outlets for their products.

The neutron bomb, on the other hand, could be a highly important accession to the armoury of a medium-sized nuclear state. It would reinforce the country's traditional defence system, make less likely the use of strategic weapons and reassure conventional military forces. Relatively cheap and simple, it would provide the best return in terms of both cost and efficiency. But the US turned against it, and so France decided not to manufacture it. And yet the motivating circumstances behind both decisions had nothing in common. For the Americans, it would serve only to accentuate their military presence in Europe at the very moment when they are gingerly trying to pull out. For France it would mean an increased obligation to defend Germany. No matter. In corporatist logic, strategy is not born of politics, it is a by-product of technology.

The space revolution is itself experiencing problems of integration with respect to French strategic planning. It is too easy to devalue the system by continually emphasizing the naivety exhibited by President Reagan on the subject of Star Wars. It is, of course, true that even a hermetic shield could never completely isolate any territory; that Star Wars will never manage to eliminate nuclear weapons, and that since its main aim is to protect the US, it will never be able to serve as an effective protection for Europe. One might think that the realization of this stark truth is significant enough in itself, but there are other powerful arguments. Let us look at some of them.

First Point: Space Weapons

Having for once applied the best principles of Colbertism on a European scale, Europeans now have considerable expertise in space matters. And yet they are still reluctant to graduate from a civil programme to one involving military technology. Inability or ineptitude? Definitely not. The traditional method of organizing personnel into land, sea and air forces would not countenance the placing of solid military institutions at the disposal of space politics. Information satellites have been long in coming, even though their importance exceeds that of outdated armoured divisions. But space anti-missile weapons do not fall within established budgetary categories, and so raise the question of whose responsibility they are. In military terms, space not being a natural extension of the atmosphere, the air force cannot lay claim to space weapons. Being no one's responsibility, they are not accorded priority status. In twenty years' time the construction of space military bases will be essential, and yet they are only a peripheral part of the French military programme. Instead of the classic phenomenon whereby civil use of any advance in technology comes as a by-product of military design, we have a situation in which European policy on space development exploits, from time to time, the results of civil enterprise. And yet, leaving aside its military potential, space technology has major possibilities for Europe. For instance, although Germany is excluded from nuclear research by the treaty of 1955, there is nothing to prevent it developing a space policy. In this field it could once again have the freedom of manoeuvre normally enjoyed by a great power. Yet another trump card is being thrown away.

Second Point: Military Spending

The mimicry of superpower policy comes up against financial limits. In order to maintain the illusion, the amount of military spending would have to be increased to the detriment of education and welfare programmes. The US and the Soviet Union are beginning to run out of steam, but France stubbornly imagines it can maintain the level of its funding of nuclear and conventional arms, as well as land, sea and air forces and a comprehensive body of specialized professionals. Out of the question. Just as unlikely is the hope of an economic revival suddenly boosting spending power. Perhaps France's partners, in particular Germany, could share the financing of a nuclear force, but in that case it would have to be designed as much for German security as for French. One answer might be the establishment of an order of priorities between nuclear power, overseas forces and a conventional land army. Clearly this could lead to real economies. For example, logistics and organization envisage the calling up of numerous divisions, whereas, as everyone knows, the nature of a future conflict would preclude such a process. And what about the amount spent on the present system of military service which provides the army with none of the skills needed in modern warfare and whose only virtue lies in keeping 600,000 young men out of the unemployment statistics? And is the maintenance of armoured divisions really justifiable, seeing that tank warfare is hardly a likely scenario in the year 2000? And why does the army insist on patrolling the whole country as though there were really the slightest possibility that attack could come from all directions at once? Why, in short, do structures, personnel and materials match in scale those used in the two world wars, as if the nuclear age had never arrived? The army is to modern defence policy what the steel industry is to an open economy, but even if one ignores running costs and budgetary deficits, a thorough restructuring is not going to take place overnight. And where will these economies come from? From those areas with limited personnel which lend themselves to blackmail by military institutions. From the nuclear programme, in which decisions are made generally on the basis of economy and which has been surreptitiously pruned. From the land army, through postponed investment rather than through a salutary reorganization of the existing system. When the state has difficulty with its priorities, it makes indiscriminate cut-backs. Defence policy is disintegrating under these perpetual excuses, these endless prevarications, this avoidance of decision-making. Shortsightedness rules through fear of the institutions and the surgeon's knife.

Third Point: Obsolescence

Technical obsolescence is a very real threat. Not in the short, or even the medium term. Since its capability was massively increased by the installation of multi-headed rockets in submarines, the French striking force affords, albeit for a short period of time, some measure of invulnerability. But looking further ahead, the risk is clear. The air force is at the mercy of increasingly sophisticated defence systems. The validity of the missiles situated on the Albion platform is threatened by the existence of Soviet defensive weapons. It is only a question of time before the presence of submarines can be detected. The superpowers face the same problem, of course, but in their case the risk is lessened by the sheer number and diversity of the weapons at their disposal. After all, the more weapons there are, the less chance there is of all of them being destroyed. The prospect of future obsolescence, however real it may be, should not have an inhibiting effect. On the contrary it should provide a context for action, just as, to a writer, the inevitability of death is not simply a limit, but a stimulus to creativity. If, in twenty years' time, the advantages we currently hold will have disappeared, all the more reason to use them to full effect now and obtain maximum political gain from the existence of our nuclear force. The defence of Europe is the 'ultima ratio', and in this respect, Germany is obviously pivotal. Current efforts to avoid obsolescence necessarily presuppose certain priorities. To spread one's energies in the attempt to remain ahead in every domain is to risk being overtaken on all fronts. It is up to the experts to identify profitable avenues of development, and the politicians to choose between them. An indiscriminate allocation of inadequate funds is disastrous.

Fourth Point: The Overseas Question

This may seem iconoclastic: the prioritizing of nuclear weaponry will make it increasingly difficult to sustain a high quality overseas intervention force. What will happen to the overseas territories if France loses its capacity to defend them? Under the pressure of local forces, harassed by internal dissent, a target of the old anti-colonialist slogans, they will soon become a useless burden on the mother country. France does not have the means to be, at one and the same time, a great European power and a minor colonial power; a choice has to be made. To leave this choice until it is too late is not to choose at all and to prejudice the chances of achieving success in either direction. If France wishes to preserve its European strategy, it will have to resign itself to losing its overseas territories, however distant the prospect may yet be, and experience has shown that it is never too early to prepare the ground for decolonization. Looked at from this angle, it is clear that naval deployment needs to be less ambitious: all that is needed is a number of armed coasters to intercept drug smugglers; tugs to clear channels in the event of an accident, and a few show vessels for the purpose of official reviews, nothing more. The bulk of available funds would be concentrated on nuclear submarines. To put it in crudely simplistic terms: the loss of Polynesia or an effective French participation in the defence of Europe – which is it to be?

Fifth Point: Nuclear and Conventional Weapons

The use of conventional forces will serve only as a threat of things to come. If the employment of nuclear weapons constitutes a last resort, then the engagement of conventional arms functions as an initial warning. It may well be that current circumstances – increasing sophistication of weapons, transformed ideologies and revised outlook – are combining to increase the likelihood of conventional conflicts which do not necessarily spill over into nuclear war, but France could only join the conventional arms race at the expense of its nuclear programme. It is up to those countries which do not possess a nuclear capacity to fulfil this role and develop top-quality conventional forces – the prime example being Germany. France's role is to maintain its strength in Germany and to build up a reserve force in the East. This will act as a guarantee of France's willingness to involve its nuclear capability, in the same way as American GIs in Germany were seen as an assurance of US intervention. Any further expense on France's part is futile. It will eventually have to accept the logical consequence of the deification of its striking force, that is, the subordination to it of all other military departments. Its nuclear programme is grafted onto a traditional and out-moded system of defence, and after a quarter of a century it is high time to put the army on a sounder footing. The whole defensive theory must be revised, with nuclear weaponry as the number one priority and everything else subordinate to its needs. Anything which detracts from this must be jettisoned.

Sixth Point: Partial Disarmament

All countries would benefit from a pause in the arms race. The Soviets, because without it they lose all hope of improving their economic situation; the Americans, because they must resolve the problem of the balance of payments deficit; the French, because if they do not urgently prioritize their means and objectives, they are likely to have to drop out of the race altogether – which would be disastrous. The disarmament talks between the two superpowers have unleashed a spate of worries and delusions in France. The worry is that the French nuclear striking force may be lost in the melting pot of Western arms reductions. A needless worry, this, since no one can force the French to comply: the US has neither the means nor the inclination to do so, the Soviets even less. All that is needed is the determination to resist. The delusion is that, by a kind of osmosis, France's strategic capability will increase in inverse proportion to the reduction of arms by the great powers. This is likely to be particularly damaging because, convinced that their deterrent is constantly being strengthened, politicians will be even less likely to make painful decisions, impose drastic cuts, or embark on an agonizing struggle with intellectual heavyweights and corporate bureaucracies. And yet partial disarmament would offer France a wonderful opportunity, provided that the pause in the arms race was viewed positively as offering the means to increase the credibility and strategic value of its striking force, rather than as a necessary evil, imposed by outside circumstances.

Seventh Point: Striking Force as Strategy

Last but not least: the striking force is not a military weapon, it is a strategic and diplomatic tool. In peace-time this is true of all arms, especially nuclear weapons, which are, by their very nature, a means of preventing war. How could they possibly be instruments of war, when war with them is unthinkable? And of course no one plans for the unthinkable. Maybe we are too prone to forget this truism in the midst of a nuclear strategy that resembles a game of 'battleships' for adults. In such a situation it is considered vital to play up the efficacy of the striking force in order to obtain maximum political benefit from the possession of it. The temptation is to go too far in this direction – beyond what is technically credible, whereas French philosophy on deterrence and on vital French interests normally errs on the side of circumspection. The characteristic of the best strategists is their ability to work wonders with the few cards they hold. De Gaulle, at the height of his power, could make Roosevelt back off with a few grunts of displeasure. Imagine such a figure today, determined to use the possession of the striking force as a bargaining counter in the restructuring of Europe: bluff, psychodrama, threats, cynicism – all would come into play. The present value of the striking force is as a lever to ensure American participation. What a superb card for a player accustomed to winning games with poor hands!

Finlandization or Leverage?

The French striking force has two possible lines of development. It can be used to accelerate the Finlandization of Europe, the shifting of German allegiance and the construction of the communal Europe that the Soviets are so keen on (because it would exclude America). Or else it can be used as a lever, in any European conflict, to oblige the Americans to intervene – except in the unlikely event that the latter had, in the meantime, become a regional power indifferent to the use of nuclear arms anywhere in the world. That this alternative is not pure fantasy is evident from the double-edged talks going on between the Soviet Union and France. On the one hand it is a conspiratorial wink from one nuclear power to another, with a touch of flattery ('We are the only two nuclear powers in Europe'), the message, in this case, being addressed to the national sanctuary element in French thinking. Proof, if one thinks about it, of the Soviet fondness for this particular doctrine: desiring influence without war, they would never opt for the concept of blackmail of the strong by the weak. On the other hand, it is a move to add French forces to the tally of the Western arsenal in order to oblige the Americans to increase their pressure on France to reduce its atomic stockpile along with its general disarmament programme. If France declined, the Americans would be forced to undertake these reductions itself. In that case the Soviets would work on the assumption that French forces would be used as the advanced nuclear force of the West, necessarily linking with US strategic forces. At the time when the Kremlin was governed by living corpses, this double message was couched in the unsubtle terms of the stick and the carrot: the carrot of friendship to persuade France to persevere with the myth of national sanctuary, and the stick of the arms tally to dissuade them from joining America in underwriting the Atlantic Alliance. With Gorbachev the message is rather more ambivalent: he has obviously lost much of his cynical Manichaeanism. But despite increasingly sophisticated rhetoric, the double message remains. To such an extent that it really constitutes a very clear definition of the options confronting France, according to the old military principle by which one's choice of strategy is based on the enemy's analysis of one's resources.

The leverage strategy would give France the status of a world power, whereas the national sanctuary option would allow it no more authority than that of any regional power. What is at stake today? The dominant impression given by the Soviets before Gorbachev was that, in the long term, they sought victory without war, or at least through a war which did not involve nuclear force. Nowadays they seem to be seeking *influence* without recourse to war. Difficult to sustain as long as any conflict was seen as presenting an immediate risk of nuclear confrontation, this strategy becomes more credible as advances in technology make more likely the recurrence of conventional armed conflicts. Anything which eliminates 'atomic poker' favours the Soviets. The all-or-nothing philosophy of French deterrent strategy allows for partial confrontations, guerrilla-type attacks and conventionl battles, with the atomic threat always lurking in the background – hence its attraction to the Soviets. If we persevere with the strategy of national sanctuary, there is the risk that it will lead to an isolationist France and a realigned Germany – two sides of the same coin. A situation will thus have been created, ostensibly based on Gaullist principles, but which in fact denies the whole basis of de Gaulle's conception of nuclear strategy. We must remember that in his day there were three major principles: any war would immediately escalate into a nuclear conflict; American superiority guaranteed their participation; sure of American protection, France could use its striking force as an instrument of political autonomy. In this context there was more to be gained from the national sanctuary approach than from any other doctrine. A more Atlantic strategy would have been too close to British defence policy, and what political advantage did Britain gain, at that time, from its possession of the atomic bomb? Mercenaries of the US, the British have been in the strange position of having military power without its resultant political influence. The French, on the other hand, endowed with the convenient ability to forget that they were protected, were able to derive maximum advantage from a striking force which was, at that time, weaker than its British equivalent.

Britain, now a prisoner of its relationship with the US, once again has its hands tied. To put its nuclear capability at the service of Europe would mean re-establishing an association with the US in which it would constantly be forced to seek American authorization for its decisions. It is hardly likely that the US would regard the British use of nuclear weapons as an automatic guarantee of its own intervention, when it has refused to offer such a guarantee to its own intermediary forces.

France, on the other hand, holds the fuse which could set the whole planet ablaze, in that it has the capacity to enforce an American intervention. This is the ace in its hand, and it must be played to full advantage. Any new situation requires new thinking. De Gaulle himself would probably have brought about such a change of direction rather more brusquely than the cautious way in which it has been introduced over the last fifteen years. But that as it may, the philosophy of forced intervention is based on three principles.

In the first place, the striking force obliges the US to bring in its strategic forces. It cannot become a kind of enormous Switzerland, distancing itself from a major thermo-nuclear conflict in Europe. Despite its return to isolationism and its increasing interest in the South and West, it still casts a proprietary eye on Europe. It is possible to imagine the US withdrawing from a conventional conflict on German territory, prepared to sacrifice GIs . . . and their honour. One could not possibly imagine it a passive onlooker in an apocalyptic nuclear confrontation fought over vitrified landscapes. Secondary damage, radioactive clouds and other unimaginable, unthinkable consequences would force it to intervene. It could not remain on the sidelines during such a cataclysm. This is why France, contrary to accepted thinking, could count absolutely on its major ally. It is simply the restatement, taken to the extreme in the nuclear context, of a very old historical principle: peace draws the US towards a policy of isolationism, while war brings it back, against its will, to one of interventionism.

But this vital leverage held by the French loses its validity in the national sanctuary context. The hypothetical situation in which France remained aloof from a European conflict is precisely the scenario in which leverage would not work. Its own isolationism would ensure that of others – particularly America. Any attempt by France to establish a clear distinction between conventional and nuclear warfare, between its own territory and that of its allies, would, in such a context, establish principles inimical to its own interests. Alliances do not operate for the benefit of one country alone. French leverage will work if it is put to the benefit of Western Europe as a whole: the latter is its legitimate field of activity, not the limited confines of the hexagon.

The use of the striking force as a lever to ensure the association of Europe and the US inevitably involves shifting the nuclear frontier from the Rhine to the Elbe. In military terms this would mean the unification of France and Germany. This truism would apply, not only in the event of conventional warfare breaking out, as the Government of Chirac thought; not only in the event of tactical nuclear weapons being fired, as French theory has had it for the last fifteen years; not only in the event of the natural boundary of our vital interests shifting Eastwards. It would apply in all contexts where such serious issues were at stake, without exception or limitation. This is not a novel theory: everyone thinks it, but no one says it out loud. In military terms, the precise enunciation of a strategy is never neutral: once formulated, a rule can never be withdrawn. So why does everyone keep silent on this? People say it is because the President of the Republic must have sufficient room to manoeuvre. But he who has most achieves least. Establishing a defensive line has never meant fighting to the death on that particular strip of land. Withdrawal is always possible; diversionary tactics are a recognized part of military strategy. History is full of these intangible, eminently changeable frontiers. All the more so, then, in the case of lines which have never been defined: militarily uncertain, their strategic value is nil. The establishment of such a zone of French nuclear influence carries no risks, since its boundaries will always be flexible. Rejection of the idea, on the other hand, would mean pushing Germany towards the centre. The revolutionary aspect of having the Elbe as a frontier would not be limited to nuclear strategy. Everything would become accessible: the fusion of conventional forces; the sharing of armaments; the devolution of authority; the unification of the command structure. A whole range of refinements have been imposed on these simple facts. The most detailed version is the Schmidt plan: this envisages a system of specialization according to which nuclear arms would be the responsibility of France, and conventional weapons that of Germany. The latter would, of course, contribute financially to the modernization of the striking force, but overall command would fall to the French because of French possession of the ultimate weapon (nuclear weaponry cannot be shared or delegated). In practical terms, there would be the reactivation of the Western European Union, the setting up of a Franco-German Defence Council, joint military manoeuvres and the first tentative attempts to standardize equipment. But more important than all that, there would have to be a recognition, at the highest political level, that the defence of one's ally is to be regarded as an integral part of the defence of one's country. Europe cannot afford to wait any longer, while Germany drifts and the US sinks into isolationism. Time is running out.

France has the choice and for once seems incapable of deciding. On the one hand there is the Gaullist litany, still surviving after all this time: the cult of national sanctuary; a narrow view of what constitutes vital interests; the naive pleasure of dealing with the Soviet Union as one nuclear power to another; a rejection of nuclear solidarity; total failure to understand how Germany is changing; the cumbersome movement of military institutions and the reluctance to make drastic budgetary cuts – in short, the heavy-footed approach which led to the Maginot Line. On the other hand, the acceptance of long-term obsolescence, the determination to gain maximum advantage from possession of nuclear weaponry, the acceptance of a hierarchy of means and priorities, the tempting possibility of being the last link in the Atlantic chain, the politics of leverage, the extending of the nuclear frontier to the Elbe, and increasing military integration with Germany. On the one hand a conservatism which accelerates the transition from Atlantic balance to continental imbalance. On the other, a last-ditch effort (based on the same principle as Pascal's wager) to block such a transition. On the one hand, the only strategy guaranteed to lose: immobility. On the other, the only valid strategy for a medium-sized state: movement. Of course the choice is not as Manichaean as that: even though freed from the concept of national sanctuary, French strategic policy will never be identical with that of Germany. But a resolute switch to the leverage strategy could be sufficient to deflect history from the route it seems to be inexorably taking, a route leading to a Europe which, beneath a veneer of friendship and reciprocity, sees the steady growth of a Soviet influence at once distant and friendly, remote and attentive, polite and possessive. Unless, of course, the East acts first . . .

5

A Wind of Change in the East?

Complexity has changed sides. The West used to be sophisticated, dynamic and unpredictable; the Soviet Union, simple, dictatorial and eternal. Its objectives seemed immutable: From Old Russia it inherited the determination to extend its frontiers to the warm seas, whilst the schism in China prompted the unlikely development of a containment policy in the East. In short, it was a strange mixture of ancient Russian aspirations combined with the Bolshevik ambition to separate Western Europe from the US. Up till now, both sides seemed to live in separate space–time zones. The West, a vibrant democracy in which demanding consumers were preoccupied with the satisfaction of immediate needs, was the 'warmest' of societies, according to Lévi-Strauss's definition of the word. The East, with its constant bureaucracy, ideological tyranny and institutional immobility, was quite definitely the 'coldest'. In that universe, time had become a variable instrument of strategy. It was to the nuclear age what space was to the age of conventional weapons: deep, heavy, doom-ridden. In the long term, the Soviet Union seemed to be on the winning side, just as, in the past, its steppes, its very immensity, protected Russia from Napoleon and foiled the armies of Hitler. Everything seemed to be obeying some sort of ground plan, in which the inevitable retreat of American GIs and the withdrawal of Germany within itself were brought about by insistent Soviet pressure.

Then came Gorbachev and suddenly everything was again in the melting pot. The Soviet Union has not suddenly become as pure as the driven snow and has not totally relinquished its ambitions, but suddenly hazard and risk seem to have changed sides. Despite its internal upheavals and the continental drift which is separating America from Europe, the West seems now to be the more stable. Its disagreements are all very familiar and kept well in hand. No one rocks the boat. Of course there are forces at work in both the US and Germany challenging accepted strategic thought, but their movement seems controlled, its direction and limits clear to a skilled analyst. This does not apply to the Soviet Union. The sceptical view which claimed that nothing ever happened in the Soviet Union is expressed less and less frequently. Those who harbour optimistic dreams of a communist world which has changed direction so completely as to become a great force for peace reveal the same juvenile naivety that characterized their predecessors when they signed the Stockholm Appeal. Western strategists are disorientated: they cannot get used to a policy of movement on the part of those who, until now, have been so adept at maintaining the status quo. In a word, the Soviet Union has become unpredictable.

What will *perestroika* lead to? What will be the future of the popular democracies? Will internal developments upset strategy? Or will these sudden strategic changes simply provide an excuse for a return to the past? Such questions will determine the nature of Europe's evolution and give pause for thought on the change from an Atlantic balance to a continental imbalance which is currently taking place. The answers to them can be reduced, roughly, to three possible scenarios. First possibility: in an attempt to impose a new liberalism, the world is taken in by the mirage of progress in the Soviet Union, Soviet ambitions are renewed and in the West the continental drift gathers speed. Second possibility: some unpredictable disaster prompts the return of the old order; the brutal effects of such an event would weigh heavily on Western opinion to the extent of slowing the continental drift, without being able to reverse its course. Third possibility: an increased openness on both sides unleashes an irresistible dynamic of change which sweeps away the old order and creates a new Europe from the Atlantic to the Urals. No longer would Europe be a glorified protectorate: its whole ethos would be continental, not Atlantic. Destabilizing factors which had previously favoured the Soviets would be replaced by balancing forces. Of course it is quite possible that none of these three stereotypes will apply exactly. It may well be that the new unpredictability of the Soviet Union will slow the continental drift, without actually reversing it.

Yesterday, Life Was Simple

After 1945, Soviet foreign policy with regard to Europe had only one aim: the domination of the continent by its absorption into a security system controlled by Moscow and the skilful manipulation of economic exchanges, with a view to reinforcing its own hegemony. Hence its obsession with the exclusion of America from Europe and its vacillating attitude towards European unity: hostility, as long as this unity seemed to go hand in hand with a strengthening of the American alliance; approval, whenever the slightest indication of European Gaullism or neutralism was detected. It was the same obsession that prompted the Soviets to play France and Germany off against each other, favouring whichever of them happened, at that moment, to be the most anti-American. It also explained the flattering approval which invariably greeted the slightest impulse towards independence from the US, as exemplified in the 1945 de Gaulle–Stalin agreement, the 1966 'détente, entente and cooperation' accord, the *Ostpolitik* of 1970, and the covert overtures to Germany in the last few years. Finally, it was behind the skilful manipulation of economic exchanges through a disingenuous allocation of contracts.

It is unlikely that the Soviets ever intended to achieve their objectives through war. Initially because they were militarily inferior; later, when they had achieved parity, because of the tremendous risks involved; recently, because there is no need to go to such lengths. Military strength is necessary for maintaining discipline in the people's democracies, whereas a mere show of strength is sufficient to bring the Western democracies to heel. The Soviet Union has always known that it was enough to have a theoretical military supremacy; the divisions and inhibitions within the Atlantic Alliance take care of the rest. War itself becomes unnecessary when you can achieve your ends by bluff, with only a negligible risk of Western European countries attempting to put up belated resistance.

Unlike the French, the Soviets have never been mesmerized by the most radical (because theoretical) concept of nuclear deterrence. They take war seriously and if it ever came about they fully intend to win. They know, too, that in equipping themselves for it they place themselves in a better position to turn things to their own advantage. This is why they developed the idea of 'dynamic stasis' (an eloquent expression if ever there was one) which states that in order to win, all that is needed is to be powerful and do nothing. Immobility is to this strategy what geographical vastness was to the old Russian policy of survival. This reliance on immobile strength ties in perfectly with their aim of dominating without occupying. If the Soviet Union wished to transform the states of Western Europe into brother countries or satellites, total conquest and occupation would be essential. But wishing only to obtain domination without occupation and influence without annexation, it is enough that the shadow of their military might should fall across the countries concerned.

In order to be fully effective, this insidious threat demands a massive superiority in conventional arms and the denuclearization of Europe. With regard to the first point, Soviet thought seems to have evolved considerably: no longer is it content to line up vastly superior numbers of divisions, battalions, tanks and planes; these forces have now been integrated into a strategy of attack based on surprise, swiftness of execution and encirclement. This strategy requires the capacity to apply a numerical superiority of five to one in key battle areas. It runs the serious risk that Western tactical weaponry might disrupt its sophisticated battle plans. The static approach of massive frontal assaults likely, in the course of time, to escalate into nuclear confrontation, is no longer valid. This is why the denuclearization of Europe is so important to the Soviets. The first zero option favoured the dissociation of Europe and America; the second guaranteed it; the triple zero option would remove all risk of nuclear force from the conventional battlefield. Possessing nuclear weaponry, Western Europe could defend itself. Without it, the battle is over before it has begun.

The Soviets have never ceased to urge the withdrawal from Europe of American medium-range nuclear weapons. In 1983 it was only their clumsiness that produced the opposite effect and prompted the deployment of Pershing and Cruise missiles. The old men who reigned in the Kremlin at the time imagined that threats would be sufficient to block the installation of these weapons. Their successors were astute enough to realize that all that was needed to persuade the Americans to take this step was to incorporate it in a give and take context, in this case the double zero option. The cosmetic effect was enough and the package received an enthusiastic reception, as if there really were parity between the US withdrawal, which was irreversible, and the Russian withdrawal, which could be reversed at any moment.

The finesse worked perfectly. Mr Gorbachev obtained through

subtlety and flexibility what his predecessors had never been able to obtain through crude threats. All that remained now was to complete the manoeuvre with the triple zero option, i.e. the elimination of short-range nuclear weapons. In attempting to assess the loss of military power that this option would impose, one discovers that (purely by chance of course!) it would result in the denuclearization of Germany – the only country threatened by the short-range nuclear weapons already in place in Europe. German politicians are, not surprisingly, disinclined to accept this option, but unfortunately they are being placed on the defensive by the pacifist movement which is gaining popularity in Germany. In fact, any reasonable person is right to be appalled at the prospect of a Western Europe totally bereft of nuclear weaponry, apart from France with its increasingly ill-adapted striking force. But there is the risk that what happened in the case of the double option debate will be repeated in discussions on the triple option, namely, that Soviet pressure for disarmament and Western pacifism will mutually reinforce one another.

For thirty years Soviet strategy has been an open book, its aims, preoccupations, tactical blunders and limitations evident to the world. Unsophisticated, it was based on simple action, backed by a simplistic philosophy. Flexibility was not its forte. One only has to look at the way it discreetly played the German card: Moscow has known for fifteen years that by building links with Germany it is luring it away from its association with America. But in spite of the obvious advantages to be gained from such a shift, Moscow always hesitated to push too hard. Fears of past dangers and the possibility that the popular democracies might, in their turn, decide to break free inhibited its diplomatic activity. When Germany was still divided, the attitude of the Soviets was one of calculated bargaining: reunification would entail neutralization. With the advent of Gorbachev the old conventions have been smashed, illustrating again the way in which the risk element has changed sides.

Until recently time had been the key dimension of Soviet strategy. Given the current state of the balance of power, time could only be a major advantage. It enabled the Soviet Union to turn its internal weakness into strategic strength. Internally, it put up with the drawbacks of being a static society: mediocre productivity, an inefficient economy and lack of innovation. On the international level, it used its immobility to maximum effect: Western edginess, instability and moodiness foundered on the rock of Soviet stasis.

Movement entailed risk. Obviously it might produce results more rapidly, but there was also the danger that ground already conquered over the years would be lost. The events of the last few years were not the result of any sudden change of mind on the part of the Soviets. It was simply that, with the increasing liveliness and awareness of their society, the old benefits of immobility could no longer be relied on. An inert society dictates an immobile stance; a society in movement demands strategic innovation. This is why Gorbachev's tactics will never be those of Brezhnev; but that does not mean, necessarily, that his objectives will be any different.

One could, in fact, argue that Gorbachev's policies are particularly well adapted to classical Soviet aspirations. On the one hand, the role of guardian of Europe comes more easily to a power that projects a sympathetic image. On the other, internal economic changes can only have the effect of strengthening links between Western countries. Then again, an apparently cooperative Soviet Union would be more likely to dissociate America from Europe simply through the effect of superpower talks and agreements on disarmament. American *bonhomie*, the naivety of public opinion and a natural tendency towards pacifism make them fall for the first hint of good humour from Moscow. In that case, one might forecast that if *perestroika* succeeds without too much drama and disintegration of the empire, Gorbachev will win his strategic challenge to the West in the process. But on the other hand, can the success of *perestroika* be relied upon? Does the term even have a meaning?

Uncertainty Changes Sides

Scepticism can no longer take the place of analysis in the face of the rumours emerging from the East, and Sovietologists in all fields are in total disarray. Since the time of Brezhnev they have stuck to three principles. Firstly, that the system is condemned to immobility as long as it is impossible to change it without losing something in the process. Secondly, that upheavals are only possible at the periphery of the empire – in the popular democracies, or in the Muslim frontier areas subjected to the pressures of Islam. Thirdly, that, in the event of such eruptions occurring, the only answer would be a repression of any initiative on the part of the Party or the army. The only point on which there is divergence of opinion among the experts is whether the

Party or the military would emerge as the dominant force. For twenty years the Soviet Union behaved according to pattern: an adherence at best to the status quo, at worst to an extreme form of totalitarianism which met any sign of upheaval with extra rigidity. In these circumstances, it is difficult for Sovietologists to understand the recent situation in which initiative has suddenly come from the top. Not from some fortuitous circumstances at grass-roots level, but by imperial decree. Change did not evolve, it was imposed. Liberalism did not insinuate itself into the system, it was ordained. Such a scenario was the least likely, and therefore the least easily comprehended. Who would have thought that the best (and youngest) leader the system has produced would become its principal adversary? The old analysis of enlightened despotism according to which the ruler was enlightened when young, despotic when old and entrenched in power, no longer suffices. Gorbachev seems to transcend such mundane motivations. But why? A belief in democratic principles? One would have to believe in a divine, smiling providence to swallow that. Machiavellianism? Perhaps: in that case *perestroika* has to be seen as a gigantic excuse to overhaul the bureaucratic machinery, while ensuring its continued allegiance to the new master. Penetrating insight? To accept that, one would have to imagine circumstances in which the leader was the only one who understood the extent of the long-term threats to the system. An understanding of the way history was moving? Such an explanation sees Gorbachev as believing he could afford the ravages that reform would undoubtedly cause, content to reap its rewards later.

For the first time since 1956, change is coming from the East. What an extraordinary turnabout! The West seemed for decades to be on the defensive, with capitalism being driven back, democracy threatened and social pressures increasing day by day. The wind of change seemed to blow in only one direction, and that was favourable to communism. Its sphere of influence grew visibly; its military might was beginning to match that of the West; its ideology continued to exert influence within the very heart of the democracies. Who could have foreseen, in the early seventies, that by the end of the decade one would see democracy rejuvenated, capitalism transformed by the injection of morality, the free market being its own moral *raison d'être*, communist parties on the verge of extinction, and Marxism surviving only as a theoretical explanation of the liberal economy. The future has been transformed; doubt has changed sides. As we contemplate the Soviet Union in the throes of *glasnost*, the future seems veiled in uncertainty. Key questions emerge, the answers to which will affect the balance of power in the coming years.

The first question is whether *perestroika* will run out of steam. A sociological movement is like a machine: it uses energy. At the moment this comes from the top, from the leader and the reformist elite which surround him, but changes resulting from such a movement are not likely to be durable. Reformism contains various elements which render it ephemeral: fatigue of the leaders, the attractions of inactivity, the comfortable reassurance of conservatism. Like a rose, it blooms and withers. Knowing this, it is up to the leaders to see that early reforms create a climate in which society as a whole can take over the running. Laws must be instituted to create the kind of self-generating movement associated with the free market and democracy. Rules and codes of conduct must allow for the formation of supple, mobile structures. The transition from right-wing dictatorship to democracy is clear cut: totalitarian structures disappear, melting like sugar in water. But *perestroika* seems to be trying to have its cake and eat it: the sole party must continue, using Leninism as an alibi and guarding its privileges through a skilful manipulation of technocracy. Such a process has no precedent. Gorbachev is clearly at a crossroads: either reformism grinds to a halt and the old system, barely dented, re-establishes itself within the state; or else society will have been given such reformist momentum that it will carry all before it: ideology, the single party system, the entrenchment in power of a hereditary elite – all these obstacles will be overcome. The possibility of a middle way – partial democracy, a watered down totalitarianism – is not really conceivable. It would be an unstable entity. Unless we have underestimated the innovative capacity of history, the Gorbachev era will eventually come down on one side or the other – probably on the side of the status quo, other things being equal. Obviously some developments would survive, and with these we would have to be content.

The second question is whether the popular democracies will survive *perestroika*. Having resisted the communist steam roller, their expectations are different. To the satellite countries, the limited freedoms acquiesced by the Soviets is negligible: what they need is not a reconstitution of basic social structure, but a reversion to democracy. Like other right-wing dictatorships, such as Franco's Spain or Salazar's Portugal, the regime has had to accommodate a rich underground society which is now so highly developed that a restoration of democracy is all that is needed to complete the picture. In Warsaw or Budapest, the man in the street views the liberal initiatives in the Soviet Union as no more than embryonic; he wants far more. This is why *perestroika* is going to be so hard to control in the popular democracies, although failure to introduce it there would be unthinkable and would guarantee trouble. To import it piecemeal from Russia is not possible: the result would be disappointing and would again risk fuelling revolt. To rely on it being carried through by the strength of local pressure might soon result in a questioning of the regime itself (that would of course suit the Poles and the Hungarians very well). Difficult to imagine in the Soviet Union, controlled liberalization seems out of the question in the satellite states. Gorbachev seems to be faced with an insoluble dilemma: in his own country he could always withdraw from rampant liberalism and revert to an enlightened conservatism, imposing it on the people. But what about the other states? Immobility presupposes an iron hand and the readiness to use it; it needs military pressure and a brutality incompatible with the image that the USSR now wishes to project. Mobility, on the other hand, opens Pandora's box. We have already seen history repeating itself in 1956, 1968 and 1980. The least relaxation unleashes the very aspirations which Moscow finds unacceptable: the introduction of pluralism and strategic emancipation. So what now? Confronted with the Hungarian revolution, a reformist Soviet power opted to protect the empire, at the expense of its 'democratic' image. Have priorities really changed? Will liberalization now be placed above the strategic imperative? Can *perestroika* accommodate a show of obstinacy on the part of the popular democracies? Can international détente replace the seemingly impenetrable obsession with defence? Legitimate questions, these, but unrealistic. One feels morally obliged to ask them, but answers to them would inevitably be based on strategic realism. If Mr Gorbachev is forced to resort to force in the event of an uncontrollable development in one of his dependent states, he will lose his freedom of action in the USSR. The idea of being a liberal Tsar at home, and an autocrat elsewhere is not exactly new, but is hardly possible in the case of societies between which real communication has been established. The time is past when mere distance allowed such schizophrenia, and Moscow's reformism might well founder on the streets of Budapest and Krakow.

Third question: will the movement towards liberalization be found to lack strategic viability? Superficially, yes, but the fundamentals of strategy will be unaffected, provided those in power remain in control of the process. On the other hand if they do not retain this control it is hard to imagine that a strategy so completely isolated from surrounding events could possibly survive intact. In democracies international strategy has to be submitted to public approval (as is defence) and is therefore not under the same threat. In changing public opinion, the Soviets have to be prepared to face the consequences. After all, did not public opinion force the withdrawal from Afghanistan in much the same way that the Americans were obliged to withdraw from Vietnam? Does it not demand more economic progress than is compatible with the exigencies of a military budget, which tends to swallow up the product of national effort? Does it not favour disarmament through the natural egotism of the consumer? At best, the leadership will simply have to clothe its traditional policies in more becoming language, as much for the benefit of the Western media as for its own public – when you think of it, do not all our refrains and variations on the theme of Europe, our common dwelling-place, serve the same purpose? At worst, it may have to compromise with its own society, perhaps dropping some element of its international programme. This eventuality may prove to be a major obstacle to *perestroika*. Are the military really likely to accept a halt in the arms race which might well be detrimental to them if the twin policies of Finlandization of Western Europe and access to the warm seas of the East were to fail? There is some risk that democratization may undermine strategy; a mere whiff of strategic failure is enough to undermine democratization.

The more the Soviet Union dreams of economic growth, the more it needs a Central and Western Europe to provide it with goods and technology. The more it turns to a Europe in the form of a discrete protectorate, the greater its chances of economic growth. The more indissolubly linked it becomes with the West, to its own benefit, the more chance it will have of exercising strategic leadership. In theory, *perestroika* is more adapted to the Finlandization of Western Europe than to the obtuse totalitarianism of recent decades, although obviously principles are not as easy to change as the pieces in a game of dominoes. Gorbachev is trying to go in this direction, but it is not clear whether, in doing so, he will improve his overall position. In his relations with the West, it has strengthened his hand, as he finds that he can achieve more through pleasantness than his predecessors did through threats. At home he still has to find the same magic formula.

With so many question marks hanging over the future, anything could happen. How extraordinary to be witnessing such an unpredictable train of events! The experts were beginning to find history boring in its banality. They need not have worried. The show is beginning and the public can choose from at least three possible scenarios, each with a different ending.

The 'Enlightened Despotism' Scenario

For Europeans this is perhaps the most potentially dramatic hypothesis. It has Mr Gorbachev successfully pursuing his vertiginous course over a long period. The essentials of Soviet tradition would be preserved: a single party, a cosmetically orientated economy, total monopoly of power, and, on the strategic level, the policy of dissociating America from Europe, the establishment of a *modus vivendi* between the great powers, and the permanence of the American–Soviet condominium.

There would be some innovation, in that Soviet society would enjoy certain additional freedoms, all granted from above, and therefore all reversible; the economic machinery would incorporate some degree of freedom in the fixing of prices and salaries. Long-term leases would serve as a pretext for the abolition of land collectivization, and, as in China, unrestricted prices would whip up production; the unofficial economy would fill the yawning gulfs which had been opened up and would become simply a valve to compensate for the lack of productivity of the official system; disarmament agreements would allow the transferral of a certain amount of the national product from defence to consumption; recruitment to the establishment would accord rather more importance to competence, rather than loyalty; young technocrats would replace the old party hardliners, and foreign policy would seek appeasement rather than confrontation, attempting to resolve conflicts rather than exacerbate them. In other words, the Soviet Union would become a kind of Hungary on a larger scale, with a new rhetoric and a kind of *fin de siècle* Leninism, ready to pay lip service to the verbal exigencies of the day without making any real concessions.

Such a Soviet Union would certainly win over Western Europe: the

Europeans, led by Germany, would use these innovations as an excuse for a new-style *Drang nach Osten*. They would justify the alacrity with which they met Soviet demands by quoting (with only minimal pangs of conscience) the need to 'encourage' the Soviet process of renovation. Any hitch in *perestroika* could then be attributed to the laggards on the Western side. Western business enterprise would lure the Soviets into running up enormous debts as it purchased Western consumer products, equipment for industry, and up to date technology for the military. For Western economies in search of credit-worthy customers this would come as manna from heaven. The West's natural inclination towards appeasement would be encouraged by Soviet moderation and willingness to cooperate. This, combined with disarmament agreements, would convince Western governments of the folly of over-arming themselves, when it was obvious that the potential adversary was being just as economical with its resources. Germany, flattered by being treated as a valued representative of the Soviet viewpoint in the West, would move further to the East. Finally, the West's in-built desire to establish good East–West relations would lead to closer links with the popular democracies, now more accessible, and with the USSR itself, which would seem far less threatening.

Such evolutions have their own dynamic; every new step taken furnishes a pretext for going further. Extrapolation is not difficult: when one sees the extent to which the West has evolved since the beginning of *Ostpolitik*, despite having to deal with a superannuated and uncooperative Soviet Government, it does not require much imagination to see how much further things would go with a more amenable and pleasant regime in power. Gorbachev has obtained as much from the West in three years as his predecessors in thirty. What will he have accomplished by the year 2000 if the 'benevolent despotism' scenario provides him with the means to exert covert pressure on the West (with all his usual charm of course)? By then, the European protectorate will have been established, the ground having been laid by the American withdrawal, the Eastward movement of Germany, the immobility of France, and the wiles of a Soviet regime sufficiently adroit to be able to avert suspicion, and sufficiently conservative to preserve what it considers the essential elements of traditional strategy.

Such a protectorate would have none of the old excesses. No occupying force, naturally: the knowledge of the military imbalance in favour of the USSR would be enough. No diplomatic supervision: Soviet ambassadors would not deign to act as glorified commissars. No verbal aggression: paeans of peace and cooperation would be the order of the day. No unpleasant authoritarianism in economic relations: credit and supplies would be coming from the West. No communist pressure from within the democracies: in fact, local communist parties would be likely to fall victim to the new détente – despised by Moscow and rejected by Western opinion they would be condemned to wither on the vine. Increasingly, people in the West would look towards Moscow, rather than Washington. The slightest frown would cause a panic; the least ambiguity would be disconcerting. Warsaw would be closer than Tokyo, Budapest than Montreal, Leningrad than Madrid, Kiev than Athens. To see history reverting to form in this way should surprise no one. The situation would still favour enlightened despotism over democracy, because whereas the former could at any time reverse what it had done and withdraw its concessions, the latter would have difficulty in doing so. The former would retain the ulterior motives of a great power, the latter is naturally credulous. The former has a strategy, the latter goes with the tide. The former would retain the advantage of military power as a last resort, the latter would have irretrievably lowered its guard. The former would be planning for the long term, the latter would be obsessed by short-term considerations. In short, the 'enlightened despotism' scenario would be the factor most likely to cause the West to implode. The Atlantic defensive system would crumble, and continental imbalance would insidiously replace the old order. Western Europe, through its own credulity, would yield to continental Europe.

The 'Restoration' Scenario

Did the dismissal of Khrushchev set a precedent? Does Soviet reformism inevitably self-destruct and lead to restoration of the old order? Gorbachev is only too aware of the danger, which is why he hastened to secure himself against a coup d'état from within the communist party. But restoration could have many origins: it could come from a crude military takeover; from a conspiracy within the Party, or from a change of heart on the part of Gorbachev himself (this would probably be the least devastating).

Unthinkable at one time, because of the Army's submissiveness with regard to the Party, a military coup d'état is no longer a purely academic hypothesis, especially since the coup in Poland in 1981. Faced with serious social unrest, the Party can do little. And when the Party crumbles, only one effective institution is left – the Army. In the case of the Soviet Union, the danger seems less likely to come from a social uprising (historically, the country is still in limbo), than from some unforeseen event in a popular democracy. The chain of events is easily imagined: society in one of the most advanced popular democracies decides that *perestroika* is not moving fast enough for it. A popular uprising, subversion from within the system and a massive takeover of the Party itself would take the Soviet Union to the limits of its tolerance. Add to this the risk that the Warsaw Pact might break up, with its members declaring their neutrality and beginning to look towards the West, and you have a situation which the Soviet military would find totally unacceptable. They would lose their lines of communication, their front line and, worse, their credibility. Either they would force the civil authorities to re-establish order, or else they would take over and do it themselves. The consequences for the West would vary enormously according to which of these courses the Army chose to follow. If they decided on the first option, Europeans could deceive themselves and, after their initial emotive reaction, would be content to put relations with the East on ice until more propitious times allowed them to resume forward progress. If they took the second option, the bloody repression needed to bring a wayward satellite state back to heel would prove too much of a shock to Western opinion and would seriously damage East–West relations. Many years would be needed to make up the ground lost. At least the Eastward shift of Germany would stop and Western Europe would turn again to the US for its protection, always provided the latter were still interested.

In comparison, a bureaucratic coup d'état would seem a storm in a teacup. The events of 1964 show the likely sequence of events: an instinctive defensive reaction from the apparat, some discreet plotting, a bending of the law in order to remove the leader and install him in cosseted retirement, and the setting up of a new team which, while promising the return of Leninism, would insidiously set about withdrawing concessions made by the previous regime. This is the immediate danger for Gorbachev and he is clearly doing his best to pre-empt it by having the office of president made virtually sacrosanct by the state: the Party, coming second in the hierarchy, would then find it legally difficult to topple him. If it did come about, the West would of course be indignant, but would be powerless before the hidden forces of history, and years of progress would be lost. Those people seeking to re-establish European identity would do their best to take advantage of the opportunities it afforded, but they would probably lack sufficient resolution and eventually the rot would begin to set in again, although not as rapidly, because of the trauma caused by the events. There would be less confidence because of the disappearance of leaders skilled in manipulating public opinion; less conviction and less enthusiasm, because of a resurgence of traditional anti-Soviet feeling. There would be no turning back the clock.

This would be even more true if Gorbachev himself were to give up his revolution and initiate a return to the old values. Many factors conspire to make him change direction: apparently insurmountable resistance, insoluble economic problems, the danger of loss of control in the popular democracies, or, on a more mundane level, fatigue, the comforting stability of conservatism, the attractions of power for its own sake. Mr Gorbachev would not be the first reformer to bring down the curtain on his own show. Such a turnabout would not be sudden, it would take place insidiously in the day-to-day exercise of power: a few steps backwards, a few deviations, freedoms no sooner granted than withdrawn, awkward people abruptly silenced, the return of forbidden practices, censors rediscovering their old zeal, policemen lapsing into their old habits, judges returning to their former ruthlessness, secret agents again filling lunatic asylums, bureaucrats and party officials breathing a sigh of relief as they felt secure again. In this insidious form, the change would be irresistible. Gorbachev would undo by cunning what he had achieved by courage; it would be a lot easier. In the meantime he would have gained inestimable advantages over the West. The latter would refuse to look at the facts, inventing all kinds of excuses and justifications for this step backward. It would be described as purely rhetorical, provisional, unclear. In its desperation to see *perestroika* succeed the West would blind itself to the truth. Then, as the Cold War set in again, it would pathetically seek to improve East–West relations. Gorbachev has built up such a store of moral credit in the West that it would take a long time for it to fade. With his understanding of Western thought, skilled in playing upon its weaknesses, he would be able to sugar the pill and disguise the true nature of the change. Long after its demise, *perestroika* would continue to fascinate the West. Like a dead star, its surface would be attractive, but its centre would be cold and all flexibility would have gone. The Soviet Union would have perfected the art of winning the international game without changing its own nature. Looked at from this point of view it is clearly more profitable to start liberal and become reactionary than to do it the other way round. Concessions effortlessly gained can be enjoyed in the full knowledge that there is no need to return the compliment. Faced with the credulous West, a Machiavellian Gorbachev would certainly proceed in this way. But if this scenario is possible, then that of the leader hoist with his own petard is equally so: the Secretary General of the Communist Party might well, like Frankenstein, have produced a creation which got out of control.

The 'Peaceful Revolution' Scenario

We cannot be sure that the outlook is bleak. Let us look at the most optimistic scenario. It shows Gorbachev as having set in motion the train of events which would sweep away totalitarianism. Freedom of expression has returned, the various economic groupings have achieved their autonomy, diverse factions have appeared within the party giving something akin to pluralism. The popular democracies have gained more than they dared hope for, without Big Brother being able to stop them. Adherence to the Warsaw Pact has become a meaningless ritual. The fragile balance achieved briefly in 1980 between Polish society and the Party has been re-established. German reunification is complete. The Soviet Union has accepted genuine disarmament agreements on conventional forces, some of which are far from favourable to them. The transfer of goods between East and West has led to the free circulation of people. In short, Europe is rapidly becoming what it should be. This scenario may be inspired by wishful thinking, but if we are considering all the possibilities, we do not have the right to dismiss it. For it to come about certain preconditions would have to be satisfied. The seemingly precarious balance between opposing forces would need to have stabilized: between the permanence of a one party system and the demands of pluralism, between economic openness and central regularization, between a weakened Russia and peripheral provinces eager for autonomy, between a reformist technocracy and a restless military, between a Soviet Union tentatively exercising new found freedoms and popular democracies hastening towards pluralism, between the façade of Soviet solidarity and the movement towards neutrality of the satellite countries. If any one of these conditions were not satisfied, the house of cards would crumble and a more sombre scenario would emerge, redolent of the classical period of Soviet strategy. This is the risk that is inherent in each of these conditions. However, statistically, the most unlikely things can occur. The transition to democracy in Spain exemplifies this: at the time it seemed to have as little chance of success as does the peaceful revolution in the East.

In this hypothetical world scene, German reunification would accelerate changes in the East; the dissociation of the US and Europe would allow a strategic balance to be established between East and West, with the latter, for once, not being exploited because of its gullibility. Eastern economies would constitute a natural expansion zone for EC countries desperate for secure outlets. Middle Europe would rediscover the cultural identity which was as important to its integrity as strategic interests. Western Europe would be replaced (successfully, this time) by the real Europe of yesteryear which stretched from the Atlantic to the Western borders of Russia. The liberalization of the West would be reinforced by its strategic drift, and vice versa. The liberalization process would take its models from the West in introducing pluralism and in increasing efficiency. The strategic drift would be justified by the increasing influence it seemed to be having on the East. As well as obvious scenarios involving the Finlandization of Western Europe, we have to deal, then, with the possibility of a new equilibrium in continental Europe.

It is clearly this optimistic scenario which obsesses the new apostles of 'détente, entente and cooperation', foremost among whom is Hans Dietrich Genscher. Each friendly gesture towards the East fuels the peaceful revolution in Moscow; an uncooperative approach inhibits it. In other words the previous strategy has been stood on its head. The enthusiastic strategists in the West hold themselves responsible for the liberalization of the Soviet Union, to the extent that they would blame themselves if it went wrong. Obsessed with their dream of a new Europe they want to pay for it in advance in order to demonstrate that progress is being made. Hence the ambivalence of the 'peaceful revolution' scenario. On the one hand, it is a hypothesis which should not be discounted, if only because it is by far the most attractive. It is also a theoretical vision which motivates many leaders today. On the other hand, it is a utopian dream which serves as a veneer to other, less utopian, ventures; as such it justifies deviations, faulty decisions and retrograde steps. As an explanatory model, it needs to be handled with care. As a real-life scenario it smacks of the miraculous.

The Remorseless Drift

The 'paradise on earth' scenario can be taken out of our calculations. Its realization would be the icing on the cake, requiring neither tactics nor strategy. It is the other scenarios which constitute the backdrop against which the destiny of Europe will be played out. The new circumstances in the East make the future somewhat less clear than it would otherwise be. American isolationism is increasing with each passing day. The power of the German dynamo is evident, even if ulterior motives – sometimes justified – prompt people to play it down. The evolution in the Soviet Union has, by a strange irony of fate, become unpredictable, but its uncertainties will not be enough to turn back the course of events. On the contrary, in most of the scenarios – enlightened despotism, conspiracy from within – *perestroika* speeds up the process, with the West giving in on essential matters, whilst the East yields only on trifles. Events could of course conspire to slow down the process. There could be a sudden slackening of momentum, or blatant repression, but these will only be momentary hitches. The curve of Western development contains various plateaux: every new stage in East–West relations makes it that much more difficult to draw back. It would need a series of increasingly violent incidents to change European reactions, and in this case, appearance and symbolism would be vital. A 'discreet' restoration of the old order would change nothing; the same process conducted in the full glare of publicity would have the effect of slowing down the continental drift; conspiracy from within would throw the West into confusion, and a bloody confrontation would reverse the train of events. The only thing of real symbolic importance which could counteract the natural tendency of the West towards *rapprochement* with the East would be an outrageous attack on liberty. The Soviets know us well: they will do all in their power to avoid such an extreme situation, which would be so harmful to their interests. If tension arose, it would be the conscious cynicism of a superpower which would motivate them to stay within the bounds of decent behaviour, not ethical considerations.

A graphic representation of the possible outcomes would show the usual curve. At one extreme, with little hope of gaining real advantage, the peaceful revolution would inevitably involve the continued drift of the West in response to Eastern 'liberalism'. At the other end of the curve, a somewhat more likely development: an uncontrollable eruption in the East followed by violent repression and the imposition (covertly or openly) of military control; in this case, the West might well slip back several decades in its attempt to put together the pieces of the European puzzle. Between these two extremes lies the area of greatest probability: the real evolution of the Soviet economy shrouded in mystery; a complex mixture of continuity and innovation, the ingredients of which would vary according to circumstances, accelerating the Western drift when *perestroika* was in favour, slowing it down when the latter was obviously under fire, using it, when necessary, to gloss over repressive measures. The West had been drifting for fifteen years, when the Kremlin was peopled by living corpses. The process will certainly continue under Gorbachev, even if he were to harden his stance. Progress might be uneven, but its direction is sure. A new form of continental drift has been invented: it is strategic, not geological, and under its influence Europe sways and shifts its position.

Many critics would refute these gloomy scenarios, quoting numerous examples calculated to demonstrate the unpredictability of history. Willing themselves to be optimistic, they ignore the significance of behavioural changes. Too respectful of current stability, they speak as though it will continue forever. For fear of undermining the Atlantic edifice, they unrelentingly proclaim lasting American solidarity. In accordance with the inalienable Gaullist convention, they exonerate France from any responsibility. Not wishing to yield to disreputable anti-German impulses, they persist in viewing the Germany of the year 2000 in the same light as that of 1950. This collective prudery is typically French. One only has to read the American press to understand that dissociation already constitutes a major cornerstone of American policy. A perusal of the German press reveals that the East and Central Europe are accorded at least as much importance as the West. How can we make these second-rate philosophers understand that history casts long shadows; that the separation of

Alsace-Lorraine contained within it the seeds of the First World War, as the Treaty of Versailles did those of World War II?

This is the backdrop against which the drama is played out. The repositioning of Europe goes back a long time, as does the process leading to its current geo-political balance. They are the dominant movements. Strategic progress, with all due respect to Marx, is not a by-product of the economy. Nations have their own dynamic, and this is unlikely to be upset by the activities of the free market economy. It is history which is redrafting the map of Europe and 1992, with all its myths, will change nothing. At the very moment when Western Europe, an accidental outcome of World War II, is about to be replaced by continental Europe, 1992 has become the focus of public attention. An admirable project, it will not have the slightest effect on the movement of Europe. Western Europe and continental Europe are not on the same plane; they lie in different historical strata; in short, they are separate in every way. Compared with the major continental developments, the common market is an epiphenomenon. How could it represent the culmination of such fundamental movements? Does it really exist, or is it simply a mirage?

PART II

1992: The Illusion

6

The Apotheosis of the
Free Market

Symbol of the incarnation of the market economy, 1992 stands like a beacon on the horizon, just when Western Europe, the embodiment of this economic system, is beginning to lose its strategic identity. Torn apart by contradictory tensions, can it really be said that Europe exists at all, other than in the rhetoric of politicians? The circles enclosing the major areas of European life are becoming less and less concentric. The first, strategic, is becoming increasingly continental. The second, economic, is limited by the conditions of 1992 to the frontiers of the EC. The third, social and cultural, encompasses the West, the US included, and parts of the other continents; Europe is no more than an important province of it. It is this progressive separation of the three circles which destroys the romantic illusion that 1992 will somehow see the creation of a definitive Europe.

To say this is not to deny the value of 1992; it simply removes some of the glittering veneer from it. In preparing for 1992, today's Europeans see themselves as forging history; they are quite convinced of this, just as, only a few years ago, they were sure that all was lost. Thanks to the ingenuity of Jacques Delors, and to the industry of a few statesmen, foremost amongst whom were François Mitterand and Helmut Kohl, the idea of Europe has re-emerged in European thinking. Whatever the motive force behind this transformation – determination, media mirage or the mysterious strength of public opinion – it is surprising that it should have been based on a double ambiguity. On the one hand, 1992 does not correspond to the strategic drift of the continent, which is a more covert, insidious and powerful movement. On the other hand, 1992, originally a political objective, represents, paradoxically, the victory of society over politics.

In a triumphal gesture to which one must pay tribute, politicians have abdicated in favour of society: this is the significance of the steps leading to the open market. The change which has allowed this European machine to go into action again must be seen as a real revolution in methodology: member states hand over control to the market; they give up the right to take action for themselves; they abandon their traditional inclination to construct, build and organize, confident that disorder will eventually turn to order more quickly than if they interfere. Beneath this unexpected humility lie both sincere hopes and ulterior motives; history will eventually disentangle them and pass its verdict. But in a world which persistently denigrates politics, we must give praise where it is due. Politicians have had the strength to engender a myth, and the courage to eliminate themselves from the action so that the myth may become reality, even if this reality is not enough to stop other, more grave movements.

A Profitable Myth

The world lacked myths; now it has one. After internal revolution, the wooing of the third world, the victory of socialism, the resuscitation of liberalism, and various associated daydreams, we now have a perfect myth: the Europe of 1992. No danger now of the Gulag giving the lie to the idyll, of communism tarnishing its own slogans, of economic incompetents taking over the means of production, while Pinochet instituted Friedman-style liberal reforms. We have made the myth in our image: 'clean', moderate, reasonable, relatively risk-free, unemotional, reassuring in its flexibility – what more could one ask. What a strange way to regard an event which will basically be the consummation of the Treaty of Rome. The idea of the free market was incorporated into the original text of 1956; now, after a thirty-five year wait, it seems set to have a highly emotional reception. And all the time, behind the economic process, is the European myth.

Not that the transformation is greeted by all the member states with the same enthusiasm. Spain, France and Italy are among its most active supporters; Great Britain (*noblesse oblige*) and Germany (force of circumstances) are the most sceptical participants. For Spain, 1992 has all the attractions of a pioneering expedition: this society in which initiative was stifled during the long hibernation of the Franco regime, has to meet the challenge of sudden entry into the modern world – which is just what it needed. The Italians, Europeans through and through, and with a natural instinct for the innovative, also have everything to gain from membership. Having anticipated it well in advance of its inception, they are able to take maximum advantage of it. French enthusiasm is rather more unexpected, since France has traditionally been the least docile of the European group. Perhaps the French see it as a more agreeable route to modernization and increased productivity, which allows them to accomplish essential tasks under cover of their customary rhetoric. Strange, nevertheless. Great Britain displays its customary lack of enthusiasm, obviously intent on adopting once again the cynical attitude which has brought it such benefits in the past, making great play of its reticence in order to obtain more than its fair share, then, after pocketing the proceeds, rejecting anything which does not meet its approval. By using this manoeuvre, the Conservative Government will be able to obtain all the advantages of financial integration without even offering the minimal compensation of taking the pound sterling into the European monetary system. The country least affected by the prospect of 1992 still seems to be Germany, perhaps because, confident of the strength of their own economy, the Germans have visions of world-wide economic activity, outside the limits of the common market. On the other hand, they may be worried about the effects of unification, or the risk of compromising their position *vis-à-vis* the East. Whatever the reasons, as far as Germans are concerned, 1992 is either a *fait accompli* or a non-event. The smaller countries are all enthusiastic about it: the richest – the Netherlands and Denmark – because they see it as a means to maximize their potential; the poorest – Portugal and Greece – because they will receive the aid and subsidies necessary for more rapid development. Whatever else one may think of the myth of 1992, it has succeeded in firing European imagination.

In this atmosphere it is not surprising that people's behaviour is beginning to anticipate the event. Bosses of industry, trade unions' leaders, directors, financial and insurance experts, bureaucrats, all those professional people grateful to have avoided the consequences of the Rueff-Armand report, are now thinking as Europeans. They draw up their plans of attack or defence with the market in mind. All are convinced that the days of privilege and private income are over; by anticipating the change, they intend to see that it benefits, not penalizes them. What a change of heart for a continent which saw oil crises as acts of God, accepted the rise of foreign competitors as the will of fate, and viewed economic stagnation as part of a divine plan! In this case, the Europeans seem to have captured the spirit of the Japanese who, when confronted with oil prices or exchange rate problems, responded with increased effort and initiative. It may be that this psychological change will have a greater macro-economic effect than will the opening up of the market itself. 1992 is deceptive. A change of style is necessary to benefit from it; a negative approach is bound to fail. But Europeans should be eternally grateful to politicians, and to Jacques Delors in particular, for this magic wand which has, after all, managed to awaken the Sleeping Beauty.

Not only is 1992 an illusion, it is also a device. It is an instrument of modernization, a means by which the economy can be painlessly reorganized, a useful apologia for change. French socialists have more reason to appreciate this than anyone: it has enabled them to bring about their own Bad Godesburg without having to use such unpleasant terms as 'laissez faire', 'laissez passer', 'market' or other liberal terminology. Reality has been transformed without there being any need to change the vocabulary; what more could any responsible establishment ask for? A few shipyards to be closed? Yesterday it would have meant arguing, displaying cost prices, revealing the extent of state aid. Now it is sufficient to invoke 1992. A banking oligopoly to be overcome? The last twenty years have seen innumerable futile attempts to do this; henceforth such a step is fully justified by 1992. Closed professions with outrageous salaries? For half a century they had scoffed at successive governments; henceforth they will have to choose, either to set their house in order in advance of 1992, or perish for lack of foresight. Modernization in order to compete with Japan or Korea was an unpleasant necessity; facing up to competition from one's neighbour is relatively pleasant. There is not a single professional body which is not planning for 1992; no business which does not take into account its implications; no bureaucracy which does not feel threatened. However, Europe as a substitute for modernization conceals certain ambiguities: people contrast the limited time available for installing the former with the infinite number of reforms that are required by the latter. And so they choose what they see as a limited period of great exertion, in preference to a lifetime of unceasing drudgery. Unfortunately, when the time comes, they are likely to find that the one is simply the prelude to the other; that adapting to the open market is the first step in adapting to the world.

By the same token, 1992 has become the magic formula for growth, the latter currently having disappeared, to be replaced by stagnation: austerity, a steady decrease in purchasing power, the laying off of personnel, and so on, each sacrifice calling for another. Zero growth, with austerity as a life style: this was how people saw the future some years ago, once the lack of realism and naivety of the seventies had disappeared. These same people now expect to see the return of expansionism, just as their parents had seen post-war reconstruction as the motor of development. Doubtless, the market does not merit either excessive praise or condemnation. It will not bring about another 'thirty glorious days'. But apart from its practical effects, it will have done us the immense service of ridding us of our inhibitions; the economy is not a limited universe, it is life itself, with all its ups and downs.

Keen observers of the European climate, the Americans have proclaimed the advent of what they call 'Euro-optimism', replacing 'Euro-pessimism' or 'Euro-sclerosis'. It appears that the outward signs of decline have changed sides: it is now they who are worried, we who are confident; they who are slipping back, we who are going forward. These changes of mood are to world economy what polls are to public opinion. The next upset will no doubt set us back in the doldrums. This burst of optimism is likely to be short-lived: long-term economic trends, coupled with the effects of a disgruntled population, do not bode well. However, after fifteen agonizing years of inexorable decline, 1992 will have given Europe back its confidence and its appetite for growth. To a society shaped more by its outlook (with apologies to any remaining Marxists) than by its infrastructures, this is manna from the gods.

At Fontainebleau, in 1985, heads of state thought that they had made two important innovations: economic, in the form of the open market; political, in the form of voting by a qualified majority. In fact, they had engendered a myth. No doubt European society, troubled by its unconscious, felt in need of reinforcement, at a time when the ground seemed to be giving way beneath it and when strategy was clearly being transformed. Logically, any strategic shift should be answered by a defensive initiative, but in fact it was to the economy that they turned for a demonstration of the European spirit. So 1992 provides an answer to another question and, in doing so, has given rise to collective emotions that a more usual, i.e. military, approach would never have inspired. It is no longer the military who mobilize the population, but economists. Patriotism has become commercial. Energy is no longer a function of the military, but of industry. The Elbe as a military defensive line for Europe would, at best, have inspired indifference, at worst fear, whereas the open market is having a galvanizing effect on dormant societies. Convention has gone out of the window, now that a premium has been placed on individuality, the profit motive and market ideology. A society based on the market needs a market ideology and enthusiasm to make it work, although the use of an economic project to unify Europe could be said, paradoxically, to be a victory for Marxism.

The Paradoxical Victory of Marxism

1992 is the legitimate offspring of the European Economic Community; reduced normally to its acronym, the significance of the full title has almost been forgotten. For thirty years, Europe has had an economic identity, and if, occasionally, its voice is heard in other areas, one can be assured that economic considerations are involved. This assumption exerts a kind of tyranny over every European ambition. Brussels, defender of the faith, jealously guards its little plot. From a Berlaymont perspective, Europe can only be defined in terms of the economy, and all initiatives must express this truism or they are doomed: without subsidies or help of any sort, they will never be more than empty ideas. Europe could have come into being in other ways, something we generally forget: politically, for instance, with an embryonic organization laying the groundwork for a confederation – since the failure of the Fouchet Plan in 1962, Europe's only political driving forces have been good will and cooperation, both of them ephemeral and undependable –; militarily, if only the abrupt curtailment of the community's defensive system had not traumatized public opinion for several decades; culturally, through transnational initiatives; pedagogically, through the convergence of educational programmes and the teaching of the same history of Europe in all the member states; judicially, through the unification of civil and penal law and the creation of a European judiciary. The fact that it evolved differently is neither a charge nor a regret. Even so, problems should not be dealt with exclusively from an economic perspective. For example, there is a major need to create European citizens, with allegiance both to Europe and to their native land. Inevitably, the chosen method of accomplishing this will be economic, involving the free circulation of people and professional mobility. A judicial approach, on the other hand, would seek to establish the same rights and duties of citizens in all its member states, rendering the geographical factor irrelevant. Both approaches are equally valid, and in an ideal Europe both would be considered necessary. But through force of habit and the dominance of established institutions, only the economic construct exists, those in charge of Europe being firmly convinced that if the economy is in good shape, everything else will follow automatically.

This total reliance on the economy makes 1992 seem a somewhat ambiguous objective. Really, it is no more than the belated realization of the Treaty of Rome through the establishment of an increasingly vast and homogeneous market. For the manufacturing industry, the disappearance of non-tariff barriers should complete the process begun by the abolition of customs duty. Services would finally reach the stage to which industry had developed twenty years previously. And that would be the sum of it. But in fact, the 1992 dynamic, although primarily economic, would impinge on other areas: the equivalence of university degrees; the right to settle anywhere within the community; competition between professionals in all fields. Important steps, these, towards European citizenship, but a citizenship which is exclusively economic and which produces a curious '*homo europeanus*' – the most Marxist of beings. This person is European through economic rights, not through culture, roots or voting rights. What a bizarre paradox it is that a Greek doctor can settle in Lyons and compete freely with French colleagues, with no prospect of being able to vote in municipal, let alone general, elections. To divorce a Greek spouse, the doctor would have to go back to Athens and attend the magistrate's court there, rather than appear before the Lyons judge. It would, however, be the latter who would punish the doctor in the event of any professional misconduct. The absurdity of it! Europe is advancing erratically towards 1992 and the schizophrenia that it will bring: economically, people will be Europeans; politically and legally they will be citizens of a member state. Only a blind believer in the European concept could imagine that a real community, in every sense of the term, would arise out of economic union.

Ignoring the fact that Europe is economically based, the idea is propagated that a civil Europe is being formed. The rhetoric surrounding 1992 does nothing to dispel this delusion, which is fostered by wishful thinking and by pro-European enthusiasm. What self-deception! What a strange return to Marxism on the part of those engaged in the most liberal enterprise ever – the establishment of a market of 300 million consumers. It is inconsistent on various counts: philosophically, because it likens the working of a society to that of a marketplace; sociologically, because it ignores the nationalism of history; historically, because it does not tackle the problem of outmoded institutions and ideologies; politically, because it refuses to accept that a political entity can be as strong as an economic one. The more astute Europeans are not taken in by this ambiguity. They are not deceived into thinking that an economically united Europe is the real Europe. Nevertheless, they are prepared to gamble on the economic momentum being powerful enough to set the rest in motion, with everything else falling into place. In doing so they fail to appreciate the importance of the strategic shift of the continent; in any case, the latter seems to fit in quite well with the idea of the market. The free circulation of products and people within the EEC is hardly likely to put a stop to an underground movement whose origins and subsequent development are completely different. Movements towards unification are always initiated by states, and usually involve the use of force. Germany was not built solely on the concept of the *Zollverein* (customs union): Bismarck used plenty of other methods. Thankfully, force has disappeared from the equation, but the will of nation states remains the key to any potential unification. The market can never take its place.

These facts are self-evident, but, fascinated by the myth of 1992, we tend to forget them. Europeans think they are building Europe, but the day they draw up the balance sheet of profit and loss they are in for a rude awakening. Of course any rational person will admit that the former far outweighs the latter, but not to the extent that people think today. They delude themselves into believing that economic unity will lead to social unity; social unity to political unity; political unity to military unity, and that Europe will have been built without drama or conflict. 1992 will not see the construction of such a Europe, for that kind of unity is no longer possible. The 'liberal Marxists' are going to have to come down to earth again: by a strange alchemy, they managed to mingle the liberals' dream of the market and the Marxist credo of the primacy of the economy. In doing so, they may have delivered the coup de grâce to the European dream.

A Stroke of Technical Genius

What a transformation for an entrenched bureaucracy: four or five years ago the Brussels machine embodied all the worst aspects of a technocracy. Presiding over fossilized procedures, shackled by immutable rules, consuming vast amounts of money, totally unproductive, it had become self-justifying. The concept of Europe was distant indeed; it did not even serve as a cosmetic device to hide the people's wretchedness. Unrestrained, pushed to the ultimate extreme, the Brussels model seemed to be omega, the final point to which all administrations gravitated. And now, suddenly, everything has changed, and this ailing institution has sprung into life again. The motive force for this change did not come from the grass roots of the organization, but from the politicians who directed it. Nevertheless, the organization followed the lead given to it and accepted with good grace the upturning of its traditional approach, which must, after all, have been as traumatic for it as the Copernican revolution had been for the Church.

For thirty years, the community's institutions had operated according to one inviolable principle: free exchange must be preceded by unification of the regulations. This is no more than one would have expected from an organization fostered in the spirit of Parisian technocracy, which had always identified efficiency with the issuing of perfectly sculpted rules and regulations, capable of dividing society up into neat sections like a French garden. It was on the basis of this philosophy that the European Coal and Steel Community (ECSC), the Community, the Agricultural Policy and other institutions were set up. Customs duty was ruthlessly annihilated by the hammer blows of a bureaucracy expert in the art of creating regulations to counter those of other people, but confronted with the obstacles of non-tariff barriers, fiscal nationalism and legal peculiarities within member states, the machine ground to a halt. The administration was just not up to the task of dismantling the vast number of commercial standards: 1,500 French, 7,000 British and 25,000 German (a good indication, this, of the clandestine protectionism practised by all parties). Whereas the rules governing customs duty were well publicized and few in number, those designed to erect non-tariff barriers were invisible and protean. The technocratic pile-driver was enough to deal with the former, but was powerless in the case of the latter. Greatest resistance came from those taxes which were state-imposed (exceptionally, VAT was not). There was not the slightest unification of judicial processes, and the project of a European Law Society, regarded as urgent by even the smallest industrialists, had lain on the table of the Council of Ministers since 1973. Even the most enthusiastic of Eurocrats gave up eventually. The Common Market seemed doomed to remain incomplete, the Community to struggle along from day to day, and Europe to go from one crisis to another, each resolved after a fashion, but not very satisfactorily.

Eventually, however, fear of death acts as a spur to institutions, as it does to people. The Catholic Church came up with John-Paul II, the world hauled itself back from the edge of the precipice, and the EEC gave up its fundamental principle of the primacy of unification over liberation. Since 1985 the opposite principle has applied: liberation now takes priority over unification. The origin of such a revolutionary change lay in the pragmatic realization that a formula had to be found which would satisfy all states. Under the new principle, all that is valid in one of the twelve member states is automatically valid in the eleven others. This means that non-tariff barriers are condemned.

The law regarding the purity of German beer which had been in force since the Middle Ages, preventing the import of French beers, has now gone. Henceforth, as long as French beers are recognized in France, they will automatically be accepted in Germany too. National regulations deciding, say, the width of an axle, or the distance between the driving seat and the steering wheel, have been around for long enough, weighing the market down. The sanitary laws whose uniformly grotesque requirements used to protect the British market have been given the death sentence. This seemingly inevitable revolution must go down in the history books as the brain-child of Jacques Delors. Its adoption was made possible by a general acceptance on the part of a technocracy of its own impotence, and its elevation above the mundane was effected by the ingeniously simple idea of a fixed date of commencement. What it required, from the very start, was the sort of willingness exhibited by heads of state and the leaders of parliament, in particular those politicians such as François Mitterand who were little disposed to extol the virtues of the market, but who nevertheless accepted this detour in order to give Europe a new lease of life.

However, this Copernican revolution has certainly not made Brussels redundant. If it had, it would have been rejected by the

European technocrats. There is plenty of room for complementary work on harmonization. But thanks to the act which introduced a voting system based on qualified majority rather than unanimity, the 300 remaining directives[1] will proceed on time. Each year brings in its new batch of texts without fuss and bother. While the old way of thinking prevailed, the single European market would have been a task fit for Penelope; with the new principles of equivalence, it is almost a *fait accompli*. While harmonization was a prerequisite, progress had to submit to the possible veto of any national administration, but with the primacy of the liberation process, bureaucratic procedure has been relegated to the sidelines. From now on, the market makes the decisions. Under the stricter approach, Europe accumulated rules and regulations at both national and community level. Under the more liberal approach, this mountain of text is no longer any use. Of course, at the moment, we can only see the virtues of this new method, its dynamism, its efficiency and its simplicity. In 1992 we will have a better idea of the price involved, the costs engendered by a Darwinian process of natural selection which seems very foreign to our carefully cocooned economies. The shock will be unimaginable, but one that we should welcome as we seem to have placed ourselves on the side of those who consider any shake-up to be salutary. Was this the intention of the Brussels bureaucratic machine, when it changed track? Did it deliberately adopt a *Weltanschauung* which had little in common with its traditions and methods of working? Would it have chosen to undergo such a metamorphosis? Of course not. But its instinct for survival pushed it towards an initiative which was unmeasurable in its scope and long-term effects. The politicians who carried it along had no way of knowing the future of the bomb they were helping to ignite. This is blindness on a classic and admirable scale, a repeat of 4 August, with the aristocrats played by politicians and civil servants who are being stripped of their privileges and powers for the sake of the market. It is a sacrifice on their part, but also an abdication of responsibility.

Political Abdication

The pre-eminence of legislation over liberation was not haphazard. In the fifties, it mirrored the policies of politicians and civil servants. ECSC and the Plan shared the same 'constructivist' outlook, according to Hayek. It was up to the State to decide on general rules, and up to economic concerns to obey them. This was the period of unlimited growth, of massive public investment and of technocracy triumphant. Strengthened by its success nationally and by the constructive efforts of its civil servants. France had no problem imposing its image on a Europe made up of six countries, of which its only possible rival, the Federal Republic, was both paralysed by its own past and fascinated by Gallic mythology. It was this utter self-confidence that paved the way for the Common Agricultural Policy, that unpredictable fruit of a Byzantine administration. This 'constructivist' approach was not merely the delight of European and national civil servants, it also perpetuated the role of the politicians. They alone would resolve points of order, settle conflicts and untangle the Gordian knots involved. They were not impervious to the image of the Brussels arena with its night sittings, its dawn orations, its gaunt faces, its sham exits and its expansive reconciliations. These were the codes and rituals of a play in which politicians took the leading roles and the public were mere onlookers. However difficulties eventually bogged the process down and when progress became impossible, a change to this European machine became necessary.

This is what lead to the thunderbolt of the single European market, the inversion of the relative priorities of liberation and harmonization. And yet this revolution is once again an abdication on the part of the political world which is resorting to the market to bring about what it has failed to achieve by itself. Such behaviour is hardly new and it is by no means the first time that the European political class, finding it impossible to advance on its own terms, has turned to the economy to give Europe a second wind. After the setback of the Economic Defence Community, politicians set in motion the Treaty of Rome and the Common Market, convinced that, once on the right track, this latter construction would advance under its own steam, and would not require politically costly and technically complex decisions at each stage of the route. Similarly, after the failure of Fouchet's plan to build a hypothetical political confederation, the economy once more asserted itself with an acceleration in the pace of the Common Market and the first steps of the Common Agricultural Policy. However, this shift of emphasis did not entail any decrease in political responsibility since French-style technocratic 'constructivism' required that each step be unanimously approved by the administration of each country.

The present retreat is of a different nature. It is a transfer from state to society, from legislator to economic agent, and, more generally, from the principle of order to that of disorder.

The change from state to society is easy to understand: once legitimately based on national regulations currently in force, exchanges will be given free run, restructuring the economy and thus society. Unprecedented upheavals will take place in terms of commercial reorganization, the disappearance of certain professions, individual mobility and a mingling of products, technology and manpower. When the various European societies were set up in the eighteenth and nineteenth centuries, alongside that creation of the market economy, they were fussed over by a vigilant and omnipresent state system; Bismarckism was anything but a gamble on the spontaneous response of German society. Nowadays, it would not be possible for any institution to watch over the interests of European society in the same way. The member states will have their hands tied, faced with changes over which they are powerless. The European Community has been stripped of all but a few of its real powers, and the Court of Justice can only have a remedial and thus marginal effect.

What about the move away from the legislators and towards consumers and the business world? Once the principle of harmonization is discarded, it is the consumer who becomes the sole monitor. It is the consumer who must choose between products which, though possessing different characteristics, must nevertheless submit to heterogeneous regulations. The balance between quality and price, which is common to any purchase, will swing tacitly in favour of price, the only undisputable means of assessment. This is not to say, of course, that consumers will not eventually evince a need for quality, but that the initial battle will be fought over prices. Standardization will be replaced by an infinity of macro-economic adjustments, and behind this abrupt change lies a belief and a gamble. The belief is that Europe is so homogeneous that regulations in the least strict country still form an acceptable minimum. And the gamble, that given a prosperous economy, consumers will succeed in exercising real pressure over producers. This presupposes, of course, an even more rigorous ban on monopolies and cartels, without which free transfer of goods would proceed at the expense of consumers. The business world, similarly, will find that the ball is now in their court. Economic prosperity will come through competition and not via the subtle balance between regulation and the market which had developed since the War. The single European market contains the seed of a battle of unprecedented violence and brutality: those who theorized about a 'pure and perfect' market would never have dreamed of such a field of experimentation in Europe. It is basically American philosophy which is beginning to prevail, but taken to ridiculous extremes. In the US national standards still exist: America does not depend on its states to the extent of following whichever among them happens to be the most lenient as regards a particular regulation. This mere detail (!) apart, the EC is making an American-style gamble on the single market or an economic motor, on competition as a regulator, and on a respect for the laws as the 'ultima ratio'. In other words, what we are witnessing is the changeover from order to disorder. Europe, which until now has been governed economically by technocrats, will now have to submit to the hotchpotch of life. Laws which concerned everyone will be replaced by the free play of initiative. The economy will be lived rather than planned. It is a belief in methodology rather than an ideological vision which shows through this comprehensive volte-face. An ideological choice would consist of either a Reagan- or Thatcher-style discourse on the market (its good side) or excessive legislation (its bad side). Current unprecedented deregulation on a continental scale does nor reflect such a choice. But it does make implicit use of the contemporary belief that order cannot exist without an initial period of disorder, that movement cannot be obtained without loss of balance. Contemporary scientific theory must have permeated our whole way of thinking for yesterday's heresies to have become today's accepted facts. Current beliefs in complexity are lurking everywhere, teaching us about feedback, knock-on effect and regulation by apparent disorder. The situation is not so far away from those physical laws which state that order is nothing but a state of stable disorder. Recent ideas on biology which have established how much the 'logic of life' owes to 'chance and necessity'[2] have also had some considerable influence. By means of scientific vulgates, general outlines and extreme banalities, a philosophy which was within everyone's grasp and which upset forever previous assumptions regarding order and disorder, began to take root. The fathers of the single market would be astonished at being charged with such a scientific vision of the world, but they, like everyone, merely adapted to a changed climate. Planning used to bear the same relationship to the economy as determinism to science; the wager on the market plays the same role as regards economic action as that of chance in scientific thought. Creative disorder has overtaken conservative disorder in the ratings; in art it happened a long time ago, in science it was more recent and it is only now happening in today's society and economy.

If the option of the single market had been presented in this way, it would doubtless never have come about. The risks would have seemed too great and its chances of success too remote. In the logic of disorder, the former must come about before the latter can triumph and politicians have a rather different attitude towards immediate and long-term future. A little hypocrisy, a pinch of thoughtlessness, a helping of courage, a dose of historic vision and you have the magic potion which has allowed politicians to turn their responsibilities regarding Europe over to society. They have ridden the crest of their enthusiasm to the point of changing the way the Community functions in order that nothing hampers the march towards 1992. They have accepted without any fuss or theoretical confrontation the principle of a qualified majority, which limits the necessity for unanimity to very extreme cases, thus doing away with the oldest spectre of European debate. This spectre had led de Gaulle to adopt the policy of the empty chair, it had served as a test to distinguish between the followers of a supra-national Europe and the disciples of a Europe of nation states, and it had brought to the surface in France the authentic Gallic stamp. European leaders have thus pushed this process of relinquishing responsibility to its very limit: not only has politics given way to the economy, but it has deliberately cut off any means of turning back by precluding the last resort of veto, while at the same time disguising its abdication as a triumph. Only political power could drive back the power of the establishment in that way; only it could make the incision which would bring it back to life according to the most ancient laws of free-exchange; only it has the right to turn the tables. It has just brought this to our attention once again.

A Gamble

The founders of the single European market can be divided into several categories. Some, in particular François Mitterand and Jacques Delors, think that a reinforcing of common policies must accompany the opening up of the market. If not, one risks creating a situation in which Darwinian natural selection gives rise to enormous inequalities. This point of view follows in the footsteps of the original philosophy behind Europe, which advocated the necessity for combined action in the areas of trade and back-up legislation. Others believe in the virtues of the market per se, fully convinced that this purge will bring forth a new state of well-being. The last group is certain that order will eventually grow out of the chaos and that, in the fullness of time, the dynamic of the market will provoke a response in terms of regulatory jurisdiction, social laws and other such realigning mechanisms. Up till now, the latter have won few battles. The Eureka project, programmes such as Esprit, and a growth in certain community funds might be important but are nothing compared to the approaching earthquake.

And yet, it is not certain that order will come from chaos, as witness the International Monetary Fund. That organization, too, was carried along by the idea of a grand market. There was no considered decision, rather the institutional breakwater had been swept away by a growing mass of floating capital. The prevailing illusion was that any fluctuations would affect automatic adjustments in the balance of payments, inflation and exchange rates. Reality has obviously not been quite so irenic: over-excesses have replaced excesses, mega-devaluations have followed devaluation and still there is no sign of remedial effects.

Mrs Thatcher was alone in preaching about the freedom of trade, in her refusal of any counter-balancing mechanisms and in her rejection of any arrangements. Even the US admitted the need for certain corrective measures. And out of this process of international self-deception, nothing was born except the European Monetary System itself. There were no substantial agreements on stability, no regulating procedures, no standards set. It is easier to reject order than to regain it. Will the single market suffer the same fate?

We are too prone to forget that law and the market are two sides of the same reality. Competition without any ground rules becomes a jungle while a legislative corset leaving no freedom of movement leads to a lack of efficiency. These obvious truisms are far too often ignored. France, especially, is more restive than other countries on the subject of regulations: the law of the market, that backbone of the market economy, is still hesitant; society puts up with regulations instead of increasing contracts and lawyers find it hard to allow the existence of standards which are superior to theirs. But at each gust of liberalization, judicial aspects are systematically ignored. Europe looks like following on its heels. To imagine the market with absolutely no regulation is to greatly underestimate the intensity of the economic battle, and the violence of the competition. Europeans are in the process of building the greatest market in the world with no real back-up institutions, to take up Michel Albert and Jean Boissonnat's[3] excellent definition. This imbalance will become quickly apparent. Will new institutions and rules have to be imposed? And by whom? When the time comes will the Community's authorities really have the strength to implement them? This is the gamble. We cannot overlook the risk of seeing the community becoming as powerless under the shock of the single European market as the International Monetary Fund when faced with variable exchange rates.

Eurocrats claim that this is not a fair comparison. The Commission has its own judicial powers; with the Council of Ministers to support it and the Court of Justice in Luxembourg to uphold the law. However, we must not forget that the International Monetary Fund – also a post-war creation – did have some quasi-sovereign powers at its disposal. At the time of the fixed exchange rate, for instance, it wielded more power through the financial security forces than the Brussels commission can in terms of surveillance of the Common Market. But these powers were lost at the time of the monetary turmoil on the larger countries. As a guardian of the weaker countries, it was unable to impose even the slightest curb on the behaviour of the dominant economic powers, least of all in the case of a US Government which systematically failed to honour the code of good management that it nevertheless insisted on enforcing in Brazil, Mexico and Poland with the aim of recycling its debts. How are we to know if Germany will be any keener about the idea of obligations accompanying the single market than the US was about the injunctions issued by the IMF? More powerful countries have no interest in keeping to rules designed to limit the advantages they enjoy over the weaker countries. If these rules match their ideas they will conform to them; if they do not yet exist, why should they help to set them up? They do, of course, accept certain marginal modulations to combat the worst excesses. Thracian Greece, for example, with a per capita spending power fifteen times lower than that of Bade-Wurtenburg, would receive a grant. But the construction of a true equalizing process would still be a long way off. The countries which have the power to establish a code of conduct have no reason to do so, while the rest do not have the means. The single market risks being in a state of permanent disequilibrium with no internal regulation or compensation.

If this is the case, the state will end up by intervening anyway, but instead of this process being at a European level, it will be the member states who will feel the need to act positively. That would be a real catastrophe since the poorer governments, forced to try and pick up the pieces left by the unification of Europe, would have to choose between an anti-European reflex response, begging from the richer of their colleagues in the community, and the threat of wrecking the whole system. The last hypothesis is not even necessarily the worst, since it would be the only possible way to galvanize the inevitable winners of the single market out of their inertia. At any rate, even with an overall rise in the standard of living, the strongest will not be able to become even stronger, and the weak even weaker, without some reaction. The Community will have to produce a minimum of rules and compensations if it wishes to avoid unbearable conflicts.

At the moment 1992 brings forth unanimous enthusiasms, but one does not have to be an expert or a Marxist to anticipate tensions in store: between countries which are winning and those which are losing (since the belief in equal productivity gain will be shown to be a dream when certain countries inevitably reap better rewards than others); between growth sectors and shrinking sectors; between consumers and agriculturalists; between the employees of expanding services and those of declining industries; between the sector which will be exposed to this new, even more chaotic international competition and the protected sector, which will be even more privileged. Such conflicts are the daily bread of advanced economies, but 1992 will give them a whole new meaning. Nowadays each country makes a reasonable job of reducing tension within its own area of influence. But at a European level, who will have the task of reducing tension? These are the matters at stake in 1992: a machine has been put into action which will generate both progress and difficulties, its irreplaceable virtue being that with any luck there will be more advantages than disadvantages. Its benefits will be happily reaped, but who will take responsibility for shouldering the deficiencies?

92, then, is not going to come about in 1992. The single market will first have to undergo some kind of regulating, compensating process which will jeopardize the unanimity of the twelve countries. All of Europe's energies are once again focused on economic matters. What about the rest? Its citizens, who feel themselves to belong to the West, rather than to Europe? Its institutions, which could make Europe into a real motive force, rather than a chapter in a history book? Its defence, which could determine the direction of certain current evolutions? Its strategic planning, which could prevent this rift forming between a strategic Europe encompassing the whole of the continent, and an economic Europe left without the backbone of the state and defined by the frontiers of the future nations of the EC? If it is the case that Europe is made up of several cohabiting identities, then it cannot exist as a single idea. With our eyes fixed on the creation and then the regimenting of the single European market, we are doing nothing to halt the slow movement of the strategic terrain. In the end it will be too late: the process will be irreversible. Gaullism is there to teach us that once unleashed, it is impossible to catch up with the march of history. Between 1960 and 1966, General de Gaulle could have constructed Europe to his fancy: the Germans were ready to recognize his authority, and the other countries would have rallied round, making the best of a bad job. He would of course, have had to temper this European construction with an Atlantic flavour which was indispensable at the time, but that would have been a modest concession compared with what was at stake, especially on the part of the most pro-Atlantic statesman of all at the threat of real danger. The cult of international independence, the desire to romp freely in diplomatic matters, old rehashed suspicions regarding the US, and an obsessive hatred of anything supra-national were enough to make sure that the opportunity was passed over. That will be the everlasting sin of Gaullism. Held prisoners by the single market, we must nevertheless not allow history to have all its own way. If it is to crystallize such obsessions, 1992 will surely need to have all the features of a daydream.

Notes

1 Directives: decisions taken by the Community's Council of Ministers at the proposal of the Commission.

2 '*La logique du vivant*' and '*le hasard et la nécessité*', are references to the titles of the first two books, one by François Jacob, the other by Jacques Monod, to propound these new ideas.

3 Michel Albert and Jean Boissonnat, *Crise, krach, boom*, le Seuil, 1988.

7

A Daydream

Spruced up and odourized with the attributes of the single market, the old economic theories are making a triumphant comeback. Isn't there a large amount of Adam Smith, Ricardo, Pareto, even of Friedman in the ideas currently in vogue? Increased competition brings prices down and radiates productivity and growth. Free allocation of capital allows for investment in optimal areas, the best gauge of a healthy economy. The disappearance of non-tariff barriers has lead to increased freedom of choice. Everything in the garden is good and the world is full of '*luxe, calme et volupté*'. Never has liberal thought sparkled with such lustre. It forges ahead, albeit disguised, hidden behind synonyms: 1992 for the market, Europe for competition and the Community for *laissez faire*. The liberal economy actually won outright on the day when President Gorbachev's closest counsellor disclosed 'We know of nothing better than the market to get the economy moving.' It has taken decades to rediscover this obvious fact: the market is not a choice; it is the natural state of society. But the transition from this reality to the present ecstasy is by no means so evident. Marxist analysis of crises, Keynesian research into global balance and the need for a corrective state apparatus have all been passed over. Nowadays Europeans expect miracles from 1992, that from the market and the process of deregulation will come new growth, productivity and dynamism. The most enthusiastic of these daydreamers are not, perhaps, those one might expect: French Colbertists, for example, rather than German free-traders, the protectionist Spanish rather than the liberal British, socialists rather than conservatives and backward rather than advanced economies. What a strange 3-card trick: the old habitués of the market are aware of both its many virtues and its few drawbacks, while its most recent converts believe that they have found the promised land. It would be an amusing exercise in style to replace 1992 by market, and Europe by deregulation in a text by Mr Solchaga or Mr Beregovay: these authors would never put their signatures to such an inflammatory piece of Friedmanism. What we are experiencing is the first economic psychoanalytical projection. We are foisting onto Europe a process of realignment that we are prevented from following on a national scale by our complexes and inhibitions. Freud is not dead. In an ideal economy, it would be better to have more deregulation on a national level, and less within the Community, but, as in psychology, an acceptable projection is worth more than a complex for life. This explains the urgent need to fantasize in order to justify the strange psychoanalytical course which over-regulated, strait jacketed economics have adopted in order to liberate themselves.

A Necessary Miracle

The patient – to continue the analogy – certainly stood in need of therapy. For fifteen years Europe has been in the grip of a lethargy shown clearly in its unemployment figures and share holdings. With seventeen million claimants, it is suffering a level of underemployment unknown in the developed world. With a growth rate which, even in the optimal conditions of a combined fall in inflation, in the price of petrol and in the value of the dollar, still has trouble rising about 3 per cent, it does not cut much of a figure against a US which has been in perpetual expansion for the past six years, and a Japan which has just rediscovered the exponential development of its post-war period. With, lastly, an export level which represents a progressively smaller and smaller proportion of world commerce, it is losing out less to the Americans and the Japanese, than to new Third-World exporters such as Brazil and the Four Dragons[1] of Southeast Asia.

Admittedly Europe has not, unlike the US, twisted the rules of the game with the help of the one-sided privileges of a standard currency. Even if it has wanted to, it could not have followed America's example of an enormous Keynesian boost under cover of the supply-side economy. It could not afford the luxury of spending years digging gaping pits of internal and external deficits, without ever paying the price. It would not have had the strength to deflect part of the cost of readjustment onto others, by means of a free-fall device. The enthusiasm exhibited by some less austere members of the Community for a European currency contains the sneaking desire to have such privileges at their disposal since they seem to have the irreplaceable virtue of putting off the day of reckoning.

Faced with this declining position, Europeans were left with only three options: to drift on, to tighten their belts within the current framework, or to shift the goal posts. For a long time it was the first tendency which prevailed. Europe believed itself to be rich enough, at the time of the petrol crises, to draw on its prosperity accumulated through the ages and to manage without any extra sacrifice. This subterfuge lasted too long and it became necessary to act. The second hypothesis would have required each of the member states to go well beyond the rigorous efforts of the eighties, according to the old saying that the crueller the purge, the greater the revival. The public, which had meekly accepted the minimal austerity needed to re-establish macro-economic equilibrium, was not prepared for this. It is no coincidence that countries such as Great Britain and Germany, which recently imposed the most extreme deflationary policies, have seen a rise in spending power from 3 per cent to 4 per cent in the past two years. In advanced economies with social protection mechanisms still intact and businesses operating efficiently, any austerity measures quickly find their limits. There remains the third option, that of turning the tables, changing the rules of the game, finding a new context in which to act. This is where the projection to the idea of the single market comes in. It is then up to the market to assure increased growth, more flexibility and to act as an expansion jar.

This approach is characterized by an ambiguity which will become evident with the adaptations and modernizations required by 1992. These developments must bring about increased growth, and yet, for the latter to be accomplished speedily and painlessly, a background of long-term expansion would have been necessary . . . a somewhat irreconcilable contradiction. This is why 1992 is different from the first steps to free the market following the Treaty of Rome. European economies then were drifting happily along to the rhythm of 5 per cent growth per annum, and they expected from the Common Market not so much additional growth as a reinforcement, should their reconstructive efforts begin to flag. This situation was obviously much more comfortable for all concerned. Profits from growth at the time were able to offset any unpleasant shocks resulting from future growth. It was a happy chain of events that paved the way for the '30 glorious years'. Protectionist barriers came down, agricultural competition was extinguished, small businessmen gave up and Poujadism, the cult of the little man, was a thing of the past, in the context of such miracles of expansion. Without this adjunct, the journey will be much rougher: there is no room for manoeuvre as regards spending power, and no spare productivity gains with which to dress the resulting wounds. Each country is braking furiously into 1992 convinced, and rightly so, that the slightest lack of control will result in a skid which will add to the price of modernization. The anticipated advantages must be very attractive to justify such asceticism.

A Macro-Economic Fairy Tale

Now that the gamble on 1992 has been made, the Community sees fit to assess its effects: a schedule which demonstrates just how much the single European market was an act of faith. At a time when macro-economic models were constructed on the slightest pretext in order to measure the effects of the most modest change in economic policy, the most important economic choice of our age is made by licking a finger and holding it up. Where are the thousand and one simulations which are regularly prompted by decisions a hundred times less important? This lack is an indication of the urgency of this fundamental decision and especially of its cathartic and mythical nature. Our masters came to this decision through a process of faith, belief, intuition or scepticism, after stripping themselves of all the technical attributes which had obstructed the smallest decree on milk quotas, the width of axles, or on balancing the budget. There has been no lack of studies into the matter, they have simply all been carried out after the event.

The European Commission in Brussels now has at its disposal a whole array of figures each more splendid than the last, which allow it to justify the soundness of a gamble over which it never had any control. The current trend is for savings of approximately 220 billion ecus (150 billion pounds) per year (one billion = 1,000 million). This manna comes as a direct result of the single market and will be shared out among the Community's consumers, enterprises and member states. This distribution is intended as a key to open the door to the future and to the possible annual repetition of this miracle. The abolition of non-tariff barriers provides the basis for this amazing yield, since its sphere of influence is so wide. The first instance would be the disappearance of internal frontiers: the suppression of border patrols, of administrative procedures and the delays that they cause, of prohibitive transportation costs and the kind of administrative spending inherent to the management of an incredibly complex machine. This alone would account for between 12 and 23 billion ecus going up in smoke. Secondly, there is the protectionism within the public markets, which have always been closed off from firms in the other member states. Due to this, 15 per cent of internal produce has stayed outside the Common Market. If this area were to be even slightly opened up, 8 to 19 billion ecus would not be needlessly squandered. Our experts[2] have compiled three types of saving to be made in this area: 'static commerce effect' will lead to public authorities buying from the cheapest source, whether national or European; the 'competitive effect' will oblige firms to lower their prices in order to remain in contention and to protect their territory, and a 'restructuring effect' will be linked to the scale of economic savings ushered in by the continental dimension. To retain an even balance, price reductions imposed on public services and the effects of training on innovation, investments and growth have been omitted from the calculations. In third place, enormous savings could be made from the financial services sector of the Common Market. In this case 20 billion ecus would be emptied into the coffers of the Community upon agreement as to the best conditions for competition, consumer credit, credit cards, commercial loans, every kind of insurance, and brokers' rates. One would expect the greatest decreases from Spain and, to a lesser extent, Belgium, France and Italy, all countries with thriving financial protectionist policies. In fourth place, standardization of the cost of telephone services would liberate 10 billion ecus. And lastly, a reduction in production costs would release 60 billion ecus simply for processing industries. This figure should hardly be surprising given the other gains. It is at the heart of the gamble on 1992: a single market would bring down production costs independently of the savings effected through the suppression of inefficient working practices, of internal frontiers, of cloistered public markets and splintered financial markets. Even an industry such as the car industry, which is already liberated, would see its costs decreasing by 5 per cent if it were released from its few remaining shackles, such as technical regulations, disparities, taxation and the splitting up of its production processes which, despite free exchange of products, remain national. Fiat, Peugeot and Volkswagen are not European enterprises directing an internal market which encompasses the whole Community, but simply national enterprises, which export to Europe. Add the odd gain here and there and the 220 billion ecus are within arms' reach.

When it comes to examining the macro-economic consequences of this manna, the experts preferred to maintain an act of extreme caution. They assessed direct impact rather than possible side effects. Even so the former is by no means negligible: a 4.5 per cent rise in the gross domestic product; a parallel 6.1 per cent drop in prices; a relaxation of internal and external constraints to the tune of 2.2 per cent of the GDP in the first case and 1 per cent in the second and lastly the creation of 1,800,000 jobs, with a consequent 1.5 per cent reduction in the cost of unemployment benefits. These consequences are not, of course, renewable; they are one-off benefits. But the degree of freedom thus gained would open the door to a whole chain of events: the loosening of constraints would encourage a boost which would inspire an instantaneous drop in prices, leading to a situation in which growth and employment would flourish. Another fairy tale in prospect.

We must not fall under the spell of figures. The end result of any analysis is only to regurgitate what the experts have chosen to cram into it. What do these analyses actually require to give the most favourable result? An improvement in supply, which will be a direct affect of the market; and corresponding savings, which is the hope behind 1992, a game unfettered by unfair advantages which is inevitable given the disappearance of non-tariff barriers; an improvement in the profit margin of businesses, the seed of which is carried in financial savings and a reduction in production costs nearer the source. Even macro-economic analyses are no strangers to fashion: following the demand for the whole Keynesian machinery came those simulation tools with a liberal flavour, based on the competitiveness of supply. Given such a process of assessment, victory on the part of the market was a foregone conclusion since it seemed to answer all the requirements of the system. However, this over-sympathetic defect at conception does not necessarily refute the macro-economic impact of the single market. Doubtless the simulation came to its conclusions only after having reached an impasse on intermediate processes. Doubtless the figures have over-estimated by 100 per cent because of the rather naive assumptions on savings in which the experts put their faith, and because the analysis is biased towards the progress of supply rather than demand. Doubtless the scenario is not taking into consideration any confiscation of these savings by a monopoly or oligopoly, as if such things did not go on in this world. But, even arbitrarily reducing it by a half, the impact of the single market still has all the signs of a financial fairy tale. Looked at from a distance and with macro-economic binoculars, 1992 exhibits nothing but virtues. Seen from close up with a micro-economic magnifying glass, some faults begin to appear.

Possible Room for Action

Leaving aside its real virtues and its fairy-tale aspects, the single European market has another advantage in that it offers a space where macro-economic action becomes possible once more. For the past ten years or so, it has been an accepted practice to laugh at macro-economic policies, always excepting those which deal with production and supply. Just think about the charges levelled at Keynesianism. Theoretically: that it ends up making erroneous claims, in particular with respect to global demand. Empirically: that it justified courses of action which were deemed failures: witness Chirac in 1976, Mauroy in 1981, Callaghan in 1978 and Schmidt in 1980. Politically: that it prompted an excessive importance of the State, which civil societies are no longer willing to support. Socially: that it served as an excuse for the bulimia of a welfare programme which had become a distribution machine for the middle class. There is obviously some truth in this witch hunt: Keynesianism has provided a theoretical alibi for state torpor. But it came to grief mainly in the area of economics, which was principally where it was put into practice by governments. It is no longer a relevant form of action at a national level. Take Germany for example. Its foreign trade represents almost a third of its national product; its interest rates are even more dependent on the international environment rather than on their central bank; the slightest aggravation in its external deficit, given floating exchange rates, accelerates a depreciation of its currency, the slightest surge in its internal deficit weighs heavily on consumer demand and so on imports, and its labour costs are fixed by international competition. What possible inroads could a Keynesian policy make?

At a European level, however, things become very different. In the first place, Europe's dependence on its exterior market is only 11 per cent, taking account of the importance of exchanges within the Community when calculating current foreign trade. The Community will become, then, a kind of semi-protected zone along the lines of the US which has a similar import rate. In the absence of a minimum of protection at the frontiers of the Community, the single market will certainly give rise to a growth in foreign trade which would lead to increased dependence. But the EC as a whole will not be in a position where foreign imports represent a third of its national product as they do for its states taken separately. In the second place, the Community will be far less sensitive to foreign interest rates. The German rate does not automatically follow impulses from elsewhere, not even from New York; a European rate would play as much of a leading role as its American equivalent. It would once again become a variable in economic policy rather than a pawn. This, of course, presupposes a European currency, but no long-term market can possibly exist without monetary unification.[3] Lastly, there will be a certain amount of play as regards inflation. The drop in prices inherent to the single market will give a degree of liberty leading to a more vital boost.

Even in the absence of the single market, Europe as an area seemed ripe for an economic boost. Albert and Ball became ardent proponents of such a course of action in 1983.[4] They demonstrated the possibility of increased efficiency in the community along Keynesian lines. The illustration was simple: any revivalist policy which was not systematically adopted was hopeless since the majority of the countries within the community exported mainly amongst themselves. However, as soon as this policy was followed at a European level, it would start to show results. Convinced of their theory, Michel Albert and Jean Boissonnat[5] started to put it into practice. They claimed that a loan by the Community of 20,000 ecus per year, for three years – 120,000 francs, a little more than France's annual budget deficit – would allow a 1 per cent increase in the rate of growth, per year. Pursued for another two years it would bring about an acceleration: +1.2 per cent in 1991; +1.3 per cent in 1993. The effect on employment would be considerable: 4,700,000 jobs created in the first case, and 5,400,000 in the second. In a context of exaggerated forecasts, these figures are even more significant than those connected with the single market. And once again this simulation was made with respect to contemporary economic structures, without taking into consideration the ultimate multiplier of the single European market.

Paradoxically, it is the very efficiency of the supply-side economics followed for the last few years that brings Keynesianism back into the picture. From 1960 to 1973 a minimum growth rate of 4.2 per cent was needed to create jobs; in the period 1973 to 1979 the rate reached was just 2.1 per cent and since 1979, 1.7 per cent, on condition that wages remain stable in relation to prices. The strengthening of the structure of enterprises, their increased efficiency, and the lowering of their 'dead points' are all factors favourable to a new economic boost. The advantages of Keynesianism have been rediscovered at European level, particularly in the context of the single market. Germany has yet to accept this principal, but that is another matter. Also Keynesianism has yet to be rehabilitated and retrieved from the disfavour into which it was cast by the dominant vulgate: all public spending is unhealthy, any boost is criminal and any artificially induced growth is a perversion.

These hypothetical thousands of ecus have to find a home and the old principle holds even better now than before: a boost due to consumption is worth less than if it were due to investment or foreign demand. In other words, the extra money must not be swallowed up merely on an increase in spending-power. Thank goodness! The old taste for infrastructures has not disappeared: once again the round table of great European patrons has given it top priority, realizing their dreams of peppering the map of Europe with tunnels, motorways and speedways. There is an astonishing tendency on the part of these active market economists not to think about public spending except in terms of the most massive infrastructures, following the example of Soviet economists of the thirties. But, over and above this hardly original area of investment hovers the idea of a Marshall plan for Eastern Europe. Its economic advantages are obvious: an increased foreign demand has none of the even moderate inflationary effects of an internal boost. The proponents of this idea also enumerate its humanitarian effects, its political advantages and its strategic impact. So by a strange detour, the economic unification of Europe, independent of the drift in the continent, will end up by joining the same path. Instead of checking the passage from a Western to a continental Europe, it will spur it on. This is one of the several reasons which help to explain the position of the Russians as regards the European Community. Implacably hostile at a time when it seemed to be an Atlantic appendage, Russia's attitude has become more and more positive as Europe has gained greater independence from the Americans. The Russians have viewed the EC in a more favourable light ever since it became obvious that a unified Europe was inevitably going to lead to an active *Ostpolitik*. The idea of a new Marshall plan was evidence enough of this. The Germans found it much harder to refuse such a boost, having themselves surreptitiously set up their own plan involving aid to the popular democracies in the name of *Mittel Europa*.

The single market readmits the possibility of following an economic policy. We can now excise that deflationist sense of doom which had become the norm in Europe due to various reasons: the severe limitations imposed by an unbelievable interdependence of the member states; the psychological effect of a gradual habituation to the decline; and our cowardice in always wishing to limit as far as possible the privations which would have provided the only answer to the petrol crises. Seen from the vantage point of Europe, this abandonment of any economic policy seems to be a matter of common-sense. But that would be to forget the fact that Japan and the US, both masters of their own economic space, never rejected the idea of controlling essential balance. An atmosphere of liberalism obscured the US Government's habit of bringing a lot of weight to bear on the larger aggregates: incredibly monetarist at certain stages and violently Keynesian at others. In the end, via one of history's classic ruses, only an authentic market can begin to open up the door of economic intervention for its member states. Always supposing, of course, that this immense market will not merely be the prerogative of goods and services but will witness a financial revolution.

The Financial Revolution

In the run-up to 1992, the financial aspect of Europe will play a decisive role. It is already on the move in principle and the most recent decisions made by Finance Ministers concerned ways of putting these principles into practice, such as including transition periods for the weakest economies. What an amazing victory for Pareto and for classic theories about the money market! All those responsible are stating as a matter of course that only the construction of a financial Europe and the consequent free circulation of assets can bring about the perfect balance between savings and investment that is a prerequisite for economic prosperity. On reading some of the declarations of the Community Council of Ministers, one occasionally has the impression of opening an economic policy manual for beginners. Lesson one: savings and investment levels must achieve a balance. Lesson two: the higher the level arrived at, the healthier the economy. Lesson three: a perfect market would allow this equilibrium to be accomplished. And on the basis of these profound thoughts, the most important financial deregulation ever envisaged has been put into action. Nothing escapes it: provision of services must be freed and capital must circulate unfettered. The European project, if realized, will instigate the most competitive money market in the world. The United States will seem, in comparison, to be enmeshed in regulations.

The freeing of services will give any financial institution installed in Europe the right to put its services directly on the market anywhere in the EC, without necessarily having to be established outside its own country, and without having to obey any other regulations and control standards than those of this country. The first of these principles, the right to supply the whole of Europe, will apply to the financial world in the same way as it does to industry: the Banque Nationale Populaire (BNP) will be able to export its credit or its unit trusts from Paris just as Peugeot will be able to export its cars. The second principle, of exclusive control by the country of origin reflects, in financial terms, the priority henceforth given to liberation and harmonization. In the case of a medium-term loan advanced by the BNP in Paris to an enterprise in Hamburg, the regulations of the Banque de France will apply rather than the standards imposed by the Bundesbank. This freedom of long-distance competition between establishments is going to run riot in the financial world, gambling on the most up-to-date systems of telecommunications at the expense of the on-site establishment. Until recently, in order to carve out a share of the market in a country, one had to set up shop, conforming to local regulations and behaving in a similar fashion to all the other banks in that area. Since 1990, a Frenchman can freely open a bank account in Barclays of London and organizations involved in collective placements, such as unit trusts, have been at liberty to place their products abroad since 1989. A Londoner can therefore build up debts in an Italian bank, place his assets in Luxembourg, subscribe to a life assurance policy in Paris and have his damages insurance in London. Anything is possible. Basic deals will not of course be done from a distance just as a Frenchman who wishes to buy a Volkswagen will go to an agent in his area rather than to his competitor in Frankfurt, but there will be sufficient movement across frontiers to bring the conditions of the Community's internal market into alignment. It is a feature of any perfect market that a few exchanges are enough to spread a balanced price throughout.

The free circulation of capital is evidently a necessary condition for this absolute competition. It means the end of exchange controls, of disguised protections, of the desire, which is as old as the states themselves, to jealously guard their national savings. The 'Belgian dentist', that mythical figure of the European market now has mimics in the other eleven member states. A Spaniard can place savings in pounds sterling in Amsterdam, a Frenchman in Deutschmarks. Of paramount concern will be confidence in a currency and its interest rates, the fiscal regime of the recipient country and the quality of service rendered by financial intermediaries. From a comparative weighing up of these diverse elements will emerge a map of the movement of capital. There will be some who claim that progress is more superficial than real and that capital circulates throughout the whole world, not just within the Community. This is true of most main economic aspects, with the exception of those which still have to submit to archaic exchange controls, but it is not true in specific cases. Neither bank deposits, personal loans, mortgages, nor savings could circulate freely until recently. For a Frenchman, unhappy at seeing his account bringing no return, could still not transfer his salary to London in sterling in order to obtain a favourable interest rate.

Consumers, once again, will be the overall winners. Interest rates will fall, particularly for individuals, who until now have been fleeced by the banks, under the protection of national frontiers. That is all coming to an end. The banking system will no longer be able to make up its profit margin, eaten away by its bigger clients, by oppressing individual clients. They will learn in their turn about the harsh laws of productivity: the charms of the sheltered sector will not take long to fade. Alignment on conditions will have to be based on those with the least regimented commerce and the lowest taxation. For the customer, this will be manna from heaven. For the member states it is a guarantee of a loss of fiscal revenue. For organizations controlling the banks, it will mean working along the lines of the most lenient system. One day we will have to pay for this lack of regulation with agencies that expand only to go bankrupt, leaving their consumers high and dry, but these are the risks that go with any rapid freeing of trade restrictions. For the consumer, the Community's most recent hero, the daydream will be perpetuated from industrial products through to financial conditions. But one day this same individual will realize that the advantages he enjoys as consumer and saver are being paid for by his concurrent roles as producer and contributor. It will become necessary to find a new fiscal system. Businesses will look for ways of rechannelling their taxes through their production costs, while individuals will have no way of passing the buck. However, at the moment, at the dawn of this financial revolution, it is still the dream which prevails, the more so since it is becoming rooted in the psychologically gratifying perspective of a European currency.

The Monetary Backbone

Without a common currency, free circulation of capital is a delusion. Instead of Gresham's old law whereby a bad currency drives out a good one, it would be a case of a strong currency laying its law down to a weak one. Take the extreme case of the Greek drachma, competing with the arrogant Deutschmark. An Athenian who wished to open a savings account would give in to the mirage presented by German currency, and there would be no legal way of stopping Greece's capital from gradually draining away. Controls in this area would be just as difficult to set up as safeguards on merchandise have become. Greece would consequently be forced to put up interest rates, for no good macro-economic reason, and would suffer the consequences in terms of austerity. That would be the beginning of a terrible vicious circle in which poorer countries would be condemned to recession because of high interest rates, while richer countries would prosper. Neophytes of an absolute market would have us believe that the wealth created in Germany would give rise to inflation, which would bring with it a devaluation of the mark. What nonsense! Experience has proved that in a universe of unstable exchange rates, rich countries get richer and poor countries are condemned to an extreme tightening of their belts. This phenomenon will be even stronger and less bearable within Europe. The European Monetary System in its present guise is incompatible with a free circulation of capital. One might claim, theoretically, that free circulation would lead to a balance between currencies by means of extensive fluctuation, but fifteen years of flexible exchange rates should have given the lie to this theory. On the other hand one cannot easily believe in stable exchange rates between currencies forced to submit to the ebbs and flows of a free circulation of capital. Such a denial is as unrealistic, in financial terms, as a denial, in chemical terms, that a solid changes form when exposed to heat. The alternative is simple, however. Either the European Monetary System will collapse under incessant compensatory adjustments (strange paradox that a previously financially disparate Europe should have relative stability as regards exchanges whereas a united Europe in financial terms sees a return to fluctuating exchange rates), or it will give way to a real currency, with all its constraints and demands. In the present European euphoria the first hypothesis seems to be out of the question and the second taken for granted. We have to accept the signs as long as the daydream lasts.

A European currency seems at first sight to be the perfect answer; it would be a gauge of the market's success, putting the minimum of constraints in the way of this European space, making macro-economic freedom once again possible, and discouraging the taste for an easy life on the part of certain of the member states. What advantage does a national currency hold nowadays for a small country? It gives it the option of the familiar cycle of boost – growth – deficit – devaluation – austerity – boost. This cycle does not now function with the same efficiency as in the time of the Bretton Woods agreements, but it does still allow the odd gust of *laissez faire* on the part of a few fugitive states. Accounts will, of course, have to be settled in the end, but in the meantime governments can let themselves be taken by the illusion of freedom. With a European currency, that illusion would dissolve and a new rigour would set in. A single currency is also the only way to rid member states of insistent external constraints which risk being exacerbated by the European market. Adjustments will not of course be magicked away completely, but instead of being accomplished through constant devaluations and revaluations, they will come about in the same way as in the fifty US states which are all governed by the dollar, that is, through spending power, spontaneous population immigration and industrial relocation. This logic matches the single market rather more than variable exchange rates which are as little adapted to 1992 as the city toll was to budding trade freedoms. An authentic ecu, not the statistical concept which is currently passing for it, would bestow on a Europe which was in control of its management in terms of political power and a central banking system, all the advantages of an international currency. It would create the capacity to print in massive quantities without having to continually check current conversion rates, the possibility of raising important amounts of capital on behalf of the EC, and the change of controlling interest rate policy. Those are simply the advantages enjoyed by the community as a whole. Each individual state would also enjoy the security of being lashed onto the most powerful economics of the community and the guarantee of a kind of economic life assurance.

However, unlike the single market, the project of a European currency is not going to be brought to fruition simply by the wave of a technocratic magic wand. It signifies a return to an 'administrated' Europe, one of complex agreements, a reluctant abandoning of sovereignty and constant power struggles. Harmonization will make a comeback, with all the sluggishness and difficulties it entails. Here are just some of the problems that need to be solved: will a European currency exclude national currencies, or will they exist side by side? Who will be in charge of it: politicians, the Commission or a central banking system? In the latter case, would this be an American style federal bank or a united bank? How will the ecu be defined? Replacing the current basket of currencies, will it forge an independent relationship with other world currencies? Who will determine the principles of monetary policy: a European organization, an interstate organization, or the governor of a central bank whose actions will be as free as those of Paul Volcker in the US? Who will look after the debt in ecus which underpins this European currency, or the corresponding budgetary credits? What will be the timetable, the transitionary steps? It is an immense task, alongside which the most complex European constraints, such as the Agricultural Policy, seem to be mere 'works in progress'. In other words, Europe's leaders will once more have to wear a different hat. Having abdicated all responsibility to the market, they will be forced to assume their old bridge-building role. Currency is close to the heart of any state – one had only to listen to Mrs Thatcher's reactions to realize that an unshakeable collective volition is needed, far greater than that required to build the Coal and Steel Community or lay to rest the agricultural monster. If a 'constructivist' Europe does not replace the current *laissez faire*, the single market will never fulfil its potential, deprived of the common currency on which it is dependent. This daydream of an economically united Europe will not merely await a miracle; it will also call for a hell of a lot of elbow grease.

Goodies All Round

Everyone is dreaming of 1992; not merely the member states but also powerful foreign competitors. It is possible that the greatest beneficiaries of the united market will be non-Europeans, but, eager not to provoke a protectionist backlash, they tread carefully. As for the European countries, they all expect different benefits from the single market. France, as usual, is the most contradictory: its particular economic structures will have to undergo the most severe processes of adaptation. Industry, banking, insurance and fiscal reform will all require massive sacrifices, as will be seen in the following chapter. The weight of its past will be felt in no uncertain manner: a fiscal structure which favours social contributions rather than taxes, and indirect taxes rather than direct taxes, is inevitably going to suffer. Behind the naive and motivating enthusiasm for 1992 is a much more sophisticated but familiar approach: that of rape with consent. This is not the first time that the French economy has been forced to adopt measures concerning modernization and productivity which it would not have submitted to of its own accord. The trading treaties of the nineteenth century, the Common Market of 1958 or the threat of undergoing the Caudine Forks of the International Monetary Fund: each time the forceps carries out its duties.

France is reacting according to its traditional habits, Britain too. Despite the very liberal philosophy behind the single market, which even Mrs Thatcher could have been proud of, Britain has, as usual, shied at every step of the way. Mrs Thatcher found it impossible to accept the aims of the market, and especially its method – role of a qualified majority – until her budgetary cheque had been cashed. Although reticent when faced with a *laissez-faire* Europe, she was paradoxically the staunchest adversary of any considered action such as an attempt to compensate for the most glaring injustices, as even wars progress towards a common currency. A reluctance to enter the European Monetary System has allowed the British Government to loudly maintain this symbol of anti-European scepticism. This policy, neither fish nor fowl, was totally hypocritical. British institutions, on the other hand, have always vigorously welcomed the idea of a free circulation of capital, since the City would be a principal beneficiary. If any proof were needed that the establishment of a single market is only a moderately important element in the construction of Europe, the British attitude would provide it. Sector-based advantages are certainly agreeable and a return to liberal principles very pleasant, but heaven forbid that this construct should pass itself off as Europe.

The attitude of Germany is much more complex and indicates that the question of Europe revolves around the question of Germany. In its single market capacity, 1992 hardly provokes any objections: either from a militant wing, embodied by Chancellor Kohl who, during the former Federal Republic's presidency of the Community, displayed both enthusiasm and savoir-faire; or from industrialists and financiers who think in terms of a world market and for whom the achievement of a European market would be very convenient, or even from the public, whose enthusiasm for Europe has cooled and who do not look on 1992 as a priority. The ambiguities only start when 1992 begins to take on a significance beyond that of a more competitive market. Projects such as that of monetary union, for example, come up against the old German phobia of losing out through the *laissez-faire* policies of other countries. Ideas of protectionism at the Community's borders provoke a fear of retaliation on the part of industrialists who are anxious about their international outlets. On the other hand, any thoughts concerning the extension of the European market towards the East are anticipated by the Germans, who are eager to exploit to the fullest the ever more porous frontier between the two blocs. Basically, Germany wants a single European market which is open to the West, so as to put no obstacle in the way of its global dynamism, and to the East, in order to reinforce its own policies. Nothing could be more natural on the part of a country which is in the process of completely remodelling Central Europe around itself. The brass tacks seem less certain, however. Germany is tired of acting as the EC's banker and of increasing its own financial efforts on behalf of a European ideal which seems less vital now than it did in the sixties. At that point it at least permitted Germany to free itself from its guilt complex and escape its diplomatic isolation. Nowadays it is no longer the kind of dream which used to prompt Germany into incredible acts of folly, through extremes of honour or of indignity.

The other members of the Community all look at 1992 from their own particular viewpoints, with their own specific expectations. For the spanish, it is the 'big bang', a consolidation of a process of democratic and economic transition entered upon after the death of Franco, and 1992 contains the promise of modernization, development and growth. It is the only unanimously accepted method forcing the pace of change. In effect, 1992 puts the finishing touches on a particularly skilful macro-economic policy directed by the socialists ever since their accession to power. They sat on salaries in order to keep their competitive advantage of 25 per cent which resulted from a relatively low standard of living. They then stepped up investment in industry by relying as much as possible on foreign investors, to the extent that in many sectors the Spanish production machinery is already first rate. And lastly, they used their relationship with the EC to guarantee outlets for an industrial base which had now become hyper-competitive. It is the success of this equation which will secure for Spain a growth rate 1 to 2 per cent higher than the European average for the next few years. For Italy, 1992 does not constitute such a clear objective, a fact that must be connected with the heterogeneity of the country itself. The heads of Italian industry already regard 1992 as a reality; faster and more adaptable, they are better prepared for it than any other country. For a myriad of dynamic medium-sized exporting firms it will come as a godsend, providing extra outlets and a field of expansion to suit their needs. For the archaic bureaucratic sectors of the economic world such as the public services, monopolies of any kind and the banking system, it will be a dramatic challenge, and state-owned companies must be having nightmares at the very thought of the single market. For people with savings, the miracle of free choice combined with Italy's interest rates will turn the country into the Japan of Europe. For the state, it is a powerful administrative crutch, since one can hardly conceive of a 14 per cent deficit in the domestic product in the context of a Europe otherwise heading for monetary union.

The other small countries of the community are getting ready to launch a 'battlement' strategy towards 1992, the only option open to them. For Belgium, then, the aim is to increase the standing of Brussels as a European capital, attracting more and more parent companies. Holland is counting on playing the best cards it has and is busy making preparations; transport firms for example, are teaching their lorry drivers to speak French to that they can take the French market by storm. Luxembourg wishes to extend its role as a tax haven and the country of holding companies when there is a truly free circulation of capital. Portugal and Greece are drawing up a sophisticated plan, involving as rapid a process of modernization as possible, the procurement of temporary transitional protections to avoid an over-dramatic period of adjustment and allocation of community grants via a mechanism of redistribution which will prioritize such countries from the outset. By striking a balance between the limitations and the advantages of 1992, they will be the initial winners.

Everyone has something to gain from the single market which should offset whatever sacrifices and difficulties they will have to put up with. Concomitant stages on the other hand, particularly those involving monetary aspects, will put an end to this agreeable unanimity. Certain countries will be afraid of losing their control over monetary decisions. Others, the single currency's first victims, will fear the budgetary transfers required in compensations. A third group, made up principally of weaker countries, will feel, on the contrary, that these subsidies are not enough to create a proper balance in terms of spending power. The last group will fear the loss of certain specifically economic aspects, such as the public deficit, which they have previously managed to turn to suit their own ends. When the time comes for construction rather than liberation, these reservations and worries will begin to mount up, and the current illusion of a united Europe, a land of milk and honey, will start to dissolve.

This image has all the disadvantages of an instant snap; it gauges the aspirations of each member state by their relative strengths, while ignoring the fact that behind this economic evolution is a demographic earthquake which is about to overturn the present hierarchy. Is it possible to imagine Germany, with an ageing population of 40 million and the consequently unbearable burden of pensions, exerting an undisputed influence over the community? What courses of action will a shrinking Holland be left with? What influence will Britain exert when its declining population is further burdened by an increase in Commonwealth immigration at the lower end of the social scale? Southern countries, whose population statistics, although by no means wonderful, seem by comparison to be extremely healthy, will be the ones to gain the advantage. Their dynamism and efficiency will guarantee a comfortable macro-economic balance, a sustainable welfare state and respectable productivity figures. With 1.8 to 1.9

children per woman, France seems positively prolific set against West Germany's 1.1 or 1.2. Two centuries on, France is rediscovering the status it used to enjoy as the European country with the strongest demography. This last occurred in the 1800s, and its economic consequences today are just as important. The single market will amplify these population developments favouring those countries with a potentially young and vigorous workforce. The long-term effects of 1992 will therefore differ considerably from its more immediate impact, with the threat of an increasing rift between countries with a stable population and those in the process of human desertification.

Conversely, Europe will undoubtedly be a land of plenty for non-Europeans, who will get the lion's share of the cake. The creation of an internal market without any form of external protection is a godsend for which they were only partially prepared by the philosophy behind the Community. It is the complete opposite in every way of the Common Agricultural Policy which made Europe into a high price zone, protected from the outside by a system of buffers, levies and compensations and where producers were encouraged into other markets, by means of subsidies. Agriculture is undoubtedly a world of hidden subsidies and covert transfers of cash. The US is well acquainted with such a system but European protectionism is more than a match for its American rival. However, as far as goods and services are concerned, European naivety is truly staggering and current anxiety on the part of foreign competitors goes no further than wondering whether Europe might one day catch on to their own ingenuity.

Competitors would derive all of the advantages of a united Europe, without any of the disadvantages. Imagine a homogeneous economic area with a population of 320 million, a high level of spending and sophisticated habit of consumerism, a quality workforce, abundant savings and, to cap it all, totally open to the outside world. What an unbelievable stroke of luck! What an incredible substitute for the Japanese, accustomed to the defence mechanism of American commerce with its 'self-regulating' import quotas. What a gust of fresh air for the States, badly in need of outlets. What a miracle for new exporters such as Brazil and Korea who were turned away from Japan and restricted by the US. The Europe of goods and services looks like becoming the Balkans of the world. The Japanese are methodically adapting their industrial armoury and making sure that it is in good working order. Countless large firms have already ordered their subsidiaries to prepare themselves for the invasion of Europe. The community will have to expect a rush of Japanese imports and a flood of investments as they seek first to carve out their share of the market, and then to fully secure it. There will be no hesitation from other countries either, although the scale of the attack might not be so great. After all, it is not every day that such openings present themselves without any price to be paid in terms of reciprocal concessions.

This time around, the financial world will not be protected from such a deluge. The freeing of services and of the circulation of capital amounts to no less than a formal invitation to foreigners. What incredible facilities for American and Japanese banks which will be able to dispense with the maintenance of a costly distribution network involving them in the same inflated expenses as their European colleagues. Instead they will install a single establishment in Europe, preferably in the country with the most lenient regulations, and will then be free to decide on their own riches in the market. What a field day! In the rush towards lower costs, areas of the market will fall one after the other. Japanese banks already dominate the Eurocredits market in dollars, which, being the only non-regulated sector at present, best reflects the future of financial Europe. When the various European banking and financial markets function along the same lines as Eurocredits, EC banks will have to pick up a heavy bill. The opening out of the Community to the outside world will harbour a triple paradox. It will further emancipate the frontiers of an area which is anyway the least protected in the world, above all when compared to other dominant countries such as Japan and America. It offers an unsolicited free gift to European competitors without seeking to obtain any reciprocal concessions, and it thus creates a situation of unfair competition between European countries and their competitors. The former, if they wish to take advantage of the single market, will have to pay a heavy price in terms of an accelerated restructuring process, the disappearance of certain firms and an entire reworking of the industrial and financial landscape. The latter, on the other hand, will be able to reap the benefits of a united Europe while having made no contribution, not even in the form of duty tax, to the establishment of this market. For Europeans the single market will show a balance in favour of advantages rather than disadvantages while foreigners can only benefit from it. One begins to understand the pro-European feeling which occupies entire foreign newspaper columns devoted to the new attitude of the Old Continent, Euro-optimism, and other such cliches.

1992: In our Heads or our Hearts?

Economic processes have a tendency to be extremely lengthy and the single European market is currently being anticipated by wholesale restructurings, inter-corporate liaisons and take-over bids, etc. Change is on the way, whether voluntary or not, but the progression from heart to head, from instinct to reason, is a long one. The author would here like to spend a paragraph discussing points brought up by his own experience of the first public purchase offer on a European scale, that of the take-over of the Société Générale de Belgique.

At the outset, the situation seemed clear: one of the most dynamic concerns in Europe, led by a universally recognized industrialist, namely Carlo de Benedetti, wished to take control of that very ancient society, the Société Générale de Belgique. The reasoning behind this take-over bid was almost simplistic: given the prospect of the single market, European holding companies would be created whose assets would be spread throughout the whole of Europe, rather than remaining in any one single country. The plan, if the bid were successful, was to bring together all these holding companies, attackers and attacked, and to put the Société Générale at their head, with Brussels, the capital of Europe, as the seat of this industrial and financial empire. A real textbook case in the new perspective of 1992. Over and above the financial battle, the judicial imbroglio, the absence of laws in Belgium and the final outcome, it is the sociopolitical dimension of the whole operation which serves to highlight the problems inherent in the constitution of the single market. If we are willing to look at this event in an objective light, there are many lessons to be learnt.

The first lesson is that nationalism is alive and kicking and informs each country's attitudes. The member states regard Europe as a battlefield and its companies as mobile armies which must be protected if necessary, by the authorities of each country. But the various states are not equally equipped to deal with this situation. Countries without a well-organized administration and a strong government are powerless. The Belgian Government, for instance, was basically impotent in the face of the battle over the Société

Générale de Belgique. But imagine this conflict transferred to France or Great Britain; the authorities in these countries could have opposed such an operation, if they had wished. It is no coincidence that the Bank of England's consent must be given to any proposed holding greater than 15 per cent in an organization, however modest, which controls a bank. The Bank of France, not to be outdone, set an even lower limit of 10 per cent, as Italian General Insurance discovered to their cost at the time of their take-over bid for the Compagnie du Midi.

The second lesson here is that public opinion is more pro-European than was previously imagined. Once the initial excitement had died down, there was no noticeable xenophobia on the part of the Belgian public. Although it was initially stunned by the idea of an Italian at the head of an institution even older than the monarchy, this incredulity soon subsided. For the mobile sectors in society, young professionals, business people in key areas, Europe represents all that is modern, and from this point of view, national preoccupations are hardly pressing. Although inclined to be more reserved, progressive unions are nevertheless on the same side; they hope that Europe will force businesses to get rid of certain archaic codes of social practice. As for investors, it is nothing new for them to ignore the call of nationalism. The Générale's shareholders in Belgium threw themselves onto the market in order to take advantage of the prices offered without worrying unduly about whether they were reinforcing the battle strength of two foreign powers. No amount of patriotic feeling was going to restrain such people from selling. So it goes without saying that given free circulation of capital in Europe, self-interest will reign, putting paid to any qualms about tradition and local enterprise.

The third lesson concerns Europe's traditional elite who experience the most difficulties in making the switch from theory to practice. They feel threatened by the inevitable shape-ups caused by the single market, and fear the loss of their power monopoly. In Belgium, and even more so in France, they reacted to the take-over of the Générale de Belgique as if witnessing the erosion of a sacred myth regarding the unassailability of the old economic feudal system, whose ancient organizations should have been protected by their own renown. 'If boundaries are transgressed, there are no longer any limits' announced sagely the Sapeur Camember, a sentiment which was shared by many powerful people. At that point a Holy Alliance of certain institutions was formed to put a halt to the operation, an attempt which, even had it succeeded, would have been about as much use as trying to empty the sea with a thimble. Witness the attempt on the Compagnie du Midi, a month later, by the Italian 'Generali' and at the instigation of the very mercantile bank that had become the hero of the establishment in its defence of the Générale de Belgique.

The fourth lesson is that this defensive reflex on the part of the establishment is not arbitrary. It demonstrates the problems confronting any organization when it discovers, to its cost, that 1992 is synonymous with competition and that in an open market, no monopoly, whether of power, of knowledge, of regulation or of customs, will last for long. The first shocks will be painful and Malthus-type restrictions will attempt to provide some sort of defence. Whether this succeeds or not will be decided by the public and by governments. Which side will the former take? And which the latter?

Fifth lesson: in a peaceful society, without generation conflicts or social dramas, the economic arena has become a kind of substitute battlefield. It is the only area where people discuss strategies and tactics, join forces or repulse attacks. The resultant epic tale of industry and finance has provoked great media interest which will continue to increase with the expansion of the battlefield now under way. This phenomenon is slightly ambivalent in its relationship with the European idea. On the one hand it draws attention to the speed at which Europe is being re-shaped, on the other, it provides a resonance chamber for negative reactions and rearguard actions.

The affair of the Société Générale de Belgique has given the capitalist world a preview of the shocks inherent in the constitution of the single market. Pliable and mobile by nature, capitalism reacts quickly and sees clearly the meaning of 1992 in everyday terms. But nothing – not even the most highly protected economic sector, profession or specialized field – will survive this resolution intact. That is what the single market is all about. To stage left, it promises an ageing Europe greater prosperity, a renewed sense of dynamism and a new economic deal: this is the daydream. To stage right, it will give rise to imbalances, back-stabbing, new inequalities and unexpected injustices, these are the inevitable manifestations of a Darwinian nightmare.

Notes

1 Expression used to describe Taiwan, Singapore, Hong Kong and South Korea.
2 *1992, le défi: Nouvelles données economiques de l'Europe sans frontières* (1992, the Challenge: New Economic Data on a Europe without Frontiers), Communautés européennes, Flammarion, 1988.
3 See the final chapters, below.
4 Michel Albert, *Le Pari européen* (The European Wager), Seuil, 1984.
5 Albert and Boissonnat, *Crise, krach, boom.*

8

The Darwinian Nightmare

The liberal enthusiasm which presides over the construction of the single market is anything but unprecedented. Every advance towards free trade has been accompanied by the conviction that such a move would bring about an economic paradise on earth. This mercantile dream of Utopia has shown its face once or twice each century since its first appearance in England in 1750. But with the coming of complex societies, such ideological flights of fancy seemed to be on the wane. The market was an excellent tool, state intervention was justifiable and regulations could be imposed; it was simply a case of striking the right balance. But now Manicheanism makes its comeback. This time it certainly has the usual elements of daydream about it, but it also exhibits nightmarish aspects, according to one's point of view or the features one chooses to exaggerate. If 'Euro-ideology' insists on promising us the attractions of all that lies in store, it is a matter of intellectual common-sense to look at the flip side of this rosy picture. It gives some indication of the problems to be tackled, it also demonstrates that once the single market is in operation, Europe will have to travel the same path as any economy abruptly liberated: it will have to invent a new welfare state in order to cushion shocks and share out sacrifices.

The Darwinian purge is both inevitable and unjust. Inevitable since the realization of the single market was the only way to stimulate Europe and since the dramatic priority given to liberalization of trade over harmonization of regulation will enable enterprise to escape the mire of European agreement efforts. Unjust, since the kiss of life given by the market in the absence of any compensating system of redistribution will have the automatic effect of making the strong even stronger and the weak even weaker. The fruit of the single market, i.e., a percentage rise in the national product, threatens to go inevitably to the more prosperous. Their dynamism does of course benefit the whole economy; that is the old quarrel between liberalism and social democracy. But in this case, the match is considerably more imbalanced than if it were simply a national matter: one country might procure immense benefits leaving another with nothing. Jacques Delors was the first to be convinced of this and called for the setting up of corrective mechanisms. But the first manifestations of the Darwinian nightmare and a fear of seeing societies rebel against each other will doubtless be required before the basis of a welfare state can be established.

The Trauma of Competition

Nothing will escape the rigours of competition from now on. Industrial products which used to hide behind non-tariff barriers, services which until now have ignored the international arena, and professions which were strictly regulated, will all have to submit to this new mode of functioning. So too will aspects of production such as capital, inevitably, since it is the first requirement of a free circulation of money, and also employment. In that area, there may be a few unpleasant shocks in store.

The battle regarding the proposed obligatory installation of catalytic converters in new cars is highly informative. It demonstrates to what an extent the market would have been thwarted if demands for a harmonization of legislation had continued. There are nevertheless three areas which still escape the primacy of the process of liberation, namely health, security and the environment. This astonishing list of exceptions seem to indicate a certain amount of political arbitration. The Germans succeeded in making sure that the environment figures on this list in order to satisfy their green contingent and thus avoid the beginnings of an anti-European feeling based on ecological factors. But if those were the ground rules, why did the French not demand an exception to be made of cultural aspects, and the Italians of fashion? Everyone has their own secret garden. Health must be credited to the British influence alongside the German lobby on behalf of the environment. These exceptions highlight internal power relations within the Community. In the absence of such specific cases of regulation, protective mechanisms on cars would have been at the discretion of the producing country, with the ultimate decision made in the marketplace. If the Germans had carried on collectively prioritizing a clean environment over cost considerations, they would have been free to choose cars which were more ecologically sound but more expensive. They would not have given in to the Sirens of low cost if this meant buying a car with no converter. This is the type of situation that will constitute a kind of communal law from now on. It goes without saying that there will be a few surprises in store, including a proliferation of 'Made in Greece' and 'Made in Portugal' labels. Previously benefiting from low production costs, these countries will derive further advantage from their lenient system of regulations. In order to attract work, governments will undoubtedly manufacture deliberately flimsy regulations in the same way as they invented loopholes in the tax system. The new order will keep some surprises up its sleeve. For consumers, for instance, once the initial charm of lower prices is over, for businesses, which will see competition arising from unexpected sources, for administrations, forced to graduate from sophistication to superficiality, and finally for businesses outside the community, which will continually discover new scope for action. Hyper-competition involves all these consequences; it is not merely a matter of reduced prices to delight consumers flabbergasted by this permanent miracle.

Alongside this financial hubbub and reorganization, the liberation of services is going to rock the boat still more violently when it begins to take advantage of the clause regarding 'the member state with the most lenient regulations'. All regulated professions are going to be prised from their protective shells: doctors, road haulage contractors and lawyers, to name but a few. They are the market's most recent pawns and are being asked to discard their familiar defensive and corporate strategies and to play a more attacking role. It is a cultural revolution that is being demanded of them. Protectionism always gives rise to rear-guard actions, mentality that is perhaps the hardest habit to break. Take French doctors. They are currently fighting about rates of consultation as though nothing had happened. Has it escaped them that, after 1992, they will suffer a level of competition which will bear down enormously on the cost of services? Their real challenge is to confront this future scenario with an improved, up-dated level of organization. Under corporatist logic, in which as many professional costs as possible are referred to the community, what they should be demanding is that the state fund a detailed restructuring project. Once the first shock waves have been felt, the medical world will undergo a shedding process far greater than has ever yet been envisaged. As for the road haulage contractors, who are currently campaigning on day- and night-time working hours, what will benefits gained now be worth come 1992, when less demanding competitors in search of freight begin flooding French roads? Maybe they will be able to achieve a minimum of protection on the pretext of security requirements, but any other elements which determine the cost of transport will be imposed on them by competition. The profession has just about enough time to modernize itself, to do some hard thinking and to provide a competitive response on this adverse territory. The question is, will it actually make the necessary effort? How will lawyers fare in the same position? Synonymous, in France, with individualism, this profession is only now beginning to accept collective chambers. With one exception, twenty or thirty lawyers in an association seems to be considered a maximum. Is any forethought going into how best to survive out and out competition with enormous English chambers? In comparison to France, these latter seem to be veritable judicial factories with a Taylor-like organization of work, and a constant pressure towards productivity. And what about pharmacists? They are too busy carrying on a political lobby against insurance pharmacies to have the time to prepare for the total lack of restrictions that is now inevitable. Insurance brokers? They still think that mutual societies pose the greatest threat to their patch, and continue to rail against them as they have done for the past twenty years. Have they not yet realized that heightened competition between European companies will oblige them to look to the shortest and most productive distribution channels? Taxi-drivers? Solicitors? Auctioneers? Do they imagine that they can preserve a restricted intake which has survived artificially since the Reuff-Armand liaison in 1958, in a Europe with free professional competition? The approaching earth tremor is going to be very violent, and these professions would do well not to waste the time and energy that they still possess in futile rearguard battles. The quality of French diplomas gives them a savoir-faire which ought to allow them to play an offensive rather than a defensive role. But through a perverse Malthusian effect, these professionals are often rather more familiar with defensive stratagems and a dependence on the State, than with open-minded and strategic dynamism.

Turning aside from products and services themselves, an equally savage competition is likely to hit the production chain. From the

point of view of investment, the situation is clear. Free circulation of
capital must be the order of the day and the Brussels Commission has
a responsibility to track down the origins of any subsidies, tax
avoidance schemes and other localized infringements which threaten
to corrupt the process of competition. Brussels is becoming more
rigorous in its execution of these duties. It now controls the Court of
Justice in Luxembourg with the result that fraud and swindling of any
kind will be much more difficult in the future: regional aid will only
be accepted under the name of the Community's redistribution
policy. But the greatest effect of competition in this area will be felt as
a pressure on the cost of labour. The Irish phenomenon of
multiplying foreign investments in Spain, and more recently in
Portugal, is only the beginning of a fierce competition to bring down
the price of labour. Countries with higher social standards will
inevitably be on the defensive. Minimum wages, average pay, hours of
work, subsidiary rights concerning training and worker representation:
all these will be in the hot seat. It is not unduly pessimistic to think
that the more socially advanced countries will be less likely to elevate
backward countries, than to be themselves dragged down. If the
unions were at their strongest the old balancing act might still be
possible through international solidarity on alignment of restrictive
and non-restrictive practices. But how can we expect unions which
are currently incapable of exerting any power on a national scale, to
find the means to do so at a Community level? In the absence of any
process of harmonization conducted by the state, a generalized
pressure will obviously lead to an erosion in social rights. The natural
and indeed healthy dialectic between the market and the social
framework will be subverted, allowing the former to flourish while the
latter wastes away. Logically, employment and social rights ought to
be transferred from national to community level. But without social
pressure, this is a task worthy of Sisyphus. Several factors are working
against such an evolution: the technical difficulties of harmonization,
a lack of experience of such matters on the part of the authorities, the
distinction, different in each member state, between contractual and
public laws, and finally the strength of the interests at stake. For once,
it is the weakest countries which are holding all the aces; why should
they squander them? This is demonstrated by the example of the
Spanish socialists, who were careful not to allow salaries to slide
towards the European norm. Social responsibilities are also involved
in this particular game, implying competition between different social

systems. The difficulties involved in elevating less favoured countries would be immense, even given a massive amount of public support on the matter. How could one decide on a fair pension for a Portuguese person who has never made any kind of contribution as opposed to a Dane who has contributed for the whole of his life. And who would pay this pension? British engineers, Belgian dentists or Italian entrepreneurs? Such arbitrations and compromises between social groups constitute major stumbling blocks. Agricultural Europe discovered as much when it suffered a thousand and one nocturnal marathons in order to establish the correct balance between a cereal grower from the Beauce and a Dutch cattle breeder, a Mediterranean citrus producer and a Bavarian farmer. This is not to say that we will see an identical repetition of this phenomenon. A return of the class struggle would be needed for such a dynamic to reappear, a hypothesis which is most unlikely in the current climate. In this context, the Darwinian-style purge could be expected to lead to an erosion of social rights – to use union jargon – rather than to an improvement.

Under the influence of the single market, the least restrictive country should force a process of readjustment on the most restrictive, the most generous firms on the least generous, the most developed social system on the least developed. Let's not be too neurotic: the German system of social security is not going to remodel itself on the Greek system, Danish salaries on Portuguese salaries, British working hours on Spanish ones, and the French minimum wage on the Irish. But to a certain extent, the advantages currenly gained have reached their limit. There will be a considerable amount of pressure to restrict them and even to gradually eat away at them. This will certainly be the only way to defend employment in the more well-off member states and to prevent excessive transfers of shares and investments. Viewed from the angle of traditional social demands, 1992 does not look like being a bundle of laughs.

An intensification of the differences between richer and poorer, advanced and less advanced countries, inevitable in a wider market, will occur from the outset. Massive current discrepancies are exhibited in the extremes of a 1 to 15 ratio between the spending power of the poorest region in Greece and the richest German Land and a 1 to 10 difference in unemployment rates between the 3 per cent in Luxembourg and the 30 per cent in Andalucia. Such inequalities remain only half acknowledged in a Europe which is not yet in a position to see itself clearly. They will be felt more keenly in a single market where mutual knowledge will progress at the same rate as exchanges of products, capital and manpower. Will this be enough to spark off compensatory mechanisms in the member states, given that a cessation of conflicts hardly augurs well for redistribution among social groups? Nothing is less certain; Europe seems incapable of instituting the maximum of social harmonization to go along with this liberation of trade barriers.[1]

An Economic Battlefield

1992 is no mere bagatelle. A war fought by industrialists and financiers will be no joke and member states will be anything but indifferent. Just as freedom of trade will give rise to competition between the various levels of regulation, the battlefield constituted by the single market will bring with it a violent contest between state–industrial concerns. However much Brussels tries to keep an eye on signs of state intervention in the name of the free market, it will never be able to confront the thousand and one understandings that provide a mutual support system between the state apparatus and the world of big business. From this point of view, the Germans have at their disposal an incredible advantage. Their government is never in the front line, and the Länder are, without exception, discreet. This oligopoly, consisting of the most important economic concerns, takes charge of its own regulation just as in Bismarck's time. Banks, insurance companies and industrial groups support each other by means of a tightly knit web of interaction, running through the entire national space; a take-over bid is not going to succeed in Germany in the near future. This web also ensures discipline within the production apparatus. What can the Commission say about a decision that has been taken in the boardroom of the Deutsche Bank or Siemens? It is hard to understand why these private societies should wish to acquire operations for reasons other than profitability, but in the economic war about to commence between the twelve member states, nothing could be more valuable than a 'self-sufficient' economic and sociological system. The French and the British are obviously handicapped by the power of the state at the heart of their state–industrial concerns. Because of this they are always on the defensive, obliged to justify themselves according to a supposedly pure market which in fact contains more than a touch of comfortable hypocrisy.

For these state–industrial complexes, 1992 has already kicked-off. They are currently obeying rule number one in the game of strategy, namely to batten down their territory. From this standpoint, the degree of integration between German businesses is impressive. This can be interpreted either as an indication of a type of bizarre industrial in-breeding, incompatible with any foreign expansion, or as a calculated rationalization prior to foreign conquests. The latter hypothesis is more likely in this case, since according to a firmly rooted tradition, German industry does not feel at ease until it has ensured domination over its own market. Such internal rationalization processes to prepare for the impact of the single market are not restricted to Germany either. Mrs Thatcher did not hesitate to hand Rover over to British Aerospace under conditions which would have made the most interventionist socialist green with envy. Spanish banks, too, are being forced to regroup amongst themselves in order to achieve the necessary internal stature, before going international. France escapes this whirlwind to a certain extent, having entered the international arena later than others. Its enterprises are currently developing further into foreign markets rather than regrouping internally except in rare cases such as Asia-Midi or Louis Vuitton-Moet-Hennessy. The battening down of the national market ultimately foreshadows transnational confrontations of a violent nature: certain latent nationalist impulses will be tacked on to the pure game of capitalism and the battle for the Société Générale de Belgique will seem like a romantic preamble by comparison.

The existence of powerful public sectors within certain countries bears down on the competition between state–industrial concerns. On the face of it they constitute a kind of Achilles heel, attracting the suspicion, even the hostility, of other member states. But although a struggling public concern might be a real handicap, a prosperous state institution will undoubtedly be an asset, as long as the country in question is discreet with its capital, behaving as a major investor rather than an outright owner. In this role, it will protect the company from external attack, allow it to run according to classic capitalist rules and guarantee it indirect sponsorship. A firm such as the Compagnie Française des Pétroles in France has a bright future. As for public monopolies, the best and most efficient, such as our transport and electricity, will benefit from deregulation. The French electricity board might even be able to export all of its surplus nuclear electricity. Technological dynamism is not going to be enough, although there will have to be a real cultural revolution before business acumen and organizational versatility take on the same imperative as technical progress. This vision of the public sector as being a possible asset in the context of the single market does not match the prevailing urge to cost the state out of the game entirely. It would of course be more natural and even more healthy, but let's not be naive. Governments will never be indifferent to the future of their large companies in a unified market. A certain amount of favouritism always remains. Even in the US, Washington State cares more about Boeing than about IBM, since Seattle's continued prosperity depends on the former. And the authorities in Texas pursue rather more intimate relations with the oil industry than with the automobile construction industry. On top of this initial motivation there are always cultural understandings and the natural desire for those in power to protect their own universe. Indeed, isn't German-style oligopoly above all a sociological phenomenon? It is thus perfectly possible to make skilful use of the public sector, as long as the state relinquishes its position of dominance. Managed by force, national enterprises will be a handicap in 1992; subtly coaxed by a discreet but attentive shareholding state, they could become an asset in the merciless struggle between state–industrial concerns.

A Fiscal Earthquake

Of all the indirect upheavals entailed by 1992, the fiscal earthquake is definitely the most profound, the least controllable and the most unsettling for certain social conventions. Tax is one of the few areas where the role of the qualified majority does not prevail. Instead, each country still has a sovereign right of veto if its interests do not happen to coincide with the majority. This leads to a truly paradoxical situation. In order to complement the single market, the European tax system needs an immense amount of adjustment and yet the decision-making processes currently in force put the system at the mercy of the egotism of a single member state. A quick glance at the situation is enough to demonstrate that diversity is the rule and similarity the exception. Initial moves towards realignment are already implying some fairly drastic consequences.

The Brussels Commission has started by tackling the problem of VAT in the light of the disappearance of national frontiers. Any perpetuation of the present system, which involves a process of de-taxation of exports and taxation of imports, would require the maintenance of frontier controls, inimical to the aims and especially to the spirit of 1992. It was thus decided that VAT should be regulated according to destination. An exporter would pay VAT at the rate of the importing country, having deducted an intermediate VAT payable at the country of origin. In this way the sacred neutrality of the tax would be preserved. But with no compensatory mechanisms, the consequent proliferation of blind transfers of fiscal receipts would lead to the establishment of a system of remuneration such that the tax collected initially would return eventually to the country of consumption. Let us pass over the complexity of the plumbing required to channel this flood: each state will calculate its accrued and deduced tax on a monthly basis and the balance will go towards a process of redistribution. Frontier formalities will thus be transferred from businesses to states, who will subsequently do their accounts with no technical worries for the taxpayer. The installation of this complex machinery will go along with a second decision involving the coordination of the rates of VAT in the twelve countries, each of which has been placed in one of two bands, 4 to 9 per cent or 14 to 20 per cent. Then the real difficulties begin. The Commission justifies this realignment of taxes on the grounds of simplicity and the larger of the bands on the basis that rates that differ by 5 to 6 per cent do not entail unacceptable distortions in competition. The US serves as an example of a large internal market which sustains deviations in local taxes of up to 9 per cent. However this line of reasoning is ultimately specious. If one takes into account the neutrality of VAT as regards enterprises, which in this case are simply acting as tax collectors, why should common rates be necessary? The rate in force in a specific country, even if it is unnaturally high, applies equally to all transactions and therefore does not disrupt competition. And to worry about the effect of very different rates of tax of the level of consumption in a particular country seems to be rather a roundabout way of justifying harmonization. Something which at first sight has all the appearance of a truism is no such thing when looked at more carefully. Here the measures envisaged are out of all proportion to their end result. Obviously countries with the highest rates will be penalized, but they will simply have to resign themselves to such sacrifices. In response to France, which is particularly worried about these rates, the Commission cites the growth in profits that the French treasury will make from the realignment, also obligatory, of excise duty on tobacco, alcohol and fuel. According to their calculations, profits and losses will balance themselves out. This is a false parallel, however, since VAT indexed to eventual consumption has the best fiscal revenue, while specific taxes are dependent on products such as tobacco and alcohol which are on the decline. For a country with particularly important indirect taxes, such a realignment of the level of VAT will be very costly. Certain malevolent tongues suspect their partner–competitors of having forced harmonization on VAT in order to restrain the budgetary freedom enjoyed by France and indirectly the support given by the state to its enterprises. Even if this is mere vituperation the result will not in fact be so very different.

As well as this initial harmonization decided on by the Community, there will be further measures imposed by the market. One such example will be taxes on savings. With the free circulation of capital, tax havens will be at a premium. Jersey and Luxembourg already provide a service whereby the anonymity of depositors is total, their revenues are exonerated and, thanks to the conventions involved in double taxation, they can normally recuperate tax credits imposed in the country of origin. That old caricature of the financial market, the 'Belgian dentist', embodies this type of saver: he pays off obligatory international contributions from Luxembourg, thus avoiding deduction at source, which in the case of Belgium is 25 per cent. In the future, the French will legally be able to manage their affairs in Luxembourg, being totally exempt from any tax. Will there be many people who respect their legal obligation to declare foreign revenue? Any country, if it so desires, could decide to become a tax haven for non-residents, shifting the savings circuit to suit itself. This is the clause of the 'country with the lowest taxation'. There is only one solution to this brain teaser: the establishment of equal deduction at source throughout the Community, on all revenues of transferable value. But since the unanimity ruling, any state which has chosen for itself the development possibilities of a tax haven can block measures which would force it to cut short this profitable side-line. In this way, a member state can impose a major constraint on the overall tax system, without danger of retaliation. A lowering of taxation on savings is therefore the only, hardly glorious, response to the hijacking of savings.

In addition to tax evasion on certain products, fiscal fraud generally threatens to become an industry with exponential growth possibilities. Take, for example, the case of an Italian jumper, made in Naples and sold in Paris. Under the present system, the product passed the frontier with no VAT and was hit in France; the tax inspectors' task was simply to prevent sale without VAT. In the new system the French treasury will have to expect a double receipt: on the one hand, the payment of the different between the VAT charged in France and the VAT collected upstream in Italy; on the other, the reimbursement of this latter VAT due to the bias inherent to the compensation chamber. The efficiency of the French fiscal system will also be largely dependent on the diligence of the Italian administration in Naples. Once again this textbook case is clear. One does not have to be a genius to invent complex circuits with multiple stages which would have the effect of increasing losses in transit and frauds of all kinds. The map of such capital transfers would obviously match that of fiscal severity and such circuits would multiply according to the mediocrity and corruption of fiscal administrations. The most conscientious will be left champing at the bit, at the mercy of less efficient or less scrupulous colleagues. In order to avoid this slide, it would require a coordination of fraud-fighting policies as well as an agreement to adopt the most fastidious, the most severe of Europe's tax directives. Happy illusion! On the contrary, what we are threatened with is a downgrading of the more respectable services via a process of mimesis. If, in addition to VAT fraud, there is an increase in fraud on tobaccos and alcohols which have unified laws and also of fraud connected with mobile tax systems, then we have a fermenting jar for cheating, evasion and embezzlement.

Fiscal perturbations linked to the single market will be all the greater since the Community has no power to design an integrated system. Direct personal and commercial taxation, social levies, innumerable limited taxes and all death duties escape its jurisdiction entirely. All it can manage to do is to coat the existing tax structures of each country with a thin veneer. An inevitable source of short-circuits, perversions and confusions, this situation will only lead to even greater fiscal injustice.

Undertaxing the Rich, Overtaxing the Poor?

It is worth unwinding the thread of the relationship between taxes and savings through the ages to its very beginning. For the first half of the twentieth century, the idea prevalent in developed countries was that capital income ought to be taxed more heavily than earned income. This was the ABC of fiscal justice. But since then, the principle has been further and further weakened. Paradoxically enough, in a period which saw the high-point of social-democracy, work was harder hit than capital; this was certainly the case in France from 1960 onwards. Then, twelve years ago, the menace of tax havens, the need to regenerate savings and an expansion which meant that every worker became a potential saver led numerous governments to tax capital less severely than income. This is what gave rise to deduction at source, whereby tax was imposed proportionally, at a fixed rate rather than progressively according to wealth; also to tax reliefs which tended to further decrease this progressivity, and to tax credits, which had the effect of levelling out the amount payable by taxpayers. France was particularly brilliant at this particular game: a 25 per cent levy on revenue from bonds, a 16 per cent tax on any transferable benefits above a threshold of 300,000 francs as against a rapidly progressive income tax with a cut-off point of 56.5 per cent! Death duties, on the other hand, only reached a maximum of 40 per cent for a direct line of inheritance, as if inherited money was more legitimate than money earned!

Bizarrely enough, it was Mrs Thatcher who gave the signal for change of direction: she returned tax on capital gains and salaries to an equal footing, the former raised and the latter lowered. But the free circulation of capital will not permit such equalizing gestures. States will inevitably be forced to adjust taxes on savings to as low a level as possible. Faced with movements of capital motivated by tax evasions – we can hardly count on a citizen's duty to declare his or her dividends and interest accrued abroad – member states have only two options. Either they can bury their heads in the sand and keep taxes unchanged, refusing to recognize that in practice the vast majority of capital, particularly that of large companies, will be exempt. Or they can match law with reality and systematically drive taxes down to the point where a kind of legal exemption is in force. In either case, capital revenue is not going to bring in very much. If, in an attempt to keep inheritances intact, certain governments introduce incentives for investment savings, capital will not even be taxed; it will benefit from a negative tax. Obviously taxes on earnings will have to carry the brunt of this lack of capital revenue and income tax will rise proportionally. What a blow for retributory justice! The European tax system will end up reducing capital tax and raising income tax, in other words giving to the rich and taking from the poor. This is not of course a deliberate course of action, but the result of a combined alchemy of the single market, the free circulation of capital and the rights of veto in fiscal matters which allows the least important member state to strengthen the tyranny of tax havens.

This corruption of a united Europe is very ill timed. It raises its head at the very moment when the balance between income tax and inheritance tax is under question. A phase of increasing parity of net income is now coming to an end. And at the same time, with the reappearance of realistic levels, the disparities created by inherited capital are once more growing. The inequality of inheritance income will be as decisive at the end of the century as inequality of income in the fifties. It will give rise to tensions, conflicts and a sense of dissatisfaction, especially in an ageing society where established fortunes have the upper hand. The return of the idle rich, albeit in Eurobonds, will be a problem. The responsibility of exorcising this ugly spectre of capital inequality lay squarely in the hands of the fiscal departments, just as it had done for wages inequality, and ordinarily pressures of society would have led in the same direction. The influence that tax havens are now exerting must be put on the debit side of Europe. If the communist party were only in a state to fulfil their customary declamatory role, what an opportunity for facile reactions this would be: a Europe of big investors; a Europe for the rich; a one-sided Europe. That others should be seizing on these themes is even more worrying. Europe is not going to succeed through a return to the archaic model of the nineteenth century.

A Defenceless France

France, with its usual sense of paradox, is at once the most enthusiastic supporter of 1992 among the twelve member states, and also the country undoubtedly condemned to the greatest difficulties. Is this a lack of awareness on its part? Or the devilish kind of intelligence by which it welcomes something that will force it into renewed action? At any rate the price it will have to pay seems very high at the moment. Let us hope that the benefits of the single market will become quickly apparent in order to counterbalance the inevitable frustrations brought about by the purge.

The most serious handicap to France will undoubtedly lie in the changes to the tax system. The French economy is about to suffer all the drawbacks of being the furthest removed from these new standards. Only Greece, it seems, will have more problems. The French system has always chosen the least painful tax options: social contributions undertaken by businesses rather than by individuals, a social levy rather than a personal tax and indirect taxation in preference to direct taxation, without even taking into account a myriad of specific taxes such as car insurance premiums. The eventual tally is a heavy one: obligatory levies are as high as 45 per cent of the national product, as against the 40 per cent of France's main competitors; social charges undertaken by businesses are the highest in the Community; income tax represents only 5 to 6 per cent of the gross domestic product as against double this in France's partner countries, while VAT constitutes the heart of fiscal revenue. This presents France with an enormous set of difficulties.

The first difficulty lies in the competitive handicap to be suffered by its businesses. This is no recent discovery: its industrialists have never ceased protesting since the creation of the Common Market, although despite this ball and chain, they have acquitted themselves well. But other sectors, such as banking and insurance, are now going to discover what it means to be French. On top of the surcharge that their firms will now have to suffer, there will be the added weight of specific taxes previously sanctioned by sector protectionism. Closed frontiers used to push up the cost of services which led to more pocket money for the state. In other words, the consumer was paying for what the taxpayer was saving. This held true for the tax on banking transactions, the exceptional levy – systematically renewed – on banking profits and the tax on insurance premiums. Either the state will refuse to renounce these facilities and organizations will have to find the money by means of a clamp-down on salaries and fringe benefits, or it will relinquish them, in which case it will not be easy to find an equivalent source of revenue.

The second difficulty is that an abnormally high level of mandatory taxes has a detrimental effect on the competitiveness of the economy in a global context. This is born out by every economic analysis into productivity and by all the statistics relating to growth. There is also an exceptionally strong correlation between unemployment levels and commercial rates of tax, with the result that the overall atmosphere in the workplace, in terms of dynamism and dedication, can be adversely affected. In a more and more competitive market, it is, strangely enough, exactly those hidden factors which make all the difference. Do we really need to seek confirmation in the studies of Carré, Dubois and Malinvaud, who discovered, after reams of calculations and mock-ups, that it was impossible to explain 50 per cent of productivity gains by quantifiable elements? Leaving aside all their ideological bluster, Mrs Thatcher and President Reagan did at least pay us the service of pointing out the obvious fact that too much tax kills off entrepreneurial energy.

The third difficulty concerns VAT, which is twice as profitable as income tax. Since the fiscal equation is already stretched by a structural deficit, any transfer would create an uproar. To rechannel it into direct taxation would be beyond any government: with the rates currently applying to each bracket, and an already rapid escalation according to wealth, it is completely out of the question. The only way around this would be to increase the number of households liable for income tax. At the moment, a third are managing to escape being taxed, on the pretext of low pay. The injustice consists in the fact that those who benefit from this exemption are much more numerous than the actual poor who should really receive these fiscal and social advantages. But to scrap such a middle-class privilege would demand an immense amount of courage. To take such an action merely to compensate for some indirect effect of the single market would be tantamount to suicide. It is an illusion on the part of the technocrats to imagine that citizens are willing to pay more tax in order to be in Europe; in fact they are expecting Europe to pay for them and refuse to accept the sophisticated reasoning which balances VAT against personal income tax. Depreciation in taxes will also have to be redressed, this time by a reduction in spending. But in what area could such savings be made? In the military budget? That would mean encumbering, for the sake of Europe, our best European card. In spending on social issues or education? Margins are narrow enough as it is. In spending on economic intervention or large technological programmes? That would mean cutting back on our greatest strengths in the forthcoming battle of the single market. In a random manner? This is one sure way to shift the border between state and society; not a very intelligent course of action. The years go by and harmonization is still as far away as ever and becoming even more difficult as fewer and fewer budgetary restructurings remain before 1992.

The French capital gains tax, the fourth difficulty, is one of the highest in Europe. There too, harmonization will be a delicate matter. While everyone silently expects a reprieve for VAT, the fate of savings will be decided strictly by the course of events, benefiting from no stay of execution. However, no pruning will occur without a more general rethink on inheritance tax. With the proliferation of fiscal laws and of those organizations that prescribe them – the state, local government, councils, communities – this tax has become a Byzantine construction without any logic or overall planning. Europe will undoubtedly be doing France a great service by forcing it to rationalize an otherwise inextricable hotchpotch of established interests and privileges. But what a politically costly task.

An old tax is a good tax. That is the fifth difficulty in a country where any rise of individualism and rejection of the state is enough to lead to real psychodramas. Witness the confrontation concerning the solidarity tax on large fortunes, which was neither as black nor as white as it was painted. Likewise the earlier battle over professional tax or the problems raised by increasing death duties. Caught in a fiscal maelstrom and at the same time having to take a battering from the unification of Europe, the authorities will be obliged to stave off any but the most urgent matters. They will hardly be tempted, in these conditions, to begin work on the kind of fiscal overhaul that France needs, one which will bring into question the sensitive balance between wage-earners and non wage-earners, individuals and businesses, income and inheritance, property and mobile assets, and all such self-perpetuating imbalances, which are taken too much for granted.

However the inventory of problems does not stop at such obviously intrusive tax difficulties. One international study (from the DRI) is rather frightening. Sceptical about the macro-economic effects of the single market, and about the idea of an overnight miracle producing instant benefits, it warns of the likelihood of enormous upheaval. Those sectors which can expect a 'non-competitive growth pattern', i.e. a rise in the level of imports, greater than the level of growth in the market, will almost all be concentrated in France. The expected boom in the motor industry will be more than compensated for by the decline in the food and agriculture industry, the aeronautical industry and the railways. This would result in an increased external trade deficit produced by a 1.9 per cent growth in exports, and a 4.3 per cent growth in imports by the year 1995. Despite a relative fall in prices (−2.5 per cent) and an increase in the GDP (1 per cent), unemployment would reach 12 per cent due to the combination of a deteriorating balance of trade, and a growth in the active population. The specialists are totally unanimous on this last point, that France is the only large European country which can expect to see a rise in its level of unemployment. But the impact of current population trends goes way beyond that of the single market, and is also a temporary problem. In the longer term, these relatively dynamic population statistics will provide France with an important advantage. The catastrophic conclusions reached in this study can obviously be contested one by one, and certain probable advances, in computer services and luxury goods, for instance, could be set against them. Nevertheless, the following features, particular to France, serve to exaggerate the impact of 1992.

In the first place, a particularly elevated position is enjoyed by those of France's most successful enterprises which depend on public orders. Aeronautics, armaments, electronics, construction and public works; all these are the fronts of a French-style Colbertism, and have become the spearheads of French industry. The opening-up of public markets will be very traumatic for these, since their private hunting-ground will at least partially disappear. National industries, which are directed 'towards' the final market, will of course be less affected: for them the shock happened long ago. But French industry generally will begin to pay the price for over-dependence on its relationship with the state. This is not as bad as it seems, as these organizations would anyway have had to survive the shock of the world market. Comfortable monopolies are a thing of the past, and it is better for European countries to have their eyes opened by heightened competition within the familiar environment of the Community than to wait a few years, only to suffer the violent aggression of competitors from the Far East.

In the second place, certain involuntary repercussions will be engendered by the fact that the French distribution network is the most modern in Europe. France's exemplary success in this area will paradoxically have an adverse effect on its balance of trade. Any direct spin-offs in terms of dividends, licences, its presence abroad and even a downward pressure on prices will apparently be more than compensated by the avenues consequently opened to imports. In a Europe without non-tariff barriers, without protectionist standards, and without shrewd customs officers, distribution networks will constitute the last bulwark of protectionism. This may be via a deliberate appeal to the historic behaviour of consumers – buy German in Germany – or by a more diffuse method, linked to the complexity and the delays in the system of distribution of a country such as Italy. French distribution networks, on the contrary, are hyper-modern and efficient; anyone can gain access to them. And there is no national bias on the part of buyers whose only concern is the price. The French market is therefore in danger of being far more exposed than others.

In the third place, the French Government tends to be characterized by Cartesianism. Its military-style performance, its obsession with abstract, impersonal rules and its clear method of working do not sit easily with the tricks, pretences and exceptions that are the daily protectionist bread of certain of its competitors. This kind of protectionism is not just going to disappear with the single market. Even if the front door has been opened, there will still be plenty of scope for economic confrontation in the general application of regulations. The French government, rigid, hierarchical and independent, is not going to lower its standards overnight and allow certain branches of industry to flood the European markets with cheaper goods of a lower quality.

In the fourth place, there is the delay in implementing certain rationalizations. Air transport for instance, is about to take European deregulation full in the face. At a time when gigantic companies are beginning to be set up in Europe, as witness the merger of British Airways and British Caledonian, French airlines are totally divorced from reality. Social structures are likewise ill prepared; squabbling between bosses and unions ought long ago to have been replaced by a common interest in new technological advances. On the level of internal organization, French transport companies are too bureaucratic; their style of administration is too rigid and heavy-handed to be able to cope easily with more open-minded competition from Europe and elsewhere. On a structural level, how can France grant itself the luxury of being the only European country to support, for example, two international branches and one national branch of the same firm?

Nowadays it is the clients who have to foot the bill and in a deregulated universe they will simply refuse.

Lastly, there is the attraction of the country itself; its central geographical position, its climate and its way of life all combine to make it a particularly welcoming space for companies and their personnel. This will of course lead to a guarantee of foreign investment and the creation of more jobs, but also to a heightened competition. There will be more Danish dentists wishing to set up in Saint-Paul-de-Vence than French lawyers attracted by the charms of the bar in Glasgow. This more acute competition would, in the long term, be an advantage, but initially it serves only to aggravate the traumatic nature of the single market.

If we insist on playing the role of '*der Geist der immer neint*'[2] we are seriously in danger of distorting reality. In France's favour one must set its immense capacity for innovative thinking which helped to create the miracle of post-war France, its amazing adaptability in the face of the Common Market, and more recently the extraordinary revolution carried through in the wake of the two petrol crises. As a result of this revolution, the French economy is now the most rigorous in Europe as regards wage settlements, with one of the lowest inflation rates and one of the most generous levels of social spending. The challenge issued by Europe is no tougher and at least has the advantage of being considerably more uplifting than that presented by the scrapping of index-linked wages. But by going to battle with flowers for bullets, France has some unpleasant surprises in store. The single market is no mere bagatelle, it is a war, demanding reconnaissance, strategy, preparation and possible sacrifices. It is presently 5 minutes to midnight.

Look Out for the Backlash

European naivety could backfire on us without any warning. If we carry on believing in miracles, we are in for a rude awakening. Instead of being a force for modernization, a much needed lever for change, Europe might well become a kind of scapegoat, shouldering the blame for phenomena which are in fact characteristic of world-wide evolution; increased competition, continual struggle and a permanent sense of confrontation. French extremist parties, the Communists and the National Front, hoping to capitalize on the frustrations and disappointments incurred by the market, are not likely to be disappointed. The risk of a backlash is considerable and could take any of several forms: economic, through attempts at protectionism; sociological, through a return to national chauvinism, and political, through the reappearance of extremist tendencies.

The spectre of protectionism seems to have been definitively exorcised. The drama of March 1983 in France represented a final confrontation between those who believed in the possibility of 'socialism in a single country' and those who supported the opening of frontiers. Since then the subject has, in principle, been closed. Both the left and right wing now share the same respect for competition and the same desire to open Europe up to the world. But when this European earthquake happens, the worst outcome, i.e. a return to a protectionist mythology, cannot be ruled out. If this were a matter of European protectionism, or rather the establishment of a reasonable balance between a totally exposed Europe and its more restrictive competitors, Japan and the US, it would deserve serious attention.[3] But what a catastrophe it would be if old defensive phantasms should surface among our partners. For one thing, they would indicate a regression in a clearly acquired economic understanding. For another, even if they were not acted upon, they would testify to an unwillingness to meet the challenge of the market. And finally, because the state would once more have to do battle with lobbies whose previous collective action amounted to a quest for import quotas. The danger does not come from industrial sectors which are used to the Common Market; for them the disappearance of non-tariff barriers implies an adjustment in the degree, rather than in the nature of competition. Nor does this risk emanate from the newly liberated financial sectors, which, although no more impressed by the market than they were by the previous oligopoly, will naturally make the best of a bad job. Any revolt will come from the direction of corporate bodies or regimented professions, whose basic nature ill prepares them for such shocks, and who enjoy being able to hold society as a whole to ransom. Truck drivers fuming at Dutch competition; airline pilots indignant at the cut-backs inherent to deregulation, doctors confronted with the sight of foreign competitors setting up in their own backyard, pharmacists whose geographical protection will be eroded by the granting of licences; architects who will have to take on the bureaux of large foreign firms; insurance brokers outflanked by direct commercialism. The natural reaction of such dissatisfied corporations will be to ask the state to make up their losses. These reactions may be isolated, sporadic, professional crises demanding the kind of emergency treatment which has become the essence of the art of governing. Or else certain groups might join forces and hinder the market, creating a new Poujadism in which yesterday's tradesmen will become todays *petit bourgeois.* An old sociological battle would unfold, just at a time when the demands of 1992 call for action of a completely different nature.

Since this protectionist threat lies in the hands of the individualistic professions, Malthusian claims could rapidly degenerate into xenophobic attitudes. At the moment, in France, anti-European feeling is largely obscured by racism against North Africans. It does nevertheless sometimes show through the occasional disturbances in rural areas such as the Ardèche, where many foreigners are setting up second homes, or in the instinctive dislike demonstrated in Alsace for 'German colonialism', that is to say, the combined effect of Alsatians crossing over to work in Germany, and Germans purchasing holiday homes in Alsace. It is discernible in the pressure exerted by previously close professions – auditors for example who went so far as to ask the Council of State to ban British officers from practising – and in the farmers' rage at the first imports from Spain. Once again, it will not be the salaried classes who rebel: the Confédération Générale du Travail[4] will make no more than a gallant last stand on the 'imports scandal'. It will be non-salaried France, the France of exaggerated individualism, of the dissatisfied middle class, which will react adversely to the situation and experience has shown this class to be neither the most pleasant, nor the most reasonable.

A few years ago, the political implications of such turmoil in society would have been a slight increase in support for the traditional right wing, certain isolated and abortive campaigns such as that of Jean Royer, one-time hero of the small businessman, and a vague pressure on the whole of the political world. In this case the Communist Party will undoubtedly try to capitalize on any discontent, although its usual veiled manner will produce an ultimately marginal effect. The National Front, on the other hand, might well do France the sad honour of being the only anti-European party capable of furnishing this new Poujadism with a framework and a momentum lacking even in the old Poujadism. Jean-Marie le Pen was obviously not mistaken when he decided, having delivered certain predictably reactionary ideas on Christian Europe, to become the champion of an anti-Europe campaign. An all too recognizable delivery allowed him to take this hatred for the market, for money, for a bloated middle class and for a cosmopolitan movement in reverse, and to link it all to the poor sacrificed French people, and the need for a patriotic impulse. These ideas, reminiscent of Maurras and of the xenophobic and anti-semitic nature of the extreme right of old, are already circulating. They might well gain real support when the single market is viewed by the general public as a disaster. It would be so simple at that point to play on the lack of awareness of politicians, their indifference to the concerns of the little people, their arrogance and the privileges they enjoy. All that this ideological flood is missing is a good dose of anti-parliamentarianism.

Fascism is not on the march; a united Europe does not have the German inflation of 1923; the victims of the single market will not be counted in millions; but even so, le Pen has won an ideological battle for racism, and he might well repeat this victory over the question of Europe. Would it not be true to say that others have taken his anti-immigration stance as a reference point, if only to oppose him? He has moved the whole of the political spectrum to the right: witness the embarrassed silence of the left, with the exception of François Mitterand, on the subject of immigrants' rights to vote in local council elections; witness the concessions made over the years by a liberal right wing which had in the past been much more sure of its ground; witness the shift on the part of those still claiming to be Gaullists towards a Boulanger-style populism. Everyone has made a step to the right compared with their natural position. Will he manage the same sort of operation against Europe? If he did it would mean the end of European enthusiasm. The most fervent supporters of a united Europe would have to recognize its negative aspects and its less committed partisans would be even more wary. 1992 would be regarded as not so much a mishap as an obligation; the single market would seem not so much fortuitous as doomed.

The Europe of 1992 is not going to resemble this Darwinian nightmare any more than it will a daydream, but in ignoring its 'debit side' – as an accountant would say – the architects of Europe are letting themselves in for some major disappointments. For this last century, countries have systematically responded to any acceleration in the pace of the market by greater redistribution of wealth. The welfare state and the market have advanced side by side, the former more rapidly, at certain times, the latter more brutally, at others, but they remain inseparable in our modern societies. Do we really imagine that the Europe currently under construction is free from this law? On the contrary, the threat of a Darwinian nightmare cannot be answered simply by miraculously increased profits, but by the construction of some real mechanisms for the redistribution of wealth. The free market impulse acts as a useful counterbalance to the racing of the egalitarian machine in each country; but in the same way the all-powerful nature of the market, on a European scale, must be balanced by social-democratic pressure. When will Europe have even a minimum of social-democratic tools at its disposal? Their absence is simply one of many proofs that Europe is still an unfinished symphony.

Notes

1 See chapter 9 below.
2 'The spirit which always denies', in Goethe's *Faust*.
3 See chapter 9 below.
4 An association of French trade unions.

9

An Unfinished Symphony

The market, as the only tool in the rebuilding of Europe, will rapidly reach its limits. Some sort of counterbalance will have to be found for its more extreme excesses in order to avoid a violent backlash, and the fundamental questions which the market is obscuring will call for some answers. Will a common currency exist? Will macro-economic unity make sense? Will there be widespread budgetary solidarity? Will the single market be exposed to the elements or at least semiprotected? These are the least of the subjects to be tackled if the Europe of 1992, an essentially economic construct, is to have any historical and strategic meaning. If this were all to be dealt with, the strategic shift of the continent would be balanced by an equally important phenomenon. But the steps that need to be taken have nothing to do with the shrewd sleight of hand that substituted liberalization for harmonization in an effort to get the single market on the move. They demand political will, a political structure and political durability. The principle of the single market is to get rid of political action, but it will soon be back because of the need to transcend the limits of free trade. In addition to these major stakes, certain ambiguities surround the Franco-German association. France's ambition is to set up an economic policy and a common currency, but it does not have the means to do so. Germany has the means without the ambition. Its priorities do not include a common currency, a macro-economic policy nor budgetary solidarity, and Germany is obviously not alone in this reflex. Great Britain, for instance, is also backing off, although this opposition is secondary, coming as it does from the least assiduous member of Europe. German reservations, on the other hand, are critical, as Germany has always been the most supportive member state, tending to take on the role of the Community's banker. These divergences are generally played down because of the taboo regarding the sacrosanct nature of the Franco-German understanding. They do nonetheless correspond to a real conflict of interests and not merely to a reversal of ideas between France, previously nationalist and now pro-Community, and Germany, which used to be militant in its support of Europe and which now wishes to conduct its own open-ended policies. National interest is by no means dead, it still informs the behaviour of each country and finds expression in a greater or lesser enthusiasm towards the Community at any given moment. But it is no coincidence that the future of a unified Europe depends on Germany, and that Germany is the fiscal point for the drift in the continent. The question of Europe is based around the question of Germany, and the old nineteenth-century precept takes on a new meaning. To recognize this is not to give way to anti-German chauvinism, but simply to live in the real, rather than the dream world. What we are left with then, is a sketched-out Europe, a 1992 in progress, a half-finished task.

The Currency Veto

The creation of a European currency is not a technical problem, and yet the leaders of the Community are greatly tempted to take refuge in a study on its practical difficulties. At the Hanover summit, a committee comprising governors of the central banks and other experts was given a year to compile a list of all the questions that needed attention. The moment of truth will come when all these differing concerns are brought to light.

The problem is basically very simple: the more reasons Germany has for maintaining the present European Monetary System, the more it has to lose from a common currency. The EMS provides Germany with all the advantages of a zone where the mark is supreme, without any of its disadvantages. Revaluation of the mark has been limited through its link with weaker currencies and the export capacity of the former West Germany has been preserved. Germany has thus maintained an enormous commercial advantage over its partners as well as enjoying many other benefits. The other member states have been obliged, more or less, to align themselves according to the severity of the dominant economy. What disadvantages has Germany had to put up with in exchange for such advantages? An obligation, in times of tension, to help currencies undergoing devaluation and the consequent excessive growth in its money supply – not a high price to pay.

Although biased in favour of Germany by the very weight of national economics, the monetary system is useful to the other member states. Each one profits from it, even if the most powerful of the group has the most to gain. The system was very useful in helping France to avoid some stupid mistakes, sparking off the turn-around in 1983 when the French people at last accepted the need for stringent measures to compensate for ten years of recklessness. It put pressure on countries to adjust their inflation rate downwards towards the lowest rate in the community; it led to a controlling of production costs and a greater rationalization of the production apparatus; it forced French employers to drop their customary easy-going attitude and to take the bit between the teeth and, last but not least, it instilled in French people the desire for a strong currency. What an incredible revolution in thinking in a country which had always gone along with the cycle of artificial boost–devaluation–readjustment and whose currency had been cut by a third, relative to the mark, in the previous twenty years. The extent of the change can be seen in the fact that a socialist finance minister can become a kind of left-wing Pinay, guaranteeing a strong France.

The EMS is a school for economic maturity. In preaching moral virtue, it helps the weaker countries, but through its own mechanisms it ends up benefiting strong countries even more. This is quite natural, of course. A monetary system is not there to shift the balance between economies, to the disappointment of those who for fifty years have dreamed of being able to depend on such manipulation to compensate for structural landscapes. On the contrary: it reflects an already existing balance of strength. When capital is circulating without restrictions, the EMS will seem even more like the kingdom of the mark. Germany will attract further investment at the expense of weaker currencies, since in this area a good currency will always beat a bad one. The only way to compensate for this natural movement would be for member states to set systematically higher interest rates than Germany, such that their own expansion would be held back or even halted entirely. This would perpetuate the existing situation and Germany's leadership would remain intact. Faced with such a prospect, some envious looks were cast in the direction of Britain, whose position outside the EMS was maintained through Mrs Thatcher's ideological obstinacy and nationalism. Britain survived only because of the specific nature of British currency: its international character, the added strength provided by North Sea oil, and the role played by the City. British industry was nevertheless required to pay the price in terms of the pound's instability, its artificial revaluations and excessive depreciations. France decided against leaving the EMS in 1983, and would find it no easier to do so now. Any rejection of the EMS at the present time would be taken to imply a return to a *laissez-faire* monetary policy. Since European markets have such a ricochet effect on each other, this would give rise to uncontrollable depreciation and, subsequently, to the undesirable necessity of more stringent measures. Whether France likes it or not, the European Monetary System is its only possible environment, it has to belong to the territory of the mark.

The French are consequently very tempted by the idea of substituting a truly common currency for the present system. In theory, they are right, because such a development would be a change of nature rather than merely a shift of emphasis. The balance between advantages and disadvantages would change for each member state, in particular for Germany, whose reservations grow at the same rate as French enthusiasm. This is nothing new, of course. From the outset, the Bundesbank has regarded the ecu with suspicion, through fear of seeing the mark contaminated by other European currencies. For a long time, too, German businesses have not been able to borrow in ecus, and their banks only intervened in the market when faced with no other option. One can pick out several reasons behind this reluctance to accept a European currency, the first of which must be a fear of witnessing a weakening of the current monetary system. Germans think that a central European bank will never carry the same weight as the Bundesbank; that it will give in to pressures from less rigorous member states and that its status will not render it sufficiently independent to put up a solid resistance. In the second place, Germans are wary of having to pay the price of this system were they to succeed in making it work. The obvious relation between monetary strength and budgetary liability is not insignificant when one considers the process of redistribution that will be required to counteract the single currency's inevitable effects in widening the gulf between richer and poorer areas.

Thirdly, monetary strength is reversible, whereas budgetary liability is not, in which case Germany risks losing out on both counts. Germans anyway nurture a natural desire to retain their commercial surplus, especially since, from 1983 to 1987, 80 per cent of the rise in the total German surplus was through trade with its European partners. They also wish to protect their freedom to place this surplus where they choose. A single currency would require this surplus to be channelled within the Community, whereas under the present system, there is no such restriction. What could be better for such a central country than to be able to divide its liquid assets between Western and Eastern Europe and the United States? German desire for a unified Europe would have to be boundless for her to willingly accept a union of currency. At one time, this was the case, but the French committed the heinous crime of blocking the process in the name of an illusory national independence and nowadays the situation has changed. Compared with German reservations, the British refusal is of secondary importance. Mrs Thatcher proclaimed that, in her lifetime, the pound sterling would not dissolve into a community currency, because the British Government wished to retain the autonomy of its monetary policy. But she was overestimating sterling. Germany is a real force in the international money market; Britain, like France, is but a pawn.

Any debate on currency drifts naturally towards a discussion on macro-economic policy. For years the French have said 'Create the currency and the economy will follow'; Germans make the following rather more circumspect reply, 'Create the economy and the money will follow.' This means shifting the onus of proof onto an equally hypothetical macro-economic system.

Differing Macro-economic Aspirations

It seems as though all of the European economies are advancing at the same speed. Their growth rates are similar, their inflation rates have drawn closer and their unemployment levels are equally high. Viewed from Singapore or Los Angeles, Europe seems to have an economic policy of its own; differences between the member states are more tenuous than between Texas and Massachusetts or between California and Maine. This visible convergence has come about as a by-product of the European Monetary System and is due to a general alignment on the economic shape of Germany.

But a communal macro-economic policy presupposes an agreement among the member states; Germany could not maintain its leadership at the same time as compromising certain of its most cherished principles. The experience of 1980 is justifiably uppermost in the minds of German leaders. In that year, through the pressure of Western allies, Chancellor Schmidt agreed that Germany should serve as a powerhouse for the world economy. However, instead of elevating the other economies, as hoped, the German economy was to offer a drastic set-back. It took several years of rigorous measures to re-establish the balance that had been so absurdly sacrificed. Germany is not currently thinking of expansion. Firstly, because it has an instinctive fear of slipping into inflation. As soon as one month's inflation happens to rise by 1 per cent, the Bundesbank sounds the alarm. Secondly, because of its population. Germany is currently in the peculiar position whereby, with an almost stagnant economy, spending power is rising by 3 per cent to 4 per cent per year, without adversely affecting other factors in the equation. These are the first euphoric effects of the population decline, in that the same income is distributed among fewer people. Similarly, unemployment will soon diminish, under the influence of a fall in the active workforce, quenching the current revival incentive. The population decline will eventually wreak its revenge and Germany will pay dearly for these fleeting benefits by the vacuum created in her interior. But at the moment a boost in the economy would be worse than futile. Germany would hardly know how to go about affecting a growth in public spending, and an additional drop in taxes combined with already generous pay rises would produce only a marginal increase in consumption. Germany's position foreshadows that of Europe in the year 2000, when the population will be in steep decline and growth will have well and truly disappeared. Its refusal of any expansion does not only apply on a national basis; according to the Germans, a European boost would create all the same problems. Money would probably be used even less effectively, and as far as the idea for a new Marshall plan is concerned, why transfer to Community level what can be achieved much more efficiently from Bonn?

The French position is diametrically opposed to that of Germany. France has a greater need for growth than the other countries, and yet it is forced into a slower growth rate than these others. It is therefore obliged to look for a foreign source of expansion. Its unemployment rate is doomed to grow in direct proportion to its expanding workforce, possibly to as high as 15 per cent according to certain analyses, where it will drop to below 5 per cent in neighbouring countries because of their free-fall population figures. The only answer to such an alarming prospect would be considerably increased growth. Other solutions are mere stop-gaps: job creation schemes, freelancing, temporary and part-time work, community programmes and Youth Training Schemes, moonlighting – even a reduction in working hours with a corresponding drop in pay is nothing but an illusion and is recognized as such by trade unions. It would require a degree of collective solidarity which is totally contrary to a listless and egotistical society which has glorified the individual. With growth as its only solution, the French economy is currently being strangled by the imbalanced state of its foreign trade. At the slightest indication of increased growth, France's foreign trade collapses, forcing a brutal change of direction and the kind of restrictive measures which are even more disastrous for employment. It is condemned to a difference of between 0.5 per cent and 1 per cent compared with its major partners. This insoluble equation forbids an escape forward but not an escape into the dream world of a collective boost, due to a common macro-economic policy. The majority of the other member states, especially southern countries, are in the same position as France, in being unable to count on population decline to bring down unemployment.

Until recently, experts plumped for the German position, convinced that sustained expansion would set inflation off again, aggravating international financial imbalances. Nowadays they reckon that, taken as a whole, Europe has a significant margin for expansion. This is the idea behind the 'gentle landing' so often referred to in the past few years. It involves a slowing down of the US economy, brought about by fiscal rather than monetary means, matched by a corresponding acceleration on the part of Japan and Europe. Japan, despite accusations to the contrary, is in the process of fulfilling its side of the contract and reproducing the growth rates of its best years, from before the petrol crises. But Europe, under the iron rule of Germany, is not keeping her part of the bargain. The differences between Japan and Germany are particularly striking because, until recently, they had so much in common. They stem from a disparity in the appetites of the two countries for consumer goods. Prosperity has not yet reached the hearts of the Japanese people, as it has in Germany. Needs connected to individual consumption, housing, leisure and services will go largely unsatisfied; the life of a Japanese worker bears no comparison with the *Gemütlichkeit* (comfort) of his German colleague's life-style. This is why the demographic influence is not as yet felt so strongly in Japan. In the long term, it may well weigh as heavily on Japanese as on German dynamism, but for the moment Japan is avoiding any policy of stagnation.

On the other hand, neither the opinion of experts nor international agreement on the subject will have any hope of convincing the Germans. For them to accept a macro-economic growth policy which goes against their aims and interests, they would have to have some much stronger motives, just as in the area of currency. In particular, it would mean pushing the Franco-German understanding towards a union which embraced more than purely economic aspects. Why should the French, who hold back from offering Germany a nuclear and strategic guarantee, expect to be granted an 'economic guarantee'? Neither of the two wishes to make any concession in the area in which they are dominant, but if one weighs up their relative responsibilities it is not the Germans who are most to blame. The French, prisoners of their Maginot syndrome, refuse to make gestures concerning their nuclear capability which would be in their own best interests. The Germans are not willing to adopt an economic policy which would go against their interests. These reservations are not of the same nature at all. Do we then have to count on divine providence, chance, faith or a sudden burst of energy for the situation to change?

Welfare State, What Welfare State?

The brains behind the single market have been wary of conforming to the principle guiding contemporary economics whereby the market goes hand in hand with a redistribution of wealth. This reluctance was strengthened by the sample of the Common Agricultural Policy, which mixed a free-exchange with otherwise strict organization and a pay policy. It has become standard practice to jeer at this enormous bureaucratic machine, at its butter mountains, at its uncontrollable skids, and the fact that it has aggravated existing imbalances in the conditions of the farm workers. But that is to turn one's back on an impressive success: that of bringing about a rapid modernization of European agriculture without major social upheaval.

Compared with such an example, 1992 is full of deficiencies. It contains no real protection from the outside, and no social policy of wealth distribution. This will have the inevitable consequences of an overall improvement in efficiency and productivity, which are supposed to justify the purge, but at the cost of excessive regional imbalances, crises in certain sectors and a transfer of labour. We will certainly have some wounds to dress. Member states will obviously apply themselves to the task with the tools of their own social system, but this kind of intervention will not produce an answer to an obvious contradiction. It will be the weaker countries who will have the most need of compensation and yet their modest national resources will prevent them from making any move towards greater redistribution. Without the slightest provision made for welfare at a community level, the Europe of 1992 will have some regressive social effects. Jacques Delors, never ceasing to proclaim this point, explains how competitiveness and cooperation are indissolubly linked and how the market calls for corresponding social policies.

The task, theoretically, would be a formidable one, calling for financial transfers from the more prosperous member states, who are set to gain the most from 1992, to those countries in their wake. Within a national framework, richer areas always subsidize poorer ones; this is the cornerstone of any social contract. So there must surely have to be some sort of a European contract, whether explicit or implicit. Can we really hope to build a union without such a contract? It has certainly never been done before. The ingredients generally needed to restore balance are incomes benefits, budgetary subsidies, increased social spending and an overhaul of the infrastructure. Even with a recent increase in its resources, the Community's regional fund can only scratch the surface of these requirements.

Such a course of action would presuppose a considerable budgetary outlay on the part of the richer states, especially – *noblesse oblige* – Germany. And yet it is precisely these countries that are most reticent on the subject. They are all, France included, caught between a reluctance to put up taxes or to increase their deficit, the obligatory financing of their national debt, and a disinclination to draw on their own national social spending programme. In addition to the general constraints which apply to the top group of countries, Germany's patience is further stretched by having been the Community's eternal subsidizer. It was Germany that financed the Common Agricultural Policy, other specific projects, and a rebate for Mrs Thatcher that was beyond the call of duty. Generosity does have its limits, especially when it has lost original motivations which stemmed more from a bad conscience and a compelling pro-European militancy than from economic causes. At the slightest hint of a European welfare state, the Germans fear a return to the agonies of the Common Agricultural Policy, i.e., the activation of an infernal machine crammed full of automatic budgetary reactions, which would be totally unstoppable and which would once again cast Germany in the role of distributor of financial aid.

This European welfare state is in limbo; not only concerning transfers of capital, but also in terms of social laws and employment rights. The US and Canada prove that a homogeneous market can be accompanied by regional differences in social matters. Indeed, nothing could be less realistic than to imagine trying to coordinate social law from Copenhagen to the Algarve, from Munich to Salonica. It would be ridiculous. At the same time, the Community did decide to reduce discrepancies between rates of VAT, and it should one day be willing to find some sort of framework to begin to encompass all the varying social legislation. Since his arrival in power in 1981, François Mitterand has pleaded the case for a European social system. His colleagues, prisoners of the prevailing mood of liberalization, saw in this only a traditional left-wing refrain, but maybe the first shake-ups of 1992 will open their eyes on the matter. A European law society whose members would have the choice of several different ways of participating? A harmonization of conditions of employment? A minimum accord on social legislation? In the current climate such ideas are simply Utopian, but while some people foresee a 'socializing' Utopia, others fear a 'constructivist' Utopia, and the rest envisage a budgetary Utopia.

Whether or not we succeed in creating a Community welfare state will be a test of the nature of the new Europe. Either the single market will amount to nothing more than a free internal trading area, without non-tariff barriers, or it will represent the first step of a more ambitious process. Can we forget that the most recent economic and political unification, that of Bismarckian Germany, created a situation in which an internal market, exterior protection and the beginnings of an innovative social policy marched forward hand in hand? Political union only came about as an afterthought. The first hypothesis of free trade, pure and simple, is a reversible phenomenon. On encountering their first difficulties, some countries will be tempted to hold back, to look into theoretically temporary safety clauses, to restrict their support to advantageous aspects of the single market. The end result of this hypothesis will be a Europe that is anything but truly united.

To rely on this Europe to swim against the tide of enormously significant strategic evolutions would be infantile. In the end, 1992 raises as many questions as it revolves; on the welfare state, and also on currency and economic union. In the case in point, ideological uncertainties are added to the practical difficulties involved. The welfare state has lost its way and its excesses in the more developed European countries demand a drastic cure. A machine which blindly distributes benefits to the profit of the middle class and at the expense of the real poor has everything to gain from a minimum of deregulation. However, just because French or German health insurance needs the stimulation of competition does not necessarily mean that workers in Oporto do not need a redistribution of subsidies in their favour. The only answer to an extreme national welfare service is the extremes of the market, but likewise, the only answer to an excessively free market is an excessive provision of welfare. This tightrope is a difficult one for politicians to negotiate, preferring as they do to work in one dimension. And on top of that, a well-off taxpayer will have to be made to pay more, not for the benefit of his fellow citizens, but for some distant Europeans. Certainly, in a Utopian world, savings from the richer countries' welfare services would guarantee resources for a still non-existent European welfare state. But in politics fantasy worlds do not exist.

Shortcomings in the Rules of Play

Even from the point of view of the market, this symphony is unfinished. No firm decisions have been made concerning to what extent the market will be open to the rest of the world, nor the ground rules involved. 1992 is approaching with a far more modest frontier tax than any other large developed zone, and a total absence of non-tariff barriers. Their disappearance within the Community makes inevitable their phasing-out as regards the rest of the world. What will remain of the clandestine measures adopted to deal with Japanese cars: 3,000 vehicles in Italy, 3 per cent of the French market, 10 per cent of the British market? Nothing. What will limitation agreements on textiles and iron and steel be worth? Much the same. Businesses wishing to export to the Community will have only to conform to the most lenient European standards in order to satisfy Community regulations. There is an agonizing wait while external competitors are busy getting ready to take full advantage of this godsend. Japan is already armed and the Dragons of Southeast Asia are manoeuvring themselves into position. If the main object of 1992 is a frenzied price-cutting, this extra competition must be welcome. But if the aim is also to build up European businesses to an international level, they are currently being sent into battle with one hand tied behind their backs. Let's be clear: there is no question of resuscitating the old European protectionism. But unilateral disarmament is no more justifiable economically than militarily. The European market is already more open to the outside world than other markets. After 1992 it will be a paradise for foreign exporters. Concessions which have been made on previously protected areas of the market could have been used as an incredible bargaining weapon to oblige other countries to open their own frontiers. But the problems posed by a Europe which is open, or at least ajar, once again expose the differences of opinion between France, with a 'constructivist' vision which is representative of all the other member states, and Germany.

The Single Market and European Industry

First difference: for France, the single market is a space for European industry to strengthen itself, while for Germany it constitutes a zone with the lowest possible prices. According to the Germans, European industry already exists in Germany.

The Single Market and the Rest of the World

Second difference: for the French, the European market exists as a space 'in itself' – a third pole alongside the two other homogeneous markets of North America and Japan. To German eyes it only constitutes the fringes of the world market. Nothing is more likely to worry them than retaliatory measures taken by the Americans in response to European self-protection initiatives. Relying more on other markets, Germany does not wish to become a victim of an American protectionism which would hit her harder than any of her partners in the Community.

The Single Market and Global Visions

Third difference: where the economy joins forces with the philosophy of international relations and strategic planning: France sees the stages of European unity as a repeat, at a rather slower tempo, of American unification. It therefore imagines Europe with its classic frontiers. For Germany, Europe is an open space. Space, that is, not entity; and open, meaning permeable to the West, but also to the East. One gradually begins to realize that positions regarding the single market merely stem from global visions which are equally distinct. These differences of perception are automatically decided in favour of the German position. Not because Germany would have won other countries over to its position in a proper debate, but because anything to do with the frontiers of the Community calls for unanimity and the reservations of the most powerful economy are enough to prevail over the vague desires of others. The question does not merely affect merchandise, it will begin to have a more direct impact on the concrete assets of each country.

The US will not escape this aspect and the basis for a confrontation will be set up. On one side, the believers in absolute free trade, indifferent to the increasing ownership of American properties and enterprises by foreigners, in particular the Japanese. On the other, the democrats and some republicans, worried by the sight of the US selling off the family silver in order to finance its foreign trade deficit. For the first time, a law has been passed which authorizes the administration to oppose foreign investments within the US, under the catch-all philosophy of 'national security'.

The Europe of 1992 will be faced with the same dilemma: whether to establish a system under which prior authorization is needed, or to leave all transactions free, with the exception of the defence sector. But the balance of power between member states will always work in favour of the dominant economy, in this case Germany, the great exporter of capitals. Any restrictive measures on the part of the Community, and Germany would fear American or Japanese reprisals applying a brake to the expansion of its foreign investments. In addition to that, the policing of German industrial and financial markets by a club made up of large institutions protects Germany to an unrecognized and unparalleled extent. Germany will thus put forward free-trade principles in order to avoid any control over investments, a protection it does not need and whose constraints would only handicap its position as a global investor. Far more open to other markets than they are in return, Europe is in danger of becoming a soft option for the main world exporters; a land which welcomes with open arms capital previously short of investment opportunities; an immense free zone. Each of the major powers has some interest in this zone: the Americans wish for export openings, the Soviets require supplies without having to pay the strategic price of a similar dependence on the US.

This uncertainty over the rules of play is not confined to an economic 'to be or not to be' – to protect oneself or not to protect oneself; it concerns the very workings of the single market. One must bear in mind that no absolute market exists without legislative principles. These are few but extremely important: some strict provisions against monopolies as regards exchanges of goods, services and assets. On the first matter, the Community is reasonably well equipped; since the Treaty of Rome, it has some well-defined powers and on such questions, the European Court of Justice is inflexible. However, if it is to be applied to the entire market this arsenal is in need of reinforcement, particularly if it wants to ensure free access to the public markets. How can the Bundespost and Siemens, France Telecom and the GCE (the French Water Board) be prevented from indecent cohabitation? How can one stop tax privileges from disturbing free competition in the financial market? How can one pursue all the unfair mark-ups which are added at the expense of the eventual customer? The litany of practices running contrary to the spirit of competition is a long one indeed, and to get rid of them sometimes seems like a Sisyphean task. As soon as they are flushed out, they find even more obscure and deeply embedded hiding places. Fear of the police is the only effective prevention. The financial penalties imposed until now have an indefinite dissuasive effect. After all, what does a fine of a few million ecus paid in arrears, at a modest rate of interest amount to, compared with the profits generated by skilful dealing? The corrective power of penal sanctions would be a deterrent, just as it is at a national level. But this would require that any infringement of the rules of the market would be automatically accompanied by penal procedure in the guilty firm's country, at least until that distant time when Community penal jurisdiction exists. Unlike in many other areas, this matter would not necessarily entail real changes, but rather a reinforcement of those powers already in force. It will come about in the end.

The principle of reciprocity is more complex to apply. For merchandise, it is inevitable. For services, it will eventually prevail although habits, reflex responses and modes of behaviour will secretly take the place of non-tariff barriers. But what a lot of obstacles in the way of this principle's application as regards assets. The position is particularly acute concerning takeover bids, since they have become the instrument of European rationalization. Member states at the moment are open to widely differing degrees, from Great Britain, the most liberal, to the most firmly closed, which is Holland. In Britain, respect for the market is absolute and intervention on the part of the Monopolies Commission, the only regulating force, is usually limited to a strict examination of market shares, avoiding any hint of the nationalist leanings that are prevalent in the German *Kartelamt*.[1] After Britain come Belgium, Spain and France, all fairly open countries. In Belgium the affair of the Générale de Belgique bears witness to this. In Spain, the investments on the part of the KIO (Kuwait Investment Office) illustrated that serious excesses were needed to jolt the government into action. In France, despite an unrivalled set of regulations designed to batten down the hatches, it is a fairly liberal practice which has eventually asserted itself, although a host of intransigent restrictions dog the footsteps of foreign investors. Italy is further removed on this particular scale: there seem to be no restraints on investment but in fact, the economy is protected by a still dominant feudalism. A small but powerful cartel commands the situation, whether in private businesses based on family ownership, or in public concerns. No take-over bid succeeds in Italy, least of all a foreign one, and has no prospect of succeeding in the near future. Even further along this scale of impenetrability is Germany. Its institutions, as we have seen, practise their own form of in-breeding, and the *Kartelamt* acts as a full-back if the 'club' has not succeeded in settling the problem itself. The final bulwark of protectionism is Holland, thanks to a subtle distinction between businesses – which are auto-regulating – and their shareholders. In this strange system, ownership of capital is not enough to assure control over society. It is possible to take infinite advantage of the voting system in which category A shares, in the appropriate hands, have n times the voting rights of ordinary category B shares.

Given such differing backgrounds, moves towards reciprocity will not have an overnight success. Both legislative restrictions and block votes will eventually disappear since they are in direct contradiction to the main thrust of the single market, but the codes of behaviour that they have engendered will nevertheless persist. Public institutions such as monopolies commissions and other similar bureaux will carry on adding a touch of nationalism to decisions which are uncontestable.

And large national consortia, in an attempt to protect their territory, will prefer the coded, parochial confrontations of old to the spotlights of the world stage. Will the most closed countries restructure themselves according to their most open competitors, or vice versa? It is impossible to tell for certain. If there is no commitment on the part of the member states to policing themselves and to enforcing this reciprocity if necessary, the impetus is in danger of seizing up in the face of impossible imbalances.

The open market is nowhere near completion. A good course was set by the outlawing of non-tariff barriers and other obstacles, but there is still hesitation over regulations which go to form any free market. Such regulations require a process of harmonization, compromise, negotiations and exchanges; in other words, political action. For all that politicians used liberation as an excuse to abdicate their responsibilities, they will still have to hurry back to finish the task. Will they be in any state to achieve this?

The Political Spectre

European politics function via a whole network of organizations. The Community Council of Ministers, the Commission, the European Parliament, the Court of Justice, national governments, national parliaments, national and European techno-structures, the Union of Western Europe and the Franco-German understanding are all elements constituting a network of power which has nothing in common with the classic systems of organization. For a single state unit, substitute a centralized political system; for a confederation, substitute a complex mechanism of opposing strengths; for a federation, a similar machine with jurisdiction as its ultimate means of regulation; for this unique and unprecedented body that is Europe a system based on interlocking networks. This latter brings the theory of cybernetics rather more into play than the traditional Anglo-Saxon 'check and balance' attitude. Boosts, short-circuits, inverse effects and feedback; such are the hardly classic features of this particular machine. This complex mixture does not detract from the importance of human action – witness the endeavours of Mitterand, Kohl, Delors and Gonzalez – nor of sudden breakthroughs such as the primacy of trade liberations over harmonization of legislation, but it is undoubtedly specifically adapted to sophisticated societies and to a vague construction. It is no coincidence that cybernetic regulations provide us with the best description of current social phenomena, replacing old sociological and political theories. The fact that, in order to create the single market, politicians have banked on disorder in preference to order, and experiment in place of agreement is a quite extraordinary transformation. Until now they were in the business of producing exemplary institutions, hierarchical procedures, and uniform laws. But now living logic has taken the upper hand and society has become the crucial force behind change, with power mechanisms obliged to toe the line. The political organization of Europe is less an accident than a foreshadowing. It bears witness, if taken to its extreme, to the new arrangements currently being adopted in more sophisticated areas. When more high-powered enterprises wish to free themselves from bureaucratic and military organizations, they also place their trust in cybernetic regulations, as shown by the explosion in communications, the endless trade circuits and the importance accorded to less centralized initiatives.

However, although capable of directing existing operations, of avoiding conflicts and initiating a kind of auto-regulation, the network system is hardly in a position to perform drastic surgery. It has no ultimate powers to fall back on, since even at the highest level the Community Council of Ministers is limited to negotiation, with arbitration dependent on the unanimous goodwill of its members. The cybernetic mechanism worked well until and including the achievement of the single market. But if Europe is to be anything other than any immense free zone, we must now begin to tackle some real Gordian knots such as currency, economic policy, the construction of a welfare state, and our position as regards the outside world. All this demands powers, laws and institutions. At a national scale, they exist. National command may be crumbling, discipline may be collapsing, and society moving at its own pace rather an imposed one, but as a last resort the state is still there. More enmeshed, more maladroit and less sure of itself, it still has the capacity to make a decision if circumstances have not already made it, to 'cut through ambiguity at its own cost' as Cardinal de Retz put it. Europe, with all its complex machinery, does not possess the minimal sovereign power that is vital in such circumstances. This is why, if we try to go beyond the current trajectory of the single market, the political spectre once more rears its head. If these Gordian knots are cut some political clout will be necessary in order to follow the process through and set up the relevant institutions. If they are not untangled, the powers needed to achieve our desired ends will be out of the realm of national governments. If these powers do not exist, then the game is almost over; Europe will have attained its peak: it will be a free-trade zone without political or strategic identity.

Hearing Mrs Thatcher insult Jacques Delors for having spoken of 'an embryonic European government', one was inclined to be sceptical. Arguments surrounding supranationality have died away in France, but are very much alive elsewhere and do not augur well for any major political breakthrough. The most militant pro-Europeans adopt a 'time will show' response to such pessimism. An array of historical reference points, such as the slow unification of France, Germany and even the United States, remind us of the rules of long-term change and serve to counter any criticisms. But time never stands still. In the sixties, France missed its chance of building and leading an integrated Europe. Now that it no longer has the possibility, of course, it would leap at the chance. Great Britain does not wish for political integration at any price. Germany is in constant danger of being wrong footed by its own logic; at the very heart of *Mittel Europa*, it links West to East, but behind all its rhetoric, is it really any more in favour than Britain?

Given the current shape of this 'unfinished symphony', 1992 is perfectly compatible with the gradual shift in the strategic terrain. This Europe, an immense free zone, a kind of gigantic Hong Kong, is well short of the threshold whereby an originally economic construct can take on a historical, political and strategic identity. Not only is this Europe not incompatible with the evolution towards a continental Europe, but it is entirely complementary to it. American isolationism will be unaffected and Germany will be allowed to carry on its development as a major supplier to Russia under the pretext of 'Europe our common home'. Of course, if 1992 were to transcend its present prognosis, everything would be different. It would mean that Germany was ready to build Europe with the same enthusiasm that she had twenty years ago when belief and self-interest were united. At present, the belief remains but her own interests have changed. The key to an economic Europe becoming a political entity lies in Germany's hands, and Germany is not likely to use it. Europe is in the midst of an internal explosion: strategically it is shifting Eastwards to be more continental than ever; its market is in the process of becoming the world's major free zone, and its social loyalties are with a West whose territory extends well beyond Europe itself. Faced with this dissociation, 1992 can never be a real means for change, unless one believes, contrary to both liberal and Marxist thought, that the market can itself give birth to the historic process.

Notes

1 *Kartelamt*: German equivalent of the Monopolies Commission.

PART III

A Breviary of the Impossible

10

The Third Circle

The first circle, strategic, encompasses continental Europe. The second circle, economic, traces the frontiers of the twelve member states with a dotted line. A third circle, cultural and sociological, follows the fluctuating, rather less distinct contours of the West. Between these circles a hypothetical European identity is at play. The dream of a political Europe loses conviction in those surroundings. It would come about of its own accord if these three circles were convergent, or at least concentric, but is out of reach for as long as Europe is torn between such contradictory positions. In this matter, the third circle is essential since it marks the frontiers of society. If there were a civil European society, Europe would really exist, eventually managing to assert its dynamism and its aspirations. When the champions of 1992 wish to give some depth to their myth, they fuel pipe-dreams: the single European market will unify society which will unify Europe. What a charming tautology! In reality, the third circle is more elusive. A European society does not truly exist; it merges into a generalized Western community whose way of life and traditions are expressed equally well in Paris as in Toronto, in Frankfurt as in Dallas, and even, in terms of desires, in Warsaw as in Mexico. A *Homo occidentalus* does exist, but not a *Homo europeanus*. Europe has none of the features of a real civil society; no institutions nor citizenship, with public loyalties which are ambiguous and an elite which is doing nothing to improve the situation.

Honour to *Homo Occidentalus*

The West, that negative myth from the time of decolonization, has come back in force. Not, this time, in the wagon-trains of colonial expeditions, in policies of economic domination or in military supervision, but as an emblem of all that is modern. What a turnaround for a world in retreat. Neither the dictatorships of the Third World, nor the Soviet Union, nor China have been able to get rid of this mythology of the West, which impregnates reality, perpetuates dreams and embodies the future that every people wishes for itself. In this area, Europe forms part of the Western community, is even in its vanguard, although showing not the slightest individuality.

This community is made up in the first place of social structures, values, codes of behaviour and specific conflicts. One is not giving in to an elementary Marxism if one looks to the organization of society for the first criterion of Western identity. If such a feature exists, indeed, it must be the omnipotence of the middle classes. The latter constitutes the perfect yardstick for judging cohesion to the Western community. Countries undergoing rapid industrialization would find themselves about half-way along this path with a situation of conflict caused by the cohabitation of a growing middle class and hitherto dominant groups desirous of holding on to their monopoly of power. It is easy to confuse society with this middle class, with the result that an almost invisible 'lumpen society' of the poor, the outcasts and those on the fringe, is totally rejected. This relationship leads on to other distinctive signs: the rise of individualism as a cardinal value along with solid corporate reflexes to protect already acquired benefits; the dying away of traditional production conflicts, only to be replaced by often more tough conflicts centring around life within society – environment, ecology, refusal of nuclear policy, surrogate mothers, abortion and immigration – all factors revolving around a moral confrontation which, unlike wage agreements, cannot be concluded by any process of fudging; a mentality embracing consumption and yet prone to sudden gusts of idealism – the cult of the supermarket is echoed by the Red Cross, Amnesty International or the welcome of the boat-people; young people with identical life-styles, dress and aspirations from one end of the West to the other; an international society of rock fans, dishwashers in restaurants, migrating tourists, jeans, trainers and pop music . . . The litany of points in common and resemblances is infinite. Sociologists construct from this the typical *Homo occidentalus*: a few adjustments here and there according to style or mood and a model is ready that stands for everyone. Where are the specifically European aspects of all this? A

French student resembles an American student as much as a German; a Spaniard is as similar to a Mexican as to a Dane.

Seen from further off, the West appears equally homogeneous. Its preoccupations, problems and solutions are all shared. The decline in the population, for instance, whose effects are not yet overt, will mean an interior implosion for less well-off countries and for the better off, serious difficulties linked to ageing, a reduced dynamism and weaker productivity. But this division will not occur between Europe and the rest of the West. In the next thirty years, France will come to bear more resemblance to the United States than to Germany, with a population that is stagnant but not in massive decline; a high level of immigration from south of the Mediterranean in the case of France, and from Mexico, in the case of the US; a chaotic 'melting pot' which is slightly harder on France than on the States; a sufficiently high level of consumption to stretch the resilience of the economy and a major advantage over their competitors, who will not have had immigration to fill the gaps left by the decline in birth rate.

The second example of this homogeneity is the phasing out of the State and of public bureaucracies. Initiated in the west of the US, the movement has swept through the whole world. This applies to Europe, of course, but also to the countries of the Third World who are not constantly privatizing, and to socialist economies who are discovering the virtues of the market. By liberating its agricultural prices, for instance, China rediscovered in the space of three years a self-sufficiency in food production that had disappeared with collectivization of farming. The ebb of this liberalizing dream will also, when the time comes, emanate from the US. It is written in the stars under the name of the good old theory of cycles, which is at least as convincing regarding ideological matters as it is in the economic domain.

Next we come to the question of control over the welfare state. The ageing of the population and the consequent increase in already explosive medical expenses is placing responsibility for financing pensions on a younger generation which is shrinking in numbers and growing more and more reticent by the minute. This equation seems to be as insoluble in Canada as it is in Germany. Then there is the protection of nature: demonstrators who violently opposed the extension of Frankfurt airport are reminiscent of the Japanese, who conducted a similar battle over Narita, rather than the French ecologists whose meagre claims to fame are limited to the odd demonstration, donkey's years ago, in front of Plogoff or Creys-Malville. The organization of cities can be a further indication: the care taken over town planning in Denmark has more in common with the architectural preoccupations of the Canadians in Ontario than with Italian anxieties about preserving their heritage. Priority given to improvements in the educational system is another: a feeling of deterioration is general and American cries of alarm are no different from French worries. The common symptom is one of the inadaptability of a system originally constructed for a privileged privileged minority, faced with the developments of mass education, the distractive competition of television, the over-abrupt cut-off between education and professional life and the difficulty of maintaining a minimum of order and discipline. Then lastly, there is the necessity to preserve the social consensus and the consequent universal need to ensure integration of immigrants and to avoid the proliferation of ethnic ghettos.

That is the West for you. Over and above its strategic interests, its democratic state and its cultural heritage, it is primarily a community of life-styles and preoccupations. Where is the European identity to be found? It is nonsense to imagine a collective unconscious, a historical resurgence, a psychological proximity or 'selective affinities' at the heart of the twelve countries, so porous is the wall that isolates them from the rest of the West. Realistically speaking, the Western circle is centred on the US, just as it was when America had real superpower status. The influence is at least as strong now as it was then, even though the US's economic domination and strategic protection has dissolved. Proof if it were needed of the erroneous nature of those old Marxist theories which saw the imperialism of American society as a by-product of its economy. *Homo occidentalus* reigns through concentric circles and Europe is in one of the innermost of these circles. But the curve is spreading to encompass Eastern Europe and even the Soviet Union. The 'Voice of America' or German television are irreplaceable, but the passion for Coca Cola, jeans and trainers is no coincidence. It is a kind of membership card, a knowing wink, an appropriation of the Western dream. In some ways, the attraction of Western Europe for the East is not connected with specific attributes, whether cultural or intellectual – only Kundera and his disciples now believe that – but comes from the fact that Europe is the nearest embodiment of the West. It is one of history's paradoxes that Western Europe is viewed more than ever as the limb of the West by societies in the East at the very moment when, on the contrary, it is slipping strategically from an occidental to a continental system.

A European Society with No Institutions?

In order to give some substance to the myth of 1992, the idea is being spread that it will bring about an economic and social identity simultaneously. This is a reassuring vision at a time when that mythological figure of the eighties, the civil society, is in the process of rehabilitation and is now endowed with a thousand and one virtues. Since she is the mother of all things, she must also be the mother of Europe. This belief has its good side in that it permits a halt in the process of political unification, the logic being that if society is commanding the State, the latter will eventually be forced to exist. The only trouble with this very pleasant sophism is that no European civil society actually exists. Do we have to remind ourselves that a society is not merely the sum of its constituent individuals? A network of institutions is required as well as the State. It was precisely a weakness in France's institutions, enfeebled by the omnipotence of the State, which prevented French society from reaching the complexity, richness and intensity of its Anglo-Saxon equivalent. But the hypothetical European civil society already constitutes a model of this type. Just as the European State is not yet showing on the horizon, the European civil society does not exist, deprived as it is of institutions and intermediary bodies.

No unions, no bosses, no lobbies. Even in the economic sphere, where indirect sociological effects of 1992 ought to feature strongly, the lack of institutions is impressive. The unions, weakened in each country, are incapable of extending themselves to a European scale; the time has passed when the beginnings of a single union could develop at the heart of multinationals. In order to protect its current benefits and hang onto its jobs, each labour organization has to battle against commercial partners at an international level and foreign subsidiaries at national level. Class consciousness, if it still exists, shows itself in a factory, possibly in a subsidiary firm, scarcely at all in the case of a large group and never at a multinational level. European social organizations wished to act as a crucible in which new

European unions could crystallize. What a waste of time and effort: everyone makes the right noises but nothing has come of it nor will come of it. The union movement is currently on the defensive, obliged to cut back drastically on its action if it wishes to survive, and forced to adapt to a change in values and in technology. How can we then expect it to expand to the scale of this new space with all the risk of following up the first traumatic revolution with another, equally disturbing?

Employers are not making any greater anticipatory efforts and their inertia is rather less understandable since, unlike the unions, they have plenty of wind in their sails. The market reigns, free enterprise dominates, power is held by the bosses and Europe is always on the agenda. But European commercial leaders are incapable of finding any means of unity at a European level. Vague attempts to some sort of organization are left straggling with no real sense of representation, strategy, vision nor credibility. There are hoards of individual European directors, but as a body they lack any cohesion. This combined lack of foresight on the part of unions and bosses in the Community forbids any formalizing of social relations on a European level. Can any society exist without such a set of relations?

Even that lower form of institution, the lobby, is not asserting itself at a community level. This is a truly bizarre situation since the Brussels Commission has control of an enormous amount of money, and at any other time, the slightest whiff of a subsidy would be enough to inspire the creation of a lobby. But specific interests continue to be pursued within a national framework, each lobby trying to reach this manna in Brussels via their own government. European farmers have also not made any attempt at regrouping. The FNSEA (the French Farmers' union) sees its German equivalent as a rival rather than an ally, preferring its traditional partner, the minister in charge of farming, to go off to Brussels in search of money. Corporations rule throughout Europe but not on a European scale. Even professions which overlap national frontiers are not yet tempted to open out this field of action. Air traffic controllers, for instance, all have the same problems and as such their profession cries out to be integrated throughout Europe. They stage more and more protests and strikes in their own area, leading to excessive criticisms levelled at the authorities, when in fact such Community organizations would arise quite naturally, if only there were some real action from European societies.

At present neither churches, political parties nor other associations are providing this impetus. For religious organizations, Western Europe is anyway a historical accident. Seen from afar and within the historical context which is the prerogative of the Church, Europe seems to be vague and insubstantial. The Catholic Church, obsessed by its desire to survive in Eastern Europe and the Soviet Union, has always refrained from giving the slightest inclination that it considered Western Europe to be a significant religious area. Its universal nature provided it with an admirable pretext for refusing to accept the division of Europe. According to the Vatican there is a spiritual Europe, but it stretches from the Atlantic to the Urals; an *Ostpolitik* that pre-dated even that of the former Federal Republic. The same tendency, even in such different areas as spiritual and strategic, leads to the same result. Where continental Europe is a significant space, no organization or feature particular to Western Europe sets it apart artificially. Judaism, for the same reasons, follows a similar course as regards the East. When a European Jewish congress was created, one of its objectives was to do away with the Iron Curtain. Protestant churches, on the other hand, are nationality-based and it was this factor that caused the Evangelical churches of the former Germanies to come to such an intensive *rapprochement*. Spiritual matters transcend frontiers, but if such frontiers did exist, they would not enclose the twelve states of the Community.

On a far less spiritual plane, political parties are nevertheless no more organized at a Community level. This is even more paradoxical on their side since Europe, while being something of a permanent gamble, is nonetheless real. The Socialist International reaches well beyond the Community, while Liberal, Conservative or Christian Democratic associations remain well short of it. Specific allegiances, shared ideologies or a common past justify countless bilateral relationships but none that encompass the whole Community. The European Parliament has not really played its part since the parliamentary groups which constitute it have never carried their influence over into their original parties. The situation is no more encouraging concerning associations in general. The Red Cross, Amnesty International and numerous charitable organizations bear witness to a real internationalism but not one is specific to the EEC, and at a national level they do not even resemble each other. What do 'Doctors of the World' and 'Doctors without Frontiers' in France have in common with the charitable associations linked to German churches which are quite naturally eager to help the inhabitants of the old Eastern provinces?

Foundations, research institutes and universities are similarly lacking, since the intellectual life of Europe ignores the frontiers of the EC. One might at least expect to find institutions favouring a certain amount of mixing at a Community level. But this would first require large Anglo-Saxon-type foundations, such as Ford and Rockefeller, which dispense money, support and prestige. These do exist in countries such as Britain and Germany which are used to such types of organization, but they have never been emancipated from their national framework. Elsewhere, they would first have to acclimatize themselves to the new conditions before attempting to change form. The member states have never created any community research centre to replace such types of institution, with the sole exception of ECNR (the European Centre for Nuclear Research) in Geneva, and even its cooperative character extends beyond the EC. Research has remained a national matter in terms of financing, organization and personnel. Cooperative links are of course on the increase but they have never attained – and with good reason – the intensity of those woven between American institutes. Even the charming 'European University' of Florence cannot in all honesty claim to be following the principle behind its name. There, too, nationalism prevails under the effects of finance, recruitment, organization, intellectual routine and conservatism. Never has a large French educational establishment had the idea of making a proposal to a German counterpart that involved not a traditional liaison, but a real fusion. What is so iconoclastic about this proposition? Why should a merger of the mining school in Paris with its German alter ego be so much more complex a task than merging ASEA and Brown-Boveri? Simply because our minds are not open to it. When it comes to building a Europe, those responsible have neither the initiative, the ambition, nor the will that they exhibit at a national level. They are waiting for Brussels or some other supranational organization to decide. They are far from being the adult actors necessary in a civil society.

With no special organization to draw it together, no spiritual or political institutions to provide cohesion, and no spirit of initiative and originality, how can a civil society truly express itself? Quick as they are with enterprise, innovation and action within their national framework, Europeans lose these facilities as soon as it becomes a question of displaying them at a European scale. This is, unfortunately, the most terrible proof of the inexistence of any European civil society.

A European Citizenship in Limbo

Citizens of the EC can let themselves be lulled by certain aspects: a passport cover with the same colour and layout, special queues at airports – except, symbolically, in the UK where British residents are treated separately. But as far as everyday rights are concerned, that is about as far as Europe goes for its citizens. A kind of citizenship is currently being established, but it is of an exclusively economic nature. This is one peculiarity of a plan to integrate Europe which is based on and will come about only through the economy. The fact that we daily confuse Europe and the European Community serves only to fuel this ambiguity, and the conviction spreads that a European citizen will exist as soon as free professional circulation is assured. This will undoubtedly, of course, be a contributing factor. A Dutch doctor established in le Gers, or a French architect transplanted to Glasgow are typical signs of the Europe under construction. But these pioneers will not be European citizens; they will be privileged immigrants, just like the British or Canadians in the US, treated as VIPs by the immigration services. Alongside the economic construction of Europe there was supposed to be a similar legislative construction, but this has never come about. This choice is not insignificant, demonstrating just how little influence Anglo-Saxon thinking has had on the progress of Europe. The latter is a hybrid cross between technocratic vision, and the cult of the market. It has never gone along with an American-type vision of society as supported by the inseparable pillars of the market and the law. Never have Anglo-Saxon political thinkers begun to imagine an omnipotent market without its judicial counterpart. In their eyes this would not create a society and they would be right. The example of the community will prove this in no uncertain manner. Here we have a space where, as an economic actor, an individual will be European, while as a private person, he will remain a prisoner of his original nationality. None of the classic elements of citizenship exist, whether political, civil, or judicial. How are we expected to believe that a Europe without citizens can have its own identity? How are we expected to hope that this hypothetical identity is in a position to complete the 'third circle'?

Political laws are out of the European game, at the moment, with the exception of the five-yearly election of the European Parliament by universal suffrage. That is to say, the electorate vote in their own country for representatives from their own country. The promoters of this operation claim that the aim was to set up a chamber along the same federal lines as the US Senate or the old German Bundesrat. But these particular 'high assemblies', representing the States or the *Länder* are balanced by a second chamber, the House of Represent-atives and the Bundestag, which is elected by universal suffrage throughout the whole country. The founders of Europe did not dare to dream of such a bicameral system and they were probably right; the time was not ripe. But given the artificiality of the ritual election of the European Parliament, the political citizen in Europe can never be a real European citizen.

The violent debate in France surrounding immigrants' right to vote has eclipsed any thoughts on the specific case of EC natives. Doesn't common-sense dictate that a citizen originating from another member state and resident in France for several years should be able to vote in local, general and even presidential elections? Would it not be logical for participation in these elections to require a graduated term of residence: three years, perhaps, for the first, five for the second and seven years – a sacred length of time – for the third? What blasphemy! A sacrilegious idea, most people will automatically think. Gut reactions against this proposal are inevitable, and their implications must be assessed. This means, for example, that Christine Ockrent can exert an influence over French opinion professionally, but has no right to express this same opinion at the ballot box. It also means that an Italian executive who has been settled in France for fifteen years has the same fiscal and social duties as a Frenchman, paying taxes and contributions and receiving services, but has none of the latter's political rights. All in all, the right to vote, and the 'blood tax' of military service betray an idea of citizenship that is closer to the nineteenth than to the twenty-first century. Debate on this subject has not cropped up in any of the member states and politicians are careful not to provoke it since the public seems indifferent. This silence can be explained in two ways, both equally distasteful. Either Europeans believe in Europe but consider political rights as being subsidiary and unimportant, or else they see political citizenship as being essentially superior while assuming, in that case, that European identity is secondary and subordinate. There ought, theoretically, to be two visions of a political Europe. The traditional one would be to build a European political system; its state of progress is well known. The other would be to set up a political citizenship, an idea which is not even on the drawing board yet. In the first case, this would mean reckoning on a hypothetical State; in the second, on a future political society in the classical sense of the term. The latter seems to be even more unrealistic, being shocking even to think of, while the former does at least exist on a dream level.

Civic citizenship is no further advanced than political citizenship; there too the law of the land prevails. If two citizens of the Community get married in France, they can only be divorced by a French tribunal; having adopted a child in Germany, they are obliged to follow German adoption rules, and so on. It is undoubtedly a French notion, distilled from centuries of State unity, to imagine that civil laws must be the same for the whole of a country. The United States serves as a reminder that within a federation, certain laws can vary from one state to another. But the debate in Europe is not identical, containing laws which would be a matter for community definition as well as laws which would be the prerogative of each member state. In reality the definition of civil citizenship does not threaten the same taboos as political citizenship. That the former is not on the agenda is due to some far more trivial reasons, namely that no community treaty has envisaged it, no European technocracy is in charge of bringing it about, no collective pressure is demanding it and no European jurisdiction is in any state to carry it from one jurisprudence to another. It is a closed subject.

The same is not true of the European judicial system, that is to say – if this expression does not appear too self-contradictory – of penal citizenship. This problem has been very much to the forefront of discussion and even acquired a certain intensity at the time of the upsurge in terrorism and the debate on extradition. Two theses are currently in vogue. The first postulates that Europe is united to such an extent that crimes and misdemeanours can be judged in the country where the arrest was made. The second maintains the inverse, still in the name of Europeanism, i.e., that extradition must be automatic, that a criminal who has committed an offence in Rennes and has been arrested in Nice will be tried by the Court of Assizes of Ille-de-Vilaine. This debate has never been definitively settled and extradition orders for political crimes continue to provoke violent clashes. Is there anyone who does not remember the extradition of Klaus Croissant? If the former Federal Republic had not been a democracy and if its judicial system had been a source of concern to our most finicky lawyers, how could these same lawyers and militant Europeans have argued the case for an integrated Europe? A democracy can only be wedded to another democracy. Can any forget the confrontation between France and Spain in 1981–2 over Basque terrorists? How could the same politicians refuse extradition, on the one hand citing respect for individual rights, while proclaiming, on the other, that since Spain had become a democracy, it should join the EC as soon as possible? In practice the problem has ironed itself out to a certain extent, and a common solidarity in the face of terrorism has led the judiciary of the principal member states to discontinue hostilities. However, although a European judiciary is at least partially established to deal with crimes of terrorism, it has hardly progressed at all on other fronts. In an economically united Europe, economic fraud is always assessed on a national basis. A person guilty of fraud in the eyes of the French tax department who pursues his activities in Luxembourg, is there regarded as an upright citizen. This is an astonishing paradox for an area where the fraud industry, as we have seen, promises soon to enjoy unparalleled expansion.

Faced with such realities, what importance can we attach to attractive proclamations on our double citizenship, European and national? Doubtless all of us, in our contemporary society, feel restricted to a certain extent by a purely national citizenship, and see ourselves in a small way as 'citizens of the world', to quote the charming expression used by Gary Davis in the fifties. But of which world? The European Community, Europe as a whole from the Atlantic to the Urals, the Anglo-Saxon universe, or the Western system? An attachment to Europe is not quite of the same nature. It should correspond with laws which do not actually exist at the moment. Will a European system of law ever be created, if member states do not implement the same processes as they have for the economy? In other words, certain fundamental texts and a bureaucracy which slowly manages to push things forward, since that is its nature, its *raison d'être* and its commercial basis. Areas without 'Eurocrats' are moving forward at a slower rate than those who are equipped in such a way: is there any better rehabilitation of the heavy Brussels machinery?

An Ambiguous Public Opinion

If we wish for a European society, the public must feel itself to be European. At the moment their feelings are ambiguous and variable as national, European and Western loyalties vie with each other. Has the public any convictions, any spirit, any identity? Nothing could be less sure.

If one can gauge public opinion through the battery of opinion polls, France is currently more pro-European than Britain or Germany. A thousand and one analyses show the French as being passionate about 1992, ready to offer Germany their nuclear guarantee, eager to see a European state established. In a word, they are now more enthusiastic than ever, through having been discouraged for decades by the combined weight of Gaullism and communism. Of course such vague and rudimentary petitions must not be taken too seriously. The interviewer is careful not to explain to those interviewed what Hamburg = Strasbourg would actually signify. But this stream of figures does leave behind it an impression, a mood, a state of mind. Moreover, these are not the same impressions that are prevalent in the UK where a still marked predilection for the US combined with the remnants of mistrust of their continental partners and the British taste for picking and choosing are hardly counteracted by a few pro-European feelings.

Opinion polls in Germany, on the other hand, correspond exactly with the strategic development of the country. But can we assume from that that the German public has any more control over decision-making than others? Mistrust of Americans is growing each year, whether or not as a result of Gorbyism, and the curves representing levels of trust in the US and the Soviet Union have crossed so that the second are now seen in a more reassuring light than the first. Even before reunification, one half of West Germans wished for their country to be neutral, and 80 per cent were in favour of a complete denuclearization of their territory. There is no lack of signs in favour of Europe in other areas, especially regarding the depth and sincerity of their friendship with France. The German public has already embraced a continental context, rejecting the US which used to be its principal ally, big brother and adored guardian. It is balanced between the West and the East and feels its role to be one of a linking territory or a kind of no-man's land.

The public of each in these three countries is taking charge of the strategic choices of their governments and expressing very clearly the different interests concerned and the slide of the continent. Taken together, they do not necessarily constitute a united European opinion. Certainly, the inspiration provided by Europe gives rise to a sense of cohesion, but this inspiration is not shared equally and is undoubtedly felt less keenly than in other member states such as Italy and Spain. It is tinged also with vague Western reflexes, with a fluid type of internationalism, with pleasant feelings of solidarity which make a Pole seem as near as any other citizen in the Community, which make the Americans seem more familiar to the French than the English, an African closer to the heart of a Dane than a Greek. These are not the sort of elements that will create a European consciousness.

Public opinion – this is almost a tautology – goes in phase with society. At the moment it reflects Western rather than European leanings, national rather than Community loyalties. It is not prone to these great bursts of momentum that take hold of the authorities. It will never exert the same pressure in favour of the building of Europe that the German public was able to muster against its own government over defence of the environment. Europe is not a new idea in Europe, at least as far as the public is concerned.

In Search of a European Elite

Unity is no more advanced at the level of Europe's elite, and one has to recognize the motivating force that this class represents. Europe will not be created despite them, or without them, but through them. At present the elite of each member state remains strictly nationally oriented as regards membership, mentality and interests. They are obviously open to the world, but to the world as a whole rather than to the European Community. They recognize an American model and a Japanese threat, but no real European identity.

The French system is possibly the most archaic of all, a terrible notion for a technostructure which, under the admiring gaze of the whole world, has ended up seeing itself as a paragon of virtue. The whole of the developed world envies France its civil servants, but does the future really belong to civil servants, given a more and more erratic situation, a more and more mobile economy and a more and more complex society? The qualities that will be required, henceforth, will involve flexibility, decision-making skills, the ability to change tack and adapt to circumstances, speed, a sense of non-hierarchical command and a certain type of charisma and conviviality. Faced with such a job description, what is actually produced in the factories which turn out France's elite? Brilliant, young ideas people, inclined towards military-style command, rooted in the conviction that France is an important power, that administration is at the heart of this power and that they will be the instruments of this administration.

Furnished with such notions and a lifelong 'officer's certificate', just as in the *Ancien Régime*, this new nobility which is made, not born, starts its assault on the ladder of power. It has won the right to achieve the summits of politics, administration or business. Power is therefore concentrated on the hands of certain Brahmins who can be certain of their perenity, their ascendancy and their savoir-faire. Are their rights and privileges matched by the services that they fulfil? In the past, most definitely. This elite effected the modernization of France, both in the nineteenth century and since the last war, by assuming responsibility and imposing it on the politicians in power. Nowadays it is following rather than leading this revolution. This nobility is not deaf to the current world situation, quite obviously. Its members are choosing to enter the world of economics at an early stage, they fully understand the realities of international politics, they feel the vertiginous effect of the market and are learning that nothing is irreversible. But what horrible arthritic prejudices are still prevalent! As for Europe, they regard it less as a new frontier than as a new space to be constructed in the image of France. The Brussels technostructure has gained much from this transfusion of savoir-faire. But the French, too inclined to regard Europe through Napoleonic spectacles, do not constitute the essence of a newly emerging European elite.

Elsewhere, the problem is not radically different. In the countries where the bourgeoisie have handled administrative affairs, such as Spain, it is the US which has provided an entree to the rest of the world. It was in the US that a generation of 'Harvard socialists' acquired a taste for the market, a sense of technology and international awareness. These typical ingredients of *fin-de-siècle* socialism have produced in Spain the same pattern of left-wing values that existed in social-democratic Sweden twenty years ago. Needless to say, those responsible are all in favour of Europe and regard 1992 as a natural evolution, and yet their formation and attitudes have been less affected by a dominant Europe than by the influence of America. The elite in Britain and Germany conform to type and historical tradition in that the European context has played little part in their education and has not formed their behaviour. The former's Atlantic horizon and the latter's continental habits, have not weakened in either intensity or durability. It must be the Italians who best foreshadow a European elite: firstly, because the market rather than the state has been their melting pot; also because of their historic and cultural importance; and lastly, due to an adaptable nature which allows them to make the new environment their own. They are thinking and living as Europeans and are equally at ease in Paris as in Milan, in London as in Madrid.

However, the overall tendency is for elite layers of society to operate on a strictly national plane. They will be conscripted from each member state, of course, to join a general European nomenclature, but this latter can not exist by itself. There is at present no large European school whose diploma allows access to the privileged channels of each country. There is no interchange of top professionals which would allow an English person to be the director of the French treasury. Why should this raise more eyebrows than the presence of a Welsh person at the head of l'Oréal? There are no thinking institutions or clubs, no European 'Siècle'[1], no Oxford Fellows at Community level capable of creating the solidarity and group practices necessary to a smooth functioning of the nomenclature. There is no career organization which gives promotion on the basis of experience gained in another country. In the absence of such structures there can be no European establishment since this type of organizational network is as vital for the establishment as water for saurians. The public authorities, for their part, have not put in place the kind of Community university institution which could have made a start at bringing forth a European elite.

Europe remains in the hands of the political world, a professional category which could hardly be more strictly national in outlook, and of state bureaucracies which are only slightly more open-minded. Any pro-European attitude on their part has been arrived at through a process of reasoning rather than by a natural inclination. This is what leads to the apparent contradiction contained in the fact that these people think as Europeans but are not European in reality. Europe for them is a beautiful idea, not a second nature. Time, of course, could do its work and, if Europe does eventually exist, an authentically

European elite would be created. But unfortunately, that is not the question at issue here. The fact is that it is not up to Europe to create its own elite, but up to this elite to make Europe. The countdown continues as the continental shift is making a community identity more aleatory each year.

The third circle, that of society, does not, in fact, close around the twelve nations of the Community. There are civil institutions, no broadening concept of citizenship, no feeling of public unity and no European elite to form a basis for a civil European society. From the point of view of a true society, the West has more substance than Europe. The latter has no set form; its strategic, economic and social circles sometimes overlap, but never circumscribe each other. There is a widening gap between an increasingly dislocated reality and a dream which has been incarnated in 1992. One last illusion is managing to hold sway, that in the absence of a true civil society, Europe will at least be a cultural community. For the French, who naively attribute to culture a capacity to mould reality and who see it as a Marxist-type infrastructure, this would indeed be a significant identifying agent. 'If I could do it all over again, I would begin with culture,' said Jean Monnet at the end of his life, appropriating the hierarchy whereby culture is placed above the economy as a means of transformation. But, if we are honest, not even culture can close this wretched third circle.

Notes

The name of a circle which brings together all the leading members of the establishment once a month in Paris.

'If I Could Do it all Again,
I Would Begin with Culture'

What if Jean Monnet in 1950 had put into action all that he later regretted not doing? If he had begun with culture? If, instead of a European Coal and Steel Community – ECSC – and a European Economic Community – the EEC – he had created an ECC, a European Cultural Community? If cross-linguistic teaching had become the role in the member states? If the school syllabus had consisted everywhere of European affairs concerning history, geography and civil education? If cultural investment had been developed in the Community as a whole? If the first television networks had been multinational rather than merely national? If universities had been regrouped along European lines? If qualifications gained in one country had been valid for all, for the past twenty years? If, if, if. No one can say that Europe would now be more advanced. Each era creates its own structural hierarchy: the Jean Monnet of 1950 began with the economy because an urgent need for reconstruction, an appetite for consumption, the shadow of Marxism and the pursuit of an infrastructure made this a more compelling matter. The Jean Monnet who, at the end of his life, regretted not having taken a gamble on culture was living in another world. Culture – vague term that it is – seemed at that moment to have become the essence of all things, a superior reality overhanging all others whether political, economic, judicial or national. If Europe had forged a cultural identity for itself, as Monnet wished in his last years, it is possible that the rest might have followed, above all, the economy. The inverse, however, is not true. The EEC has never given rise to a cultural movement, and 1992 has not the slightest implication for culture. At a time when Europe is torn apart between several identities, strategic, economic and social, it is no use looking to culture to provide a backbone. This absence makes itself felt over a wide area covering not only traditional culture, but also education, language and, last but not least, audio-visual aspects. Europe has not found any overall identity on any of these fronts. Nothing is ever definitively lost, but likewise, history never retraces its steps; positions freeze, rules become fixed and people entrenched. This is particularly true of audio-visual culture. The ground is currently being restructured and if Europe does not now ease her way through the eye of the needle, she will have an even tougher job tomorrow. The same goes for education. If culture is unable to seal off the third circle, what means of identity is the European Community left with in order to create a true role for itself in history, given a strategic earthquake which is threatening its very foundations, and the cult of a pure market which cannot deliver anything but increased productivity?

Europe is not a Cultural Community

Faced with the indomitable universe of the complex world of culture, and with the gifted progeny who guard the sacred temple with their own talents, humility is the rule. It leads to several conclusions (seven, in this case, to surrender to the dictates of the golden number), by which a diagnosis becomes a starting point: the European Community is forbidden any cultural identity.

A Divided Culture

Firstly: Europe is made up of a number of disjointed cultural spaces. Its current frontiers have had no significance since the break-up of the old European circle of *Mittel Europa*. Behind the resurgence of the Viennese myth and the commemoration of Vienna 1850–1917 through celebrations, exhibitions, lectures and books, lies a nostalgia for the cultural Europe under display, a sacred territory marked out by Munich, Berlin, Vienna, Prague, Warsaw, Trieste, Venice. This European spirit is dead. On the other hand, the slow reappropriation of its identity by the centre does open the door slightly to a cultural renaissance. It is not purely by chance that signs of a *Mittel Europa* have often been culturally based: commemorations, exhibitions, lectures, etc. In that world, culture is fighting on the same side as the strategic drift of the continent: it has everything to gain from it and takes pleasure in anticipating and thereby forcing the pace of change. The Latin circle, France, Spain and Italy, hardly participate at all in this movement. They also are rediscovering their cultural identity and the myth of a Mediterranean culture is once again seeing the light of day, as if these countries had an unconscious need to set themselves apart from the recomposition of Central Europe. This Latin aspect is so obvious on a day-to-day basis, however, that is not strictly necessary to draw attention to it in this way. Finally, beyond these two circles rises the immense world of Anglo-Saxon culture, omnipresent, fluid, regenerative and dynamic. We have heard enough naive statements about American cultural imperialism to last a lifetime. And yet the shadow cast by the US is certainly now more pervasive in cultural matters than in anything else. The US is no longer the dominant political power – its strategic withdrawal is visible to the naked eye – but its cultural expansion is more real than ever. Gilbert Comte, Régis Debray, Philippe de Saint-Robert and Claude Jullien must all come to terms with it since it is not a voluntary hegemony but a natural dynamic. It is futile to criticize and rail against something which is here – maybe till the end of time. Under such a heavy burden of influence the European Community has no cultural identity of its own. It is an artificially divided space, carving up authentic cultural areas, and immersed in an occidental atmosphere which lacks both substance and identity.

Culture and the Consumer

Secondly: the cultural growth of the last few decades testifies to the opulence of the West, but Europe plays no specific role in this drama. Ever-increasing numbers of concerts, crowded exhibitions, the growth of mass tourism are as true of Japan as of France, of Australia as of Italy, of the US as of Spain, and the same kind of revolution is spreading through the communist world. For the middle classes, the representatives of a Western life-style, cultural consumption has become a means of identification. They revel in it, as a means of self-discovery and self-reflection. Europe has to accept that it has become, quite simply, one of the great exporters of cultural symbols.

Culture and the Past

Thirdly: what Europe has to offer, principally, are symbols of the past, since it no longer exerts any global influence. In the plastic arts the energy is coming from the US, and Europe has lost its dominance in music, literature, philosophy, previously an exclusively European domain, and the human sciences. One hears *ad nauseam* that the European intellectual died with Sartre; unpleasant, but true. Our society is without a nerve centre, delocalized, impulsive and in perpetual motion, and the world of ideas has lost its old landmarks. The time of an omnipresent German philosophy, of an existentialism carried to the four corners of the earth, of a structuralism which traumatized everything including the human sciences and of the Annals which crushed traditional research for decades is definitively over. Where is the Heidegger, the D'Annunzio, the Gide, or the Sartre of the eighties? Europe had invented a magnificent product for rich societies: intellectual magistry. It is not managing, to use the jargon of seasoned exporters, to replenish its range, not because the products are worse, but because 'the market no longer requires them'. It is not an expression of a decline, but of a changing universe. With all due respect to the Spenglers of this world, who prophesy the decline of Europe with as much conviction as ever, Europe is in fact more cultured, more active and more lively than ever. One can say about culture what Foucault thought about power, that it is everywhere and nowhere, insidious and exclusive. But seen from the outside, Europe is achieving no such identity compared with the period when, lining up Picasso, Sartre, Malraux, Moravia and Russell like an army on parade, she occupied the world stage and seemed to exist through that fact alone.

The Competition for Culture

Fourthly: culture has become a kind of gigantic industry, a pretext for mass tourism which is enough to stabilize or destabilize balances of payments. Monuments, museums, exhibitions, spectacles provide ammunition to encourage visitors, currencies and capital. European countries compete with each other in this particular game. Does Spain really want the 500th anniversary of 1492 to be celebrated in Europe rather than on home ground? Does France wish to export the bicentenary of the Revolution? Madrid is staking millions on obtaining the Thyssen-Bornemisza museum for itself, just as Ford and General Motors used to. Paris is incessantly promoting its great works and Rome is accelerating its restoration projects. Cultural values, ethics and grand principles, do, of course, forbid open expression of this egotism but all countries obey the law of necessity. Foreign accounts have to be settled and culture is more effective from this point of view than technology.

Culture and Diversity

In the fifth place: European cultural policy goes hand in hand with state action and in this area there is scarcely any resemblance among the various countries. Neither Great Britain nor Germany are centrally administered. Culture therefore, is left mainly up to local authorities or *Lander*, and is out of the hands of the government. In Italy, too, initiatives are decentralized and the minister is merely in charge of overall supervision. Spain resembles France the most, quite naturally, since in both countries culture has long been an instrument of international influence. To a certain extent, 'Hispanicism' and Gaullism share parallel ambitions. But nowhere does there exist a Culture Minister quite like in France whose post derives from a strange alchemical mixture of technocratic efficiency, state protection of arts and literature, the mysterious power of the word and the contemporary 'transsubstantiation' offered by the media. It is traditional for more militant liberals to remind us that only the USSR and France have appointed powerful ministers for culture. Rubbish! The Soviet post has neither the prestige nor the importance of the French Minister. At a time when the State is losing powers each year, this Minister is anchoring himself more firmly in the tradition of a creative protective state; there, at least, he is free to act. In a country which is still bold enough to initiate large-scale projects, the state remains the main motive force. What possible dialogue could one imagine around a table which involved a French Minister basking in his glory, his Italian colleague who is short of cash for restoration work and the respective British and German Ministers who have no political clout? They have no language, no vision and no projects in common. How can we expect actions requiring political will, determination and resources to be taken by such a diverse circle?

The European Dream

In the sixth place: even if political conditions were miraculously reconciled, the very idea of a European cultural community is nonsensical. What would be its draft? To amalgamate all the various systems of subsidy? To insure an equal spread of resources? To help the most depleted countries in the protection of their heritage? To facilitate exchanges between theatre groups? To subsidize works branded with the European seal of approval? What would they offer, these mausoleums erected to the European dream? National reflexes are expressed in cultural material; the European reflex is pure artifice.

Culture and National Identity

In the seventh place: faced with a more and more permeable world, culture remains one of the last vestiges of national identity. Just as provinces rediscovered their dialects when faced with urban acceleration, the member nations, those provinces of the twenty-first century, will try even harder to cling on to their 'cultural ego'. Inundated by television, music, fashion and the whole gamut of signs and symbols, they will tend to place more importance on their own national culture as if it were the ultimate proof of their identity. Faced with the unfolding of Western or world-wide culture, the European Community is not a valid cultural space. It has never been so in the past, is not currently and will be even less so in the future. If Monnet's retrospective dreams were of beginning with culture in its classical sense, they were way off the mark. But maybe he was thinking of education.

Education: A Powerful Lever Overlooked

With its policy of equivalent qualifications, Europe has made a great step forward. In the first place, because this guarantees free circulation of people and new competitiveness in the area of skills. Secondly, because it allows courses to alternate more easily, with a student starting his or her course in one country, and finishing it in another. Lastly, because it provides universities with the spur of international competition. The French system, for example, which forbids competition between universities on a national scale, will be forced to accept it on a European level. It will be an essential weapon for change, sounding the knell for interior monopolies. This drop of acid will eat away at any unifying, centralizing machinery. This system could only have been set in motion by external forces, since the political price of any reform coming from within had become exorbitant, as Savany and Devaquet's plans demonstrated. Equivalent qualifications constitute a shock-wave whose effects go well beyond its supposed aims, jolting the most rigid state bodies in each member state into action. European unity is thus repeating the effects of 1958 and 1992 and puts into question both established habits and funding. But this advance alone is not enough to constitute a hypothetical European education system, least of all in Monnet's sense of the term. A communal culture can be born from a communal education system; without this shared education, it has no chance of existing. A European pedagogical matrix is needed, involving shared syllabuses, regular exchanges and the beginnings of a European university system. This Europe has not progressed one iota in thirty years.

Identity lies principally in memory, as Pierre Nora superbly reminded us.[1] In which case, a cursory reading of scholarly manuals would be convincing enough proof of the inexistence of Europe. French history resounds with military triumphs and an omnipresent, victorious state; German history, with nostalgia for unity and a reaffirmation that a nation carries on existing despite division into states; Britain retains a wistful memory of its Victorian empire and Spain of its great conquests. This reading exercise is a revelation. Even if the most extreme features of nationalism and xenophobia have been erased, the atmosphere has not changed. Texts, illustrations and captions are all in step with national feelings. Europe is merely being grafted artificially onto certain pages. No country has ever tried to replace its own history by a history of Europe seen from a multiple viewpoint which does not seek to depict any one country as perfect. When young Europeans look on 1914–18 as a civil war as Spain does of its own civil war, Europe will have progressed far more than in five years of the single market. But this is not imminent: without coordination on syllabus and perspective and a revolution in method, Europe cannot exist. The typically French debate on whether to teach new-style history or factual history has never given way to a much more essential discussion on whether to teach our children the history of France or of Europe. Does the one necessarily exclude the other?

Geography is no different. National territory represents the basic area for study, surrounded by a vague space which is Europe. In France, knowledge about Mount Gerbier-de-Jonc still appears to be more essential than recognizing the Community's capital cities, and French geological resources constitute a more decisive element than the economic map of Europe. Civil education, with its outmoded title, is quite naturally centred around France and its pyramid of power, from the state to each local authority. Would it not be more worthwhile for young French people to know some rudiments of the political processes of Germany, Britain or Italy, than to be familiar with all the subtleties of local government programmes?

Literature inevitably follows the same pattern. The only literature that exists in France is French, and that resilient monument to intellectual conformism, Lagarde et Michard, has the distinctive odour of cultural nationalism. Shakespeare, Goethe, Kafka and Joyce are as nothing when set against Racine, Beaumarchais, Anatole France or Gide. That *King Lear* teaches us more about the complexities of the human soul than a sentimental tale about the *Cid* is not the point. Literature, culture and the needs of the pupil are all placed within a hierarchy. Viewed from London, the process would evidently be the same: Proust was nothing but a dirty continental and Flaubert, a writer from Normandy. Ethnocentricity, a typically European complaint, does not even extend to include the frontiers of Europe: as far as pedegogy is concerned, it is blinkered, nationalist, parochial. Beginning at primary school, the order of the world is fixed, and culture and knowledge are limited to a strictly national framework. That the founders of Europe, both past and present, have not registered these facts remains highly disconcerting.

The conservatism of the education syllabus is not due simply to ideological pressure. It is affected by tradition, by its own past, by technical procedures and by the immobility inherent to such bureaucratic monsters as the education systems of each country. But we cannot pin the blame on the teachers. They have undergone real revolutions in subject programming in France (for example the sudden dictates of modern mathematics and the invasion of new-style history) and have adapted to them without any difficulty. At least the appearance of a European dimension would call for a greater spirit of motivation than the incorporation into the syllabus of the classic confrontation in teaching circles between the Ancients and the Moderns. But such an action would only have any meaning in a European context. Are Community Education Ministers making any real effort? What inseparable obstacles are blocking their path? What mountains have they had to lift? Would such a project really be more difficult to initiate than the single European market of 1992?

The 'Europeanization' of syllabuses does not augur well for further demands on behalf of a European education. Educational exchanges are still limited and haphazard. The concept of a compulsory year of study abroad as being basic to a course has never been mooted, either at secondary or at tertiary level. Neither has a period of study in another member state during the school year been envisaged: is this less vital than the round of nature classes and snow trips? Neither have summer stays abroad been made obligatory. There are considerable technical difficulties, of course, to do with finance, organization and obligations imposed on teachers. But for goodness sake, as a project it is no more taxing than the Common Agricultural Policy or the creation of a chamber to deal with compensation of VAT receipts. When will the Minister of Education tackle this subject properly, instead of elaborating on his thousand-and-first school reform motion? When will the Federation for National Education for once seize this progressive idea? When will Brussels feel the need to act on the matter? Since the formation of the original but limited Franco-German Youth Office twenty-five years ago, nothing has been done by France or by any other member state. Educational exchanges would provide some substance to the present pro-European climate of opinion, and would therefore have a significance far greater than that of fiscal alignment.

This desert extends to cover tertiary education. Here it is not merely the State which is at fault; universities are largely to blame also. Abbeville school can hardly follow a European course by itself, but Paris IV could. Oxford has more latitude than a school in Kent, and Heidelberg has more scope than a technical college in Hamburg. By concentrating any outward reflex towards the US, universities have not bothered about extensive interuniversity exchanges within Europe, nor about associations or mergers. After thirty years, the map showing the continent's universities has not changed – it remains irredeemably national. The new equivalent degree structure is not, on its own, enough to offset this situation: it is like a tiny drop of acid. What is needed is action on a completely different scale, and on the initiative of the universities themselves. If not, their aspirations towards autonomy will be shown to be nothing but corporate bluster.

The inanity of the present European policy on education has not come about through lack of ideas; there has never been any dirth on that score. But the absence of any institution in the Community which deals specifically with this subject has definitely been felt; one of the best arguments for the Brussels bureaucracy. Without an organization straddling the whole of Europe, nothing is possible; national preoccupations are not counterbalanced and politicians are neither lobbied nor petitioned. As far as education is concerned, the EC can only mount a guerrilla offensive – a few lightning raids such as the equivalence of degrees, followed by a retreat, leaving aside any attempt at integration. Education is the Community's black hole, a situation which has become even more paradoxical since it is now a major concern in each country. Europe has not, in this case, the happy possibility of waving a magic wand and thereby resolving externally the internal problems of each member state. But this 'freezing point' is totally incompatible with any ambition on the part of the Community. Without education, identity is unattainable; even with it, it is not assured. Could this logic one day lead to a Monnet-style Utopia, an indissoluble link between the task at hand and the wherewithal to bring it about, a European Educational Community? Have Europeans the strength not only to accomplish the work in progress, i.e., the single market, but also to open up new avenues? Are they ready to create new organizations; is a European Educational Community any more revolutionary now than the European Coal and Steel Community was in 1950? Time is running out: with no cultural identity, Europe is split between a strategic and economic space; with no education project, cultural identity is still-born.

The Sole Contribution of the English: Their Language

Language has normally accompanied, even preceded, any process of unification. Countless empires have been constituted by the sword and the word. No political entity has ever survived a plurality of languages; towers of Babel simply do not last. Experience is not necessarily truth though: Europe is not like any other ensemble; its unification is following an unprecedented route; the situation is not one of confrontation between one language and several dialects, but of a co-existence of a group of major languages. Modern translation techniques are now providing a solution to a hitherto insoluble problem. This familiar refrain allows us to evade a question which nevertheless remains as vital as ever: can a Europe without a single European language exist? Does any European language other than English exist?

For countries such as France and Spain, whose languages constitute one of their last instruments of international influence, this statement is intolerable. What would it mean to be Francophone if, within the European Community, French had become a secondary language? There is therefore a kind of linguistic war being fought in the EC. Several official languages, an army of interpreters, texts translated and retranslated to the point of losing all their flavour like a continually reheated dish, Lilliputian battles; whimsical actions, principles brandished like clubs . . . this is all an act to deny reality. There is only one European Esperanto – English – and this language is perhaps the only major British contribution to Europe. Businesses recognized this fact long ago with a business jargon supposedly resembling English. A Dutch, German or Italian firm may well communicate with its foreign subsidiaries in English rather than in its mother tongue.

In the essentially practical world of business, linguistic imperialism is inevitable. Certain countries understood this long ago: the multilingual Italians, for example, with a generation of under-forties who are Anglophone and an older Francophone generation; the Dutch, the Danish and even the Germans who have abdicated all linguistic ambition but continue with an unexpressed idea that their language might become a second Latin, half-dead, but full of pedagogical and cultural virtues; even the Spanish have admitted the need for a shared language. Only the French remain strangely inflexible: older industrialists do not use English at all, in the hope of protecting themselves behind a linguistic barrier in any business discussion; English is not obligatory in schools; whole generations reach adulthood hardly capable of emitting even odd mumbles in English and there is a widespread feeling that French is all one needs to go around the world, and certainly around Europe.

Europe will not exist until the day when, legitimately or effectively, English is truly its language and when Europeans live with two natural languages; their own, and English. India brought about such a unity by adapting Hindu. Will Europe be capable of it? Will the member states dare to ignore this reality? Is it more difficult to accept the *fait accompli* of English than it was to grant Algeria its independence? Will the French understand that the Francophone Utopia is incompatible with European realism? The omnipresence of English will come about in any case and, as with any inexorable phenomenon, the choice is between submission or anticipation. Submission means forever fighting a rearguard action and creating for oneself innumerable handicaps within the Community. Anticipation means an enforced process of adaptation: making the study of English obligatory from a primary level; only allowing the choice of another language once English has been mastered, reinforcing teaching resources; making knowledge of this language a prerequisite for further studies, similarly to mathematics and spelling. Europeans must accept the idea that mastery of two languages, their own and English, is essential.

This is no trivial subject. If Europe has no unifying language it has even less chance of finding a specific identity. Linguistic nationalists, especially in France – a strange bunch who span the range of the political spectrum – thrust forward the sledge hammer they use as a counter argument; that opting for English will mean favouring a Western as opposed to a European identity. The real extremists even go one step further; that in order to distinguish itself from the Anglo-Saxon world, the European Community must adopt French as its language. QED. They are making the same mistake as the Count of Chambord, who let the chance of a return to the throne in 1870 slip through his hands because of his attachment to a white flag. Regardless of Europe, English is now vital in a world that is ever more internationally oriented. If English were not to become its natural language, Europe would be nothing but a strange tower of Babel; with English, it holds an ace up its sleeve which might even help in closing the third circle, that of a hypothetical European society.

Is Audio-visual Europe Already Dead?

There can be no Europe without a cultural identity, and no cultural identity without television: the principle is incontrovertible. In the incessant quest for integrating forces, the fate of education may also be decided by television; a chance missed for ever, an ignored imperative. The game is being played at the moment and any delay will cost us dearly. The problem, however, is immensely difficult. What exactly does a European television system consist of? Viewers?

Broadcasters? Creators? Regulating authorities? The European dimension further complicates objectives which are rendered complex enough by the following three tangled phenomena: firstly, that the market is bursting in at both a national and an international level; secondly, that the essential but elusive requirements of quality are incompatible with classic economic roles; and lastly, that the socio-political echo-chamber conditions the slightest movement on the part of governments or other interested parties.

Larger sectors, on the whole, are lucky enough to experience two successive deregulations. The first while their frontiers are still closed, allows them to re-establish stability after the initial impact of new competition. The second, which will occur after the opening of frontiers, will therefore affect enterprises which have already learned the basic roles of competition. When 1992 looms into perspective for a bank, an insurance company or the public sector, the impact will be felt within a context of national firms who are used to fighting, at least amongst themselves. The situation is not the same at all as regards broadcasting where the two ruptures are separated only by a few years. We are seeing a widespread disintegration of the outdated sixties order, which was based on a small number of channels and programmes, as a real tornado leads to a new power structure. Faced with the unchecked eruption of the market, oligopolies and monopolies are appearing on the horizon. Vertical oligopolies, which control the whole production chain, and horizontal ones, which are securing shares in the market, seem to have leapt straight from a first-year economics course. Initially, the horizontal type was more prevalent. Berlusconi, for example, controlled all of the private Italian channels, challenged only by RAI, and TF1 carved out an exorbitant part of the French market for itself. Nowadays, we are witnessing more vertical oligopolies and a situation in which large clients control advertising, advertising controls broadcasting and broadcasting controls production. The sector is rife with abuses of power. It is therefore absolutely necessary to create institutions which will enforce the basic rules of free competition at a Community, and not just a national level. This is a fundamental requirement for a healthy economy. Then there are some specifically audio-visual demands, such as a refusal of any concentration of capital, which would be a threat to pluralism, and the need to preserve a minimum of quality in a space where culture is important. All of these tasks are linked to the closing off of the circle, determining the relative positions of the public and private sectors, the extent of regulatory powers, the limits of market quotas, the maximum degree of concentration of capital, creative aid and so on.

Where is Europe to be located in this eruption? Nowhere, because the first reflex of government is to deal with the matter within a national framework, imagining that it is more easily mastered in this way. This is doubly wrong. For one thing, the evolution of technology and of the market will upset national equilibrium in a few years as surely as the deregulatory acts of 1980 completely smashed the old order. For another, community regulation can only be useful to those countries such as Italy which have permitted the establishment of such dominant positions that they no longer have enough political power to rein them in. This absence is decisive since, without community action or networks, the European market simply provides an overflow mechanism for American products, and European cultural identity will be drowned in the US, just as Canadian cultural identity has been. The strategy of those in power speaks volumes as they act within the framework of a single, homogeneous Western market, ruled from American territory. From the point of view of Maxwell, Murdoch, Berlusconi, Bertelsmann, Hachette or Canal Plus, the West is the only possible horizon. Only at such a scale can they hope to afford existing products, which are becoming more and more dear to acquire – witness the increase in broadcasting laws – and new programmes which are becoming more and more costly to produce.

For Europe to throw in the towel would once more serve as proof that it is not a significant force in an area which has a fundamental impact on society. Whether we like it or not, the subject is of a different magnitude to that of the harmonization of taxes on tobacco etc., within the Community. A Community initiative in this area, unlike that of education, does not depend on a new European institution and so should not necessarily fall into the same inertia. Problems of a strictly economic nature can at least be dealt with in a Community context and a monopolies commission would find plenty to keep itself occupied. Why, then, is there so little action at the moment? This remains a mystery. Maybe the rate of change in this sector has ruled out any overall view of the situation. Maybe the victims of monopoly take-overs have still not acquired the maturity which makes of contention a weapon. Maybe Community regulatory bodies have an unconscious fear of touching such a potentially explosive material, affecting politics, culture and various irrational and unquenchable myths. All their present economic rules would anyway go nowhere near to resolving it. The problem of protecting pluralism will soon become a European rather than a national question, through a whittling down of the actors involved. Any attempt to support creativity will be at a Community level, taking into account the international nature of production. This will be equally true of the number of new programmes as of the financial support entailed. Even the granting of broadcasting rights will come from Europe once our countries are equipped with dishes to pick up satellite television.

Once again, Europe is a decade behind hand; the authorities hardly dare offload onto the Community problems that they are unable to resolve on the home front. As a result we are seeing the emergence of powerful groups, determined to divide up the ground before the desire for regulation begins to grow; American television culture is fast becoming the point of reference. Young Europeans, like their American counterparts, will have seen 15,000 murders before the age of 15. They will enjoy the same films and series as those born in Nebraska. The law of 'Prime Time' television will be supreme, leading to a universal cocktail of inferior games shows, advertising and serials, which apparently expresses the aspirations of the market. Without a rapid change of direction, a unified European culture is even less likely to come about through television as through education. In twenty years, a founder of a single European market may well say, in his turn: 'If I could do it all again, I would begin with television.' If so, he will have less excuse than Monnet and history will have been content to stumble along blindly.

Europe's cultural identity is no further advanced than its social identity. The Community of twelve member states simply does not exist seen from this third dimension; it is merely one of several territories within the West. The latter, on the other hand, does have an identity of its own whose influence over cultures and societies, which in principle have treated it with some reserve, is spreading. There is no third circle, at least not one that is bounded by the frontiers of the single European market. What conclusions can we draw then? A Europe with at least a nascent society could possibly have discovered a sense of strategic identity. Don't let us forget that strategy is not, in fact, constructed by strategists. It is determined, conditioned and anticipated by movements in societies. America's growing isolationism is not an automatic result of changes in the military situation. It actually has more to do with the changing balance of East and West, an indifference to Europe, the rise of ethnic minorities and the vagaries of public opinion. It is because Germany is profoundly changing that German strategic planning has naturally rediscovered its old place at the heart of Europe. The strategic slide, akin to a geological movement of Europe, results far more from evolutions in society than from a fully fledged idea hatching in the brain of some leader or other. This is why the best method of putting a brake on this drift would have been the emergence of a European society with enough dynamism to transcend the changes in any one country. Neither the single European market, nor cultural, educational or audio-visual pressures are causing the formation of this society. Given such conditions there is no natural brake to apply to this slide. Europe is certainly at the intersection of three circles: a strategic circle which is becoming more and more continental; another, exclusively economic, which is limited to the borders of the Community; and the last, cultural and social, which is being lost within a West whose frontiers are becoming more and more flexible. Pulled in such different directions, Europe is condemned to a continental drift which exerts by far the most powerful pull. Its long-term import is of a totally different nature to the kind of productivity benefits ushered in by the market. Unless, of course, the member states rediscover their positions as major actors, which would be to go against the mood of their societies – a 'happy ending' which raises certain vital questions.

Notes

1 *Les Lieux de mémoire*, ed. Pierre Nora, Gallimard, 1984.

12

Questions

Post-war Europe is in a state of decomposition, although fortunately, with the advent of peace, the age of great ruptures has disappeared. In our nuclear age, the eruptions and spasms of a terrible war have been ruled out as a means of producing a new world order. Nowadays, the phenomenon is a natural, slow, insidious and irresistible flow which is both intangible and invisible. The days no longer bring in their share of riotous decisions; governments no longer proclaim their contradictory aspirations; societies no longer display either spirit or enthusiasm. In short, nothing seems to be happening in terms of action, ideas or even ulterior motives. The map of Europe is static and passive and seems to have kept to the same design for centuries. A slight breeze in the East and a touch of Europeanism in the West are mere appendages. All the same, a new law of gravity is in the making and any attempt to thwart its effects seems doomed to failure. However ready we are to risk a landing, it would nevertheless be wise to employ some runway lights. This raises questions of time, fact and principle which must be confronted by every European power.

Questions of Time

Faced with the evolution of Europe, there is no time to waste time. Absurd, some will say: France was not unified in half a century; Germany, like Italy, had to wait several hundred years for its unity. Europe is moving at its own pace and, given the complexity of the process, is going as fast as it can. A *rapprochement* between adult countries, brought about by negotiation and agreements, cannot compare with the kind of bloody chopping up of the map that Europe has known only too well in the past. Time is always related to the scope of an ambition and its difficulties. It appeases, arranges, helps and circumvents. This peaceable vision has nourished the European dream for decades and each stage cleared has merited an entry in an indefinite calendar. This deep-seated optimism is not tied to reality. Two different Europes oppose each other; a continental and a Western Europe, and time is in the process of deciding between the two. Without a massive recovery effort, it will choose the first by its very nature.

Time becomes the fourth dimension of strategy in the nuclear age. It takes on the same role as space in classic military confrontations. The Soviet Union is playing on it today just as it has played on its territory in the past. Missiles have abolished distance but time has now taken its place as a key strategic variable. Time is not identical for East and West.

Firstly there is the difference in time between a cold and a warm society, to use Lévi-Strauss's definition of primitive societies. On one side, a relative immobility, a slow evolution of social structures, the wielding of power without electoral sanction, strictly internal regenerative processes within a profoundly historic context and the remains of ideological messianism. On the other, a pulsating world, in the clutch of a versatile public opinion, which is eager for immediate results and which imposes on an already perpetually tense political system its changing moods, frustrations and fads. Then there is totalitarian time versus democratic time: on the one side, an irrepressible, if occasionally erroneous, belief in its eternal nature; on the other, the feeling of a future dogged by elections and the consequent difficulty of imposing a long-term plan faced with the incessant demands of the moment. Reality may not correspond with this image and democracies tend to have a more stable future than dictatorships, but this is not how the countries view themselves, since they do not inhabit the same timescale. In addition, we have military time as against civil time: one society which devotes 15 per cent of its national product to defence, whose army constitutes the most efficient economic sector, whose military exert significant pressure on the political apparatus and whose long-term vision contains a military imprint with its easy certainties, its indifference to the moment and its strategic and technological overview; another society whose military budget attains at most 5 per cent of the GNP, whose defence during any normal period becomes a secondary preoccupation, whose army trails at its tail rather than at its head and which is essentially civil. Lastly, this is the time of bureaucracy against the time of the market. In the East, bureaucratic power without external regulation that is slow, ungainly, and an end in itself; in the West, the insistent pressure of the market, its pirouettes, its emphasis on the moment, its blindness in the long term and its refusal to make any sustained effort. The Eastern world is therefore alone in mastering this fourth dimension and has been making the most of it since the War. It has already reaped the benefits in Europe and will continue to do so. Soviet strategy towards the West has hardly changed since Koutouzov, since duration has taken over from space. The aim is to impede, frustrate and wear down one's adversary.

Time therefore lends its advantage to continental rather than to Western Europe, even given the latter's economic union. If nothing is done in the coming years to transform the single market into a real economic space, with a macro-economic policy, a proper budget, a welfare state and a currency, it will become the Balkans of the industrial world, a gigantic free zone open to anyone wishing to enter and set up shop. What a shot in the arm for the other economic powers, who will carve out empires, concessions and shares for themselves. Unification will become more difficult as time goes by, requiring authoritative measures and a willingness to protect the frontiers of the EC, weapons which will have become blunted during the years of the free zone.

For thirty years, time has taken its toll. Three snapshots are enough to sketch out the whole film. The most yellowing, from the end of the fifties, shows Europe huddling under the wing of the US; France is exhausted, and Germany full of shame. The following one, in black and white, is from the beginning of the seventies. America is more distant, France is stubbornly nationalistic, and Germany's *Ostpolitik* is a syrupy version of nineteenth-century *Drang nach Osten*. The third, colour photo, taken just today, depicts an American ally turned more and more towards the Atlantic, a Western Europe hoping that its identity will miraculously be born out of the single market, and a Germany reweaving the threads of *Mittel Europa*. The fourth or fifth snaps are left to our imaginations.

Each era believes that history is knocking at its door. And yet we must not let a fear of ridicule prevent us from believing what we see. Time has completed at least a half of its task, the transition to a continental Europe is well under way, accelerated by Germany, and the bell is tolling for the French strategic doctrine. The map of

Europe in the year 2000 is being shaped under our very eyes: a few years to accustom ourselves to the sight of it and we will be able to make out its contours, its features, even its colours. Either we choose to accept it, a justifiable decision which could nevertheless do with some elucidation, or we can lead a final battle on behalf of the European Community. In the latter case the very urgency of the situation would demand a measure of irrationality, of imagination and that ounce of poetry which makes for a truly great political strategy. Were this question of time to be resolved, it would raise some infernal questions of fact.

Questions of Fact

There are basically four such questions. Why is continental equilibrium perverse? Why is 1992 a good answer to a question which is not being asked? Why, in a world that is more and more open, must we dream of Europe as being a real force for action? Why should we, at great risk, extricate ourselves from the current ambiguity?

Raymond Aron's old refrain on the convergence of industrial systems was mistaken. On the contrary, it is strategic spaces which converge in the first place, with any *rapprochement* of economies coming as a simple consequence. But in any case, is the prospect of a continental Europe so worrying? It would mean peace throughout the continent and a much freer flow between East and West; it would be accompanied by a desire to end frictions and conflicts; it would increase economic exchanges to the mutual benefit of a producing West and a consuming East; it would allow cultural exchanges once more . . . in short, it could lead to a new mood of tranquillity. This irenic vision will be thrust in our direction more and more often by the Soviets and, backed up by a USSR which is itself more attractive, might even begin to seem plausible. In fact the continental system could take on a truly charming aspect, pushing aside the remnants of the Cold War. But there, too, the instant snap is deceptive, taking no account of the plans, feelings and actions that lie hidden in the background. There can be no lasting balance between partners whose strengths and very natures are different. The military superiority of the Soviet Union is enough to scupper this myth, even though it has reduced its astronomical number of bombs, aeroplanes, tanks, weapons and other hardware which belong to an ultimately inefficient system. The main obstacle, however, lies in the fact that the Soviet Union does not possess the same nature as other powers: its responsibilities, its ambitions and its dynamic do not obey the same rules. This has nothing to do with morals, with hackneyed catch-phrases about the good and evil empire. It is a simple sociological statement, like the distinction that a zoologist would make between one species and another. However, it we accept this distinction, we cannot rule out the possibility of the USSR, for whatever reason, deciding to go beyond this continental pseudo-equilibrium and to capitalize on its advantage. It is not probable, certainly, but who, in all conscience, can prove that this hypothesis is completely out of the question? Democracies function on a ratchet basis; once a revolution has come about, there is no going back. Once the Americans have pulled out of Europe, they would not find it easy to return. Accustomed to the charms of continental equilibrium, European countries would no longer have the energy to oppose such a development. This is not a question of military capacity, nor of mobilization time nor other such technical nonsense, but of a different spirit and code of behaviour. Rigid positions do not come easily to democracies, even as a last resort, and continental equilibrium cannot be attained while a dissymmetry between the sides means that any risk is unilateral. As long as we are aware of this!

1992 provides no solution to this problem, but the mythology surrounding the event gives the opposite impression. Europe is under construction and is ready to change from an Atlantic balance to the continental equilibrium which has always been its more natural state. This belief, whether explicit or implicit, is common to the public, the authorities and also to economic thinkers and actors, who have the added incentive of increased outlets in the East. This vulgate seems to have nothing but virtues. It allows for a kind of conciliation between the European Community and continental Europe, between the single market and the opening of the East, and between solidarity among the twelve member states, and *Mittel Europa*. This fantastic collective alibi reassures us that the achievement of 1992 will place us within the natural progress of history. The reality of the situation, of course, is far removed from such naiveties. The single market is a wonderful productivity tool which, as experience will show, is surrounded by some very murky areas. It is not about to give birth to a real economic entity, nor to a true society, nor to a proper strategic identity, and as such is an illusion. In attracting all of the attention, energy and dynamism of the member states, it is overlooking important underground phenomena which in time will come to maturity. The Soviets are not participating in this illusion which was dreamed up by Europeans alone, but they were quick to see the advantages of it. They are now as violently pro-European as they were bitterly hostile in the past.

One fundamental question: does this ambition towards a united Europe really make sense? It has some economic advantages, which must be utilized, but has Europe the slightest reason to wish to see itself, in addition, as a world actor? In a more and more independent world, where strong positions can rapidly turn fragile, one can be prosperous, peaceful and insignificant. 'If you want to stay happy, stay hidden' is by no means the most absurd strategic choice at the moment. Seen from such an angle, the continental system obviously has qualities which were not provided by the Atlantic system: a greater sense of well-being, the disappearance of unpleasant tensions and new relationships with sister countries which had been artificially separated by the Iron Curtain. Against such monochrome temptations, there is no conclusive reply, but simply the conviction that these countries will not emerge from the process unscathed. History now wreaks its vengeance externally, rather than internally. The French should know better than anyone to what extent international cowardice goes hand in hand with internal problems of democracy. One would have to be very daring to consider Petainism simply as a statistical accident. It is possible to imagine the oldest European countries turning into gigantic models of Switzerland or Austria by the year 2000? To think that prosperity could constitute the exclusive backbone of society? To believe that such a revolution will take place without tension or drama? To see the UK, Germany and France becoming a kind of enormous Finland, without even the latter's capacity to safeguard fundamentals, and given an imposed and unwanted situation which will be totally unlike that known by our former power? In this context, the reply is hardly original: a pessimism of the intelligence, an optimism of the will. It is, however, the only one.

But taking into account all these facts, is it necessary to break out of this state of ambiguity? Might it just be a case of out of the frying pan and into the fire? Nowadays the temptation is in the other direction. Everyone is careful not to advertise their fears or hidden motives, to the point of refusing to acknowledge them even in private. Germany is juggling multiple loyalties, apparently convinced that they are not contradictory, and that they do not carry within them the seed of potential conflict. France is pretending not to notice Germany's drift and is even closer to Germany than before, ready to go along with this movement to a certain extent. The United States keeps harping on about its commitment to Europe while in fact its only desire is to withdraw. To tear down this veil, as always, entails an element of risk, since one has to play blind. Does France really wish to hear Germany articulating its true priorities? Does the latter want to show its true colours as regards the East? Experts would counter this natural and iconoclastic desire to clear up any ambiguities by talking of the dangers involved in 'strategic straight talk'. They would even go so far as to cite Talleyrand, who reminds us, in words of one syllable, that a treaty is not an accord struck for principle but for ulterior motives, that untying Gordian knots is a reckless enterprise from which one has more to lose than to gain. Apart from the odd exception, of course, these experts are perfectly right. This is the case today, all appearances to the contrary. The evolution in the continent is in danger of arriving at, and even of passing, a point of no return, in which case the ambiguity option acts as a sort of pledge. It prevents any spectacular action by directing the course of events, it encourages those in charge to play above their hand and to leave any remaining work to be completed by time. Very shortly, one of the large European players will have to come out of hiding, lay down its cards and force the others into self-discovery. It will certainly not be Germany, since she is the principal beneficiary of this veil which is cast over her contradictory aspirations. It cannot be Britain, whose marginal position in Europe has left her unable to exert the weight of which she is capable. It is therefore up to France to call the other countries, and itself, to heel. Leaving aside matters of chance, an exercise such as this would resemble a military mock-up, lacking control mechanisms and a professional basis, unfolding unconsciously and naively and throwing up whole stacks of questions of principle.

A Few Questions of Principle

For Germany

To give Germans their due, any question of Europe inevitably boils down to a question of Germany. There are several areas to be cleared up on this subject, now that reunification, an aspiration written into the fundamental law of 1949, is at last complete. Firstly, would it not be true to say that the former Federal Republic has found in reunification and in its closer relationship with other countries of the East an answer to its own population decline? The population decline in the former Federal Republic was unprecedented in peace-time Europe. Even the fall that France suffered in the nineteenth century and which played a not inconsiderable role in its loss of leadership, was insignificant in comparison. For the Federal Republic to go from sixty to forty million inhabitants in a matter of thirty years was an unparalleled trauma, whose economic, sociological and cultural implications could have been enormous. Was not its opening towards its sister country the most natural and straightforward means of avoiding these consequences?

On an international plane, isn't Germany hoping for a position of equidistance between East and West? On the one hand, without trying to change the guiding principles of the Atlantic Alliance, it is preparing itself for a time when the latter will have disappeared; it likewise goes along with the construction of Europe, while doing nothing to force the pace. On the other hand, its policies towards the East are as dynamic as possible, growing from the most tenuous relations to arrive at a position of equidistance. This analysis has not been plucked from the sky; it is merely one way perhaps not the only one, of reading current German diplomatic activity. One sure way of winning this match would obviously be to enlist French support for the new *Ostpolitik*. This would guarantee greater efficiency, the certainty of being cleared of Western suspicions and the possible acceptance of the idea of compatibility between the continental dimension and the reality of the Community, a conviction which is already firmly held by the Germans.

What about Germany's strategic aspirations? Does it wish for complete nuclear disarmament in Central Europe? Is it pretending to believe in the American nuclear umbrella? Does it dream of a French guarantee? Public opinion inclines towards the first hypothesis, wanting a triple zero option which would put an end to the risk of Germany's being the only nuclear territory in Europe. Politicians, or at least the right wing, favour the second hypothesis. They wish to avoid any ill-considered gestures which would lead the United States to align legislation with fact and officially acknowledge the disassociation. As for the third possibility, it has difficulty mustering even the support of Helmut Schmidt, a few intellectuals, some zealous Francophiles and militant pro-Europeans.

How great is Germany's commitment to Europe? What does 1992 represent: almost an end in itself, or a means to an end? The former case would imply that Germany wants Europe just enough, but not too much. Just enough, in order to be faithful to its traditional European stance, because it has an interest in opening up the market, and because it wishes to keep the Community healthy. Not too much, so as not to overburden its freedom of action and its implicit desire for equidistance with the weight of its irresistible loyalties to the West. The second case would involve Germany in taking steps that until now she has hardly favoured: a single macro-economic policy, a common currency and a massive budgetary outlay. Germany would have to pay two very unfamiliar surpluses on behalf of the European Community: a little monetary laxity and a lot of budgetary expense.

These are the choices currently facing Germany, although she has more or less taken her decisions: reunification, for both spiritual and demographic reasons, diplomatic equidistance, a desire for nuclear disarmament, and a qualified enthusiasm for the Community. But she has never been asked to account for her position and only France can exact such a response. Not to trivial verbal cross-questioning but to concrete proposals which could be quite staggering for certain parties.[1]

For Great Britain

Britain cannot escape this truth game. As long as the Atlantic system survived all by itself, the answer was simple: the high seas against the continent. No pussy-footing around, no room for ambiguity or remorse. But now that the continental system is on the ascendant, Britain can no longer be content with her traditional position. She is in danger of ending up with as much control over strategy reality as Saint-Exupéry's Little Prince over the stars. Britain's Atlantic rhetoric no longer conceals the fact that the second French Maginot line cannot obscure Britain's own strategic uncertainties.

In strategic terms, the British are facing an alternative. On the one hand they could hang on to the status quo, i.e., the role as a back-up force for the States that they have held for thirty years. On the other, they could put their nuclear capability at the service of the Community. This would obviously have to be with the full agreement of the United States, since it has both a judicial and a technological say in the use of these weapons. The Americans could discover that this situation contains certain advantages. It would be one way of staying in the European nuclear game, half-way between a dissociation heavy with diplomatic consequences, and a direct commitment which goes against present public opinion. This choice leads on to many more for the British. By not facing up to this question, they are effectively deciding in favour of an illusory status quo, a decision which implies some serious consequences. It will not assure the long-term security of Great Britain, it eliminates Britain from European action and condemns it to a peripheral role alongside either the States, or the new continental situation. Without a strategic adjournment, pro-European gestures by the UK will remain very grudging.

This goes for the economy too. Britain is already lagging behind, with sterling still holding aloof from the European Monetary System and Britain's mechanism for budgetary restitution, although accepted by the other member states, remaining a stumbling block to Community solidarity. 1992 is heartily welcomed: as a windfall for the City? This is neither a myth nor a temporary step, and Britain has responded until now by inveighing against any monetary or budgetary reinforcement of Europe, fearing contamination from the continent, from social democracy and humanism. Only a complete transformation of its strategic vision and a different understanding of the world could create the context for active rather than passive participation in the Community. Another such upheaval would be necessary before the British could accept possible new paths for Europe: progress towards citizenship, which would oblige Britain to put an end to laws allowing residents of the Commonwealth preferential rights of naturalization in Britain, and therefore in Europe; some movement towards a judicial Europe, which would force the most isolationist of English institutions to align themselves with common articles and jurisprudence; any steps, however symbolic, which might lead to a political supra-nationality and against a Gaullism which seems to have emigrated from France, crossing the English Channel on one side, and the Rhine on the other.

For the Others

Italy, Holland and some others do not escape the truth game even though they themselves submit to history, rather than shaping it. Only the new members, Spain in particular, do not have to ask themselves questions of principle. With all the fervour of a recent convert, the Spain of Juan Carlos and de Gonzalez is European by vocation, Atlanticist on occasion, and internationalist according to circumstances. Each country sees Europe according to its own sense of geography; the same tropism that is pushing Germany towards a continental Europe, is pushing Spain towards Western Europe. Unfortunately, it is likely to carry less weight on the other side of the Pyrenees.

Italy and Holland both have a multiple perspective on the situation, not surprisingly since they are the most open trading countries. Their faithfulness to the Atlantic cause is shown by their acceptance of Pershing and Cruise: the socialist government of Italy put up no opposition and so gained for itself a certificate denoting good and faithful service to Washington, while Holland had to wrestle with the pacifist pressures of a public who, like the Germans, believed in 'better red than dead'. They have always both been strongly pro-European; partisans of the Community, they used 1992 as they will use the single currency, as an expanded field of action. They have a natural taste for détente. Under the role of Giulio Andreotti, who was as open to the East as Edgar Faure in France, Italy developed its relations with the USSR and the popular democracies at the most lifeless moments of the Brezhnev regime. Italy is therefore a *pasionaria* of Gorbachev. Add to that an Arab policy, good relations with the Third World, and a respectable commercial relationship with China, and Italy and Holland emerge as the 'good pals' of the European class. They nurture no sense of grievance and have no questions of principle to contend with except for one. As a result of not establishing their own priorities, these countries lay their own stone on the prevailing ambiguity. They enjoy using it to enhance their worthy sentiments and to provide them with a role as the wise and moralistic guarantors of this state of mind. They would undoubtedly be among the most reticent countries if faced with a wide-ranging attempt at clarification, out of fear of losing the small area of freedom which they exploit so effectively.

This type of position excites envy in Austria and even maybe in Sweden. The former has anyway put itself forward as a candidate for the European Community. Vienna is no longer the centre of the world, and the Waldheim affair has exhausted foreign interest so that this act went largely unnoticed as an everyday diplomatic occurrence. But this apparently insignificant event is in fact crucially symbolic, coming as it does from a secondary country. Since 1955 Austria has had three distinct characteristics: a democratic regime, a market economy tempered by a solid social democracy, and a neutrality guaranteed by a State treaty signed by all four of the victors of the war. No one has taken umbrage at the thought of a neutral member state within the Community. Are democracy and the market the only requirements for entry in this case? Is neutrality compatible with 1992? Does an equidistance between the two blocs sit well with the market? There was hardly any reaction from the United States and Germany, and even less from the Soviet Union which a few years ago would have hit the roof at what it would have considered to be a violation of the post-war order. Would Austria be no more than a possible thirteenth member of the Community? A foretaste of what several countries wish to be; a model of the future Germany? A neutral Austria in the Community as vanguard to a Germany which had rediscovered its place at the heart of *Mittel Europa*: what an ironic reversal of the *Anschluss*.

And France?

Watch out for a collective narcissism: the change towards a continental equilibrium does not give France the excuse to see itself once more as a great power. This continental lark in fact has a familiar ring to it: the French have gone along with it for centuries, with varying success, and to give in to this feeling of vertigo would be totally ridiculous. It would be a mistake for France to see itself as a major actor providing a counterweight to the West and ensuring equilibrium. This would be playing into the Soviet's hands by acting as a stable camouflage to an unbalanced system. France does nevertheless occupy a key position, the most important for forty years. It is one of history's little ironies that de Gaulle aped a historic role in the sixties while Mitterand actually has the means to carry it off. France has not moved on the world map, but the world has slid from West to East and France now holds ring-side seats.

In order to play its part it must fulfil three preconditions, strategic, economic and political, of which the last two can almost be taken as read.

The strategic prerequisite is problematic. It involves getting rid once and for all of the Maginot syndrome, in other words, accepting that France's defensive frontier is in fact the Elbe, not the Rhine. As far as conventional forces are concerned, this is already the case and the first steps have been taken regarding tactical nuclear weapons, but strategic nuclear weapons are lagging behind. This taboo lifted, the game would be wide open to a whole host of reckless initiatives. But a collective taboo does not give up the ghost any more easily than an individual complex. What a lot of hidden motives to eliminate. What a tide of unspoken suspicions to stem. What a set of precious porcelain to be broken. It means accepting that strategic nuclear arms can be used where, until now, theory has cleverly relied on the principle of non-use. It also means putting an end to the unconscious but sacrosanct link that has developed between national sanctuary, nuclear force and the divine responsibility of the President of the Republic. And lastly, it means a commitment to Franco-German solidarity to the point of accepting the ultimate sacrifice. Such a choice does not come easily and no political act could be more decisive. It has required several years to mature, but the moment has now come: it is now, in the next few years, or never.

Compared with this question of principle, the rest seem ludicrous. Political supranationality was ratified long ago by the public and more recently by politicians, with the exception of the communists and certain paleo-Gaullists. The constraints of a truly united economic Europe are a small price to pay for the market next to the problems of a single currency and a communal welfare state. But since 1980, the French have brought about such a revolution in their economic behaviour that these efforts appear trivial by comparison. The desire to extend the concept of Europe to embrace law, education and television presents no problem for France, which is never happier than when inventing new constructs. Its technological imagination would be given free rein and it would have immense satisfaction of helping along a worthy cause.

Once its unconscious motivations were revealed, France could assume this responsibility. With a will to survive, a taste for action and a gambling sense, what has it to lose? In a state of weightlessness, released from all terms and conditions, it could take the initiative.

Notes

1 See chapter 13.

13

A Decalogue

Let us yield, for a brief moment, to an old principle from 1968 and let our imagination take over. Dreams, excesses and exaggerations have cathartic value. Delivered fleetingly from our constraints and weights we are free to trace the omega point of a policy, a horizon which is often inexpressible, never attained and always desired. Reality will ultimately take care of the business of depicting it in its true proportions. Professionals can just shut their eyes. Diplomats can look away. Sceptics can distance themselves. Cynics can snigger. Realists can withdraw. And the power of the imagination can put the imagination in power, without criticism or self-criticism.

In this ethereal world, France would play its part. It would back a communal Europe over a continental Europe and would squeeze the last drop out of the cards it holds with the conviction that it is better to try and fail than not to try at all. Its initiatives, like the Tablets of the Law, would be ten in number. This decalogue would be based on a philosophy of relations with the East: it would introduce a different nuclear concept and in the same spirit would move to a situation of total solidarity with Germany, while retaining fall-back possibilities in the event of the latter shying away. It would attempt to put an end to the totalitarianism exercised by the economy over the European idea, opening new avenues for improvement and reaping internal benefits. This is a wonderful programme in ten dream-steps which assuages the conscience rather than weighing on reality. Decalogue, proclaim your ten truths.

1 Thou Shalt Keep Thy Head

Hans Dietrich Genscher, the German Foreign Minister, was right when he suggested that we take Gorbachev at his word. But words are merely words: they cannot change miraculously into concrete concessions, especially given the difficulty democracies have in turning the clock back. And so emerges a complex game with the following three ground rules. Firstly, do not take any irreversible steps; support anything which is pushing for change in the East, but do not get carried away. Secondly, ensure that the Germans do not play this game alone, since they are in danger of going too far. Thirdly, do not get pulled into camaraderie with Germany beyond a reasonable limit. Behind these simple ideas a real three-handed trick can be made out.

On a military level, in the first place: it is necessary to refuse to accept anything which would lead to total nuclear disarmament in Central Europe; the French must not withdraw their tactical nuclear arms, even if German territory is their field of action. Any logic of retreat would restore the principle of all or nothing which, as we have seen, is synonymous with defence of the national sanctuary at the expense of European territory. However, Gorbachev-style pacifism stretches equally to embrace conventional weapons: has he not made the rather too transparent proposition of a reduction in this area, even an asymmetrical reduction on the condition that it would be discussed without American participation? The shrewdness of this ploy is obvious: the USSR allows in principle a more significant reduction on its side, considering the balance of strengths, but in exchange it wants this peace-offering to be conducted in Europe, under the roof of this 'communal home' which it holds so dear. The Germans are not far off making a positive response to this apparently tempting proposition. There is only one possible conclusion on this point: conventional disarmament can only be strongly asymmetrical and can only be discussed within the framework of the forces in situ, Americans included. In the absence of such an attitude, Europeans would only fuel the isolationist drift of the US and would encourage its withdrawal from Europe, an eventuality which is making fast enough progress on its own. Such, at least, is the French position; this assurance is hardly surprising coming from someone who, in 1983, delivered the *Bundestag* speech. In this diplomatic concubinage with the Germans, France simply has to lose some of its frankness; any concessions should be informal rather than formal.

Vis-à-vis the countries of the East, in the second place: *perestroika* must not lead to a rehabilitation of the governments in the popular democracies at the expense of their civil societies, a risk which is very real. The member states tend to hold proper dialogue only between themselves, and the West will be tempted to believe that the opening up of real relations with the communists will do more to encourage the latter to make useful concessions than will an exaggerated support for the people, which could end up having the opposite effect. This is the trap which is sprung for us. Enthusiasm for Solidarity was weaker than it might have been in the West out of hope that if the Polish authorities were more reasonable, they would be able to raise the lid of the social cauldron without running such an enormous risk. Governments are always suspicious of movements in society, even those in opposing societies. The rule on the contrary should be simple: the better the relationship between governments, the more cohesion there should be between societies.

Finally, in the economic domain. Capitalist democracies can rarely resist the temptation of new outlets, a factor which goes to explain the excessive enthusiasm exhibited in the West towards *perestroika* and towards the establishment of some kind of market substitute in the East. Credits and merchandise are going to fall like rain and the Germans are already way ahead, led by the Deutsche Bank which is eager to recycle any excess deposits in the West in the form of loans to the East. And yet some form of discrimination ought to operate. On the one hand, Europe must increase its distribution and credits related to consumer goods. This would work to the advantage of the Eastern societies while also relying on the dynamic of consumerism to exert pressure in favour of democracy. On the other hand, it should be more circumspect than ever as regards exports with a possible military use. In this way a subtle balance would be achieved between support for *perestroika* and a mistrust of the military order. In reality, however, there is a great danger of the protective dyke being carried away by the flood of eager trade from Europe.

Such a policy towards the East has nothing to do with omega points or over-excessive flights of the imagination; it simply makes good sense diplomatically. In fact, relations with the Soviet Union, even when simulating a state of weightlessness, do not call for any spectacular initiative. Through a natural incline, such gestures anyway get translated into disproportionate unilateral concessions. Unlike a host of other subjects, the dream concerning the East, today more than ever, must be to manage to 'keep thy head'.

2   Thou Shalt Operate the Lever

In freeing itself from the syndrome of the second Maginot line France would have to put its defence doctrine spectacularly under public scrutiny. As long as evolutions in French strategic thinking are progressive, modest and secretive, they will not strengthen its European hand. Strategy is a confrontation between societies far more than between states, especially in a nuclear world which rules out the possibility of conflict. It is therefore necessary to publicize one's colours loud and clear, above all in the case of jettisoning the doctrine of national sanctuary, which has always provided the French with an illusory but pleasant sense of comfort. The striking force now only has any power if it acts as a lever to begin an earth tremor from which the States would have to extricate itself if it did not want to be consigned to a position of regional power. By an unexpected paradox, it is the country which for so long was the least assiduous of the Atlantic class which now has the means of forcing Atlantic solidarity. This statement generates four consequences: an affirmation that the French defensive frontier is on the Elbe; a recognition of the importance of tactical nuclear weapons; the trumpeting of an implacably European and Atlantic spirit; and the proclamation of the new doctrine.

The lever cannot be used solely for France's benefit. This would be tantamount to admitting that the US would be obliged to defend France, even unwillingly while being indifferent to the fate of Germany or Holland. How absurd! If there is a forced nuclear solidarity, it must be to the benefit of the whole of Western Europe. The French defence line is therefore fixed by the simple application of the equation Hamburg = Strasbourg. This commitment goes well beyond the already existing initiatives on a common defence area. It puts strategic, tactical and conventional forces into play under the same terms as the current protection of national territory beginning at the Rhine.

From this perspective, tactical nuclear weapons regain all their importance. They provide the head of state, that nuclear demiurge, with a flexible instrument which he or she can use for the good of Germany, and therefore avoid the all or nothing aspect of nuclear destruction and the need for a global earthquake. However, this doctrine brings into the picture a double solidarity, both European and Atlantic. It is an absolute negation of the continental drift, since the latter is based on the split between the Atlantic defence system and the evolution of Europe. Under the lever principle, the Hamburg = Strasbourg equation is expanded into Western Europe = Atlantic Europe. Faced with the temptations of a continental equilibrium, France's lever is a major asset. At the moment the latter is carefully tucked away in the background; it undoubtedly underlies the minds of strategists and decision-makers, but its provocative nature disposes them to silence. The United States would detest being openly manipulated, the Soviet Union would suspect a resurgence of bellicose tendencies, and Germany would feel like a pawn pushed around at the whim of its partners. The publicizing of a new ground rule under these conditions would be very disturbing, but while such an action would have been ill-timed during a period of stability, it assumes a real importance at a time when the pitch is shifting.

An exceptional moment calls for an exceptional clap of thunder; absolute urgency, for absolute necessity. One does not change fate with half-measures.

3 Thou Shalt Play Banco on Germany

If the lever is the strategic reaction, the Franco–German banco must be the institutional response. There too, faced with the shifting of Germany to the centre of *Mittel Europa*, there can be no half-measures. Empiricism, human friendship, daily relations and routine agreement have done all that they could. The only remaining choice is institutional: the proposition of a true union with Germany, even a fusion. This idea appears to be ridiculous given the present European understanding which, despite its Community flavour, still bears the imprint of the Europe of Nations. The last initiative of this kind, not a good omen, was the still-born project of a Franco–British union proposed by Churchill in June 1940 in a last-ditch attempt to dissuade the French from signing the Armistice.

This crazy hypothesis would possess three considerable advantages. If it was followed through, German policy towards Central Europe would be different. Could there be any more effective brake on the continental drift, or at least a stronger assurance that it would not go beyond certain limits? Germany would be obliged to discard all ambiguity and prioritize its aspirations. It would act as a truth drug for both sides, clarifying France's feelings towards Europe, and the authenticity of the supposed priority of Germany's attachments to the

West. The European Community would thereby win a marvellous boost. An institutional mechanism would have been created, moving gradually to encompass all the other countries. The integrationist taboo would be broken in the only possible way: by example.

This institutional *rapprochement* would follow more or less set patterns tracing the progressive passage from dream to reality. The dream version first. This would involve a confederal approach, whereby the institutions issuing from the two states would have control over the domains traditional to this type of construction: defence, diplomacy, currency and rules of citizenship. The half-way house version would appoint a communal authority to take charge of the various decisions between now and the year 2000, preferring harmonization to fusion for these ten years and constitutionally committed to succeeding, come what may. In the realistic version, a monthly Council of Ministers, along the lines of that agreed in 1963, would accompany a Franco–German defence community and a unified diplomacy. The hyper-realistic version would see a judicial commitment on the part of the two foreign ministers to act unanimously, the decision of two ministers such as Depont–Dupond to function together, and the creation of unique diplomatic representation in other countries. The hyper-hyperrealist version would contain the activation of a Franco–German Defence Council and the creation of a similar diplomatic organization. Let us break off there since the following version bears a strange resemblance to the status quo.

The seriousness of such an initiative, even in its most ambitious formulation, depends on the prognosis on the pace of the continental drift. It is a mere trifle to those who view the drift in terms of a twenty-year process. It is a real idea for those who hold to a ten-year span. It is a matter of urgency as soon as the point of no return is seen as being crossed in three to five years' time. At the risk of repeating ourselves, we subscribe to the latter view.

4   Thou Shalt Enforce Security

Germany can always say no to the institutional banco in which case the burden of proof would be exposed. However, its reservations could still be graded into a hierarchy of refusals. The first level, of least commitment, would be for Germany to reaffirm its attachment to the West, its links with the Community and its relationships with France, while at the same time emphasizing that the restructuring process entailed by reunification would prevent it from anticipating its institutional future. None of its partners, least of all France, could hold this against Germany.

Such a qualified response should not turn France back to Aventin and the delights of the Maginot syndrome, since it could still exhort an 'enforced' security. Accepting that it would be impossible for Germany to sanctify an institutional alliance, France could still be flexible on the defence front by taking certain remaining initiatives, such as a determination as regards its defence frontiers. (The lever theory would still be valid since it is independent of the question of Franco–German institutional unity.) France could also try to make some real breakthroughs in military cooperation with Germany, such as unit integration, standardization of equipment, combined budgetary responsibility – with France mainly taking care of the nuclear side, Germany the conventional side – creation of a communal state organization, however vague its powers, and even the more weighty establishment of a Franco–German defence community.

On this level, Germany could not argue from a historical or institutional point of view. It has always been very clear in its commitment to Western security and has been a bulwark of communal defence organizations. In the truth game, the ploy of enforced security would lift the veil from any remaining ambiguities. To refuse this option would put Germany squarely on the side of complete disarmament, equidistance and even neutrality. The most commonly heard argument in Germany – that, since the Americans are not ready for nuclear death in order to defend Hamburg, the French would be even less so – would no longer be admissible. Even if such a suspicion were legitimate, why should this lead Germany to refuse the French umbrella? Better a hypothetical protection than no protection at all. But this principle brings forth a counter-argument from the other side of the Rhine: why should Germany have its hands tied by a nuclear guarantee it does not believe in? If France were to take upon itself the burden of proof, and Germany were to respond by reaffirming its desire for freedom of action, then the multi-dimensional nature of German strategy, its difference from that of other Western countries, would be exposed. In such a case, the advent of continental Europe would be inevitable and it would only remain to accept the consequences.

Handled in this manner, the truth serum could smell of Germano-phobia. But let us be clear: for France to apply this test with such spectacular initiatives, it would first have had to take this serum itself, in order to clear up its own ambiguities. As long as France cultivates a shadowy strategy – a pinch of Atlanticism, a dash of Europeanism, a strong dose of Gaullism – it has no right to interrogate others. Indeed its own uncertainties only fuel theirs. But once it has publicly cleared up its own strategic ground, it will have not only a right but a duty to require the same honesty from others, in particular Germany.

5   Thou Shalt Prepare a Retreat

If Germany shies away from enforced security, proving that continental Europe has established itself at the expense of Western Europe, France will have to adapt its strategy. The greatest risk will be that, having extricated itself with difficulty from its Maginot line, the French will try to fall back on it, persuading themselves that they are safe in their solitary protection. This would be the worst possible outcome, heralding an inevitable slide from a continental balance into the complete Finlandization of Europe. With France huddled up behind its striking force while the USSR kindly allows it to join the summit dialogues between continental nuclear powers, the other countries will be completely in the shadow of the East. They will be effectively neutralized without any chance to protest and the USSR will have definitively attained its historic objective.

Faced with such a situation France would have to follow as open a strategy as possible if it wanted to limit the damage. The best solution would obviously be some sort of *rapprochement* with Great Britain, although such a possibility seems extremely unlikely. If the US, through its isolationist policy, allowed this evolution in Europe to come to fruition, the UK would feel even more cut off from the continent than it does at present. It would be content to take part in an economic Europe, which would be independent of the above series of events, since 1992 is perfectly compatible with the continental drift of Europe, but it would never risk its own security. It would thus become the fifty-first US state on a strategic level and the defence frontier of the United States would be seen even more clearly than today to extend beyond the coast of Dover.

France's only alternative would be a retreat southwards, i.e., the development of links with Italy, Spain and even Portugal. These would have to be so strong that between them they would make up a homogeneous strategic area. Given the inevitable shock-waves caused by continental Europe triumphing over Western Europe, our partners in the south would undoubtedly be favourably disposed towards this move. However, this type of strategy cannot be constructed in a time of crisis, of shared disappointments. Mediterranean solidarity has to be built up when other possibilities still remain. At the moment, our Mediterranean partners feel excluded from the Franco–German duo and relegated to the second division. To gain even minimal strategic liberty in the future, these countries will have to be assiduously cultivated. Greater osmosis between the member states is, anyway, precisely what their civil societies favour. Southern societies have never been closer than in the current perspective of 1992. They are taking the same short-cut from a pre-industrial to a post-industrial age; they share a mobility and a flexibility which is helping them to get in step with the demands of contemporary economics, and they are more and more aware of their cultural proximity. The Community's economic motor is in the process of slipping southwards as a Mediterranean identity surfaces after centuries of lethargy. Once more, strategy is a by-product of movements in society. The emergence of a southern society makes strategic identity possible. It is then up to the member states themselves to set this to music, and up to whoever possesses nuclear arms to be the band leader.

6 Thou Shalt Reject the Totalitarianism of 1992

Whilst a communal Europe is not, in itself, an answer to the continental drift, there can certainly be no response without its backing. These words, once iconoclastic, are now greeted in France by a touching unanimity. But this feeling is not enough. It even produces some perverse effects, such as the belief that an economic Europe is an end in itself and that 1992 constitutes its realization. Under such a vulgate, Europeans will be able to drop everything on 1 January 1993 in order to congratulate themselves: Europe will be made. It is time to put an end to this pleasant auto-suggestive procedure. The French have not helped by being the most enthusiastic and the most credulous as regards 1992. To put an end to the 'totalitarianism' of 1992 is not merely a case of addressing the authorities: it would assume a less naive attitude on the part of the public, some real analysis from the media, and a capacity for initiative from those who have not yet been mobilized by 1992. The paradoxical nature of the situation consists in the fact that economic agents are the only ones to be directly concerned with the single market and yet, for once, all other parties involved in this development in society are happy to go along with it. We can only hope that the bottles containing the following two messages will brave the seas to arrive at their destinations. The first is a reminder to the economic world that an economic Europe is not going to exist on the 1 January 1993: the advantages of a united market will not compensate for the lack of certain trifling attributes such as a common currency, a common budget, an emerging Community welfare state, clear working rules and exterior protection mechanisms. The second message is addressed to everyone else, repeated *ad nauseam* to drive home the point that a united Europe presupposes a united citizenship, education and society and, last but not least, the basis of strategic and political identity. It is necessary to rid our minds of an absolute philosophy which for once has charmed us all; the illusory dictatorship of 1992.

7 Thou Shalt Open New Avenues

For the past thirty years, Europeans have been accustomed to thinking of economic union as being the prerequisite for institutional union. A political monster was born which surfaced regularly in the form of shrewd agreements, sympathetic motions and pious wishes. The Commission's cellars must be full of these decisive contributions. And yet refusing the myth of 1992 does not mean mounting that old war-horse again – that would be worse than useless. What it really involves is an acceptance of the work being achieved behind the scenes of the single market. The economy will not bring forth a State, but it might give birth to a European society. Instead of taking the advent of such a society for granted, another pair of forceps must be added to that of the economy which is, after all, no miracle worker. Alongside the European Economic Community, there are places set for other communities: of citizenship, education and audio-vision.[1] Since we have assigned France a prophetic function in this dream, it is her task to set forth any ambitions, projects and matters of urgency.

Communal Europe will be no substitute for continental Europe if it only advances on one front. Time is running out and it must open up new avenues, new sectors and new subjects. If, just to temper the dream-like delirium, it was necessary to set some priorities,[2] a

European Educational Community would have to come first, since it would require plenty of time to settle questions of syllabus. The working-out of a communal pedagogical matrix, its installation, the training of teachers and the slow impregnation of tens of millions of pupils – what an incredibly long haul. Add to that certain institutional *rapprochements* and it becomes obvious that this other EEC – the European Educational Community – would be facing an immense task. After that would come a Common Audio-visual Policy; there, too, time would be the main argument, although in this case the urgency of immediately applicable regulations would need to be addressed rather than the demands of a long process. Positions are currently being defined, situations acquired and habits setting in. If an audio-visual Europe is going to exist, it is now or never. The pressure is obviously not the same for citizenship. Nothing irreversible is threatening and Europeans are well used to the current state of things. A civil society without citizens can hardly exist, of course, but we must not start dreaming in the middle of our dream. Nothing can happen overnight and, for the moment, civil law, commercial law and maybe even political law must just be kept on hold. By numbering future objectives, i.e., the gaps in Europe at the moment, one can see what a store of optimism the real pro-Europeans have to keep.

8 Thou Shalt Cry Hurrah for the Commission

Every new perspective, every opened avenue, obviously poses a question about the administration which would be responsible. Since the powers of the Commission are generally economic, although it does make occasional sorties into other fields, it is not, strictly speaking, permitted to take these extra responsibilities on board. At the same time, and through a cynical self-protecting reflex, many governments can be tempted not to dwell on the merits of this organization, which from time to time seems to be rather intrusive. For a long time, Brussels technocrats have irritated ministers and high-ranking civil servants; the former through fear of seeing an embryonic European Government develop, and the latter because they see some of their responsibilities slipping into the hands of stateless colleagues, who are not only better paid but, being of a different nationality, do not have to go along with respective clan rites. There is therefore a great temptation on the part of the member states to confine the Commission to its present activities, so that it can carry

them out properly – in other words, to fob it off. This is absurd,
unproductive and contrary to the idea that, in a dream-world at least,
the member states would like to reinforce the communal nature of
Europe.

The Commission is a gigantic bureaucracy; true. It is totally
unaccountable; true. It represents an unmanageable Tower of Babel;
true. It embraces a technocratic vision; true. What a lot of justifiable
grievances. On the other hand, the Commission embodies European
legitimacy, whether we like it or not. Like any administration, it needs
a political spur from time to time and someone to hold the reins. But
under the guidance of high-calibre officials and activated by the kind
of shake-up that Jacques Delors inflicts on bureaucracies, it has
rediscovered its confidence and efficiency. The single market has
brought it back to life and, inasmuch as there exists a productivity
index for administrative bureaucracies, the Commission would seem
to be one of the best, whatever prejudices the French technocratic
citadel may have.

It is the only administration capable of taking on these new
responsibilities, but also – and more importantly – the only
imaginable embryo for a European government. Any other idea
regarding the creation of a supranational seat of political power
hinges around the idea of a hermaphrodite body, half administrative
and half political. Most governments fear that such an organization
would not be able to turn its ambiguity into an advantage. The rest is
a matter of detail, subsidiary preoccupations and gut reactions. With
the Commission, a true European Community is still in limbo;
without it, there is no hope.

9 Thou Shalt Condemn any Delay

The ground rules of our daydream designated France as the
promoter of communal Europe. However, it would be advisable for
France to rid itself of certain very familiar arthritic features.

In the first place, its linguistic imperialism: French-speaking
communities are a reality in Africa, a rarity in America and non-
existent in Europe. French is a European language but is no longer
the language of Europe, and to contest this is about as effective as
emptying the sea with a thimble. From this point of view, the daily
struggle to claim the same attributes for French as are held by English
is counterproductive. It amuses and irritates our partners and

demonstrates imperialist tendencies which go against the role of the 'saint of Europe' in which France has been cast for a brief interlude.

Secondly, France's taste for political gadgetry: it is exclusively in France that one hears about the election of a President of Europe by universal suffrage, as if French statespersons were the only ones to need redeployment. Given the kind of movements which are changing the face of the map of Europe, there is some sense in institutional initiatives regarding Germany, at least in theory. But they make no sense on a community level. Cartesianism has to go. A system of government is not put in place like a formal garden. It is a process of trial and error, of which only the first stone, the Commission is laid.

Thirdly, a mistaken impression that France is a world power: in order to play its part as a great European power, especially within a context of continental imbalance, France needs all its energy, particularly in the area of defence. It does not possess the means to ape the United States with its diversified and up-to-date nuclear arsenal, its powerful conventional army and credible forces for overseas intervention. France will have to give up its international policing activities, which means that, in the long term, the very fate of its overseas territories is under question. Not because they consume a large amount of the military budget, but because these possessions have to be defended and their defence requires a type of military protection which is very costly, while not conferring the slightest benefit in terms of the European arena. The DOM-TOMs (French overseas departments and territories) give other powers the excuse to reason as if French lines of defence were on a world-wide scale.

Lastly, the exorbitant pressure exerted by agriculture: the establishment of an embryonic Community welfare state, which is a condition of economic union, is incompatible with the continuation of present agricultural policies. It is financially impossible and politically untenable. The French are no longer the only champions of the Common Agricultural Policy as they were in 1970, at a time when their partners practically bought their agreement for other Community-based advances which were incompatible with Gaullist ideology. Everyone nowadays derives enormous benefits from this budgetary sleight of hand, in particular German farmers, which makes it difficult for Germany to pipe up with its refrain about being an eternal creditor. Likewise, the idea of agriculture as a backward and corporalist sector which would have to be subdued before economic harmonization was possible is now obsolete. However the Community cannot carry on devoting 90 per cent of millions from the member states, France in particular, if increased social spending is necessary to offset the effects of 1992. There will be no single market without a social policy, no social policy without a community redistribution policy, and no redistribution policy without a reduction in agricultural spending. This fatalistic logic could be offset by a fiscal windfall but an increase in taxation is not to current taste, nor is it consistent with the single market. Where once we were faced with a choice between bread and guns, it has now become butter or everything else. Agricultural de-escalation is only possible at a Community level if France has already gone some way along the path.

The arthritic features that the French ought to get rid of tend to have historical roots in France's ancestral past. In other words, if it wants to be leader of the Community, France will have to lose some of its identity. Nothing could be more normal in fact: one can only be a good leader of that which one resembles. In the present world, it is not grandeur but banality which constitutes a condition of leadership.

10   Finally, Thou Shalt Set Things Moving

Nuclear lever, Franco-German institutional banco, European Educational Community, dissolution of global illusion, decline of the Francophone myth, agricultural sacrifices – could the dream turn into a nightmare? Wouldn't this be an excessive price to pay for an outside bet on slowing down the drift of the continent? Could there be any political equation in France that would simultaneously throw down so many cherished temple columns? Add the inevitable opposition to each subject and you are left with a vision of the Apocalypse. As well as a refusal from the traditional European front, blending extreme left and right wing, a challenge would be mounted by traditional Gaullists, hostile to the lever theory, nationalists on all sides, whether overt or not, ready to love Germany but not to marry her, teachers reluctant to see the education system overturned under cover of Europe, the agricultural world, not particularly anxious to have to finance the emergence of a Community welfare state. The list would be almost infinite, including just about all of the French, who are schizophrenic at heart, torn between a real belief in Europe and a residual nationalism. But a political equation is not a mathematical process; it harkens back to the old Baudelairean dream of a 'movement which shifts the lines'. It is still necessary of course to find an authentic movement.

The concept of a truly united Europe, especially in its most ambitious manifestation, is unique in proposing a change to our traditional ways of thinking and acting. Given the scale, this formidable instrument underlines the only real split between the side of order and that of movement. These two survive the comings and goings of political life, but their boundaries and contours move according to fundamental questions. Neither the rules of the economic game, nor the level of redistribution, nor relations between social groups constitute real splits nowadays. The concept of Europe, paradoxically, provokes such a split. Not because of the unanimist trivia which accompany the single market and the myth of 1992, but because of the wish to see communal Europe triumph over the path of least resistance which is leading to continental Europe. Nothing can get in the way of this ambition; neither military taboos, institutional prejudices, illusions of grandeur, nor the most isolationist corporatism.

Politics is once again holding its head up high: it is interpreting a vision of the world, realizing an idea and pulling out all the stops to do so. Because it is rediscovering its true virtues, it alone has the capacity to explode the habits of politicians. It alone can triumph over itself. Such an explosion will totally reconstitute the game. Who can light this fuse? Historical legitimacy points to the President of the Republic. Who can be the main motive forces? The most flexible and least inhibited of the statespersons who exist within that immense sector of politics which is the middle classes. Who can be its beneficiaries? The party for movement, on the left, the party for movement, on the right. At the moment, their energies are more taken up with survival, faced with their own camps' obsession with order, than with joining forces. What is the reason for such a revolution? Common-sense? That has never governed the world. Internal demands? One puts up with sectorial splits. The will of certain people? Such things do not start moving all by themselves. In fact, there are only three motivations. The first: urgency; the second: urgency; the third: urgency.

The complexity of our world gives us an excuse for faint-heartedness. Faced with a confusion of aims, with the force of habit and with the innate conservatism of structural organizations, public matters progress a millimetre at a time. But a complex, self-regulating society can never simply dispose of history, of its balances of power and its silent insinuating evolutions.

Tact in the daily running of affairs dissolves into passivity when the continent begins to drift. Hardly perceptible, because of its slow progression, this development can only be checked by brutal means. In terms of principle, that means trying one's hardest to promote communal Europe at the expense of continental Europe; in terms of action, it means giving power to the imagination while allowing oneself to make gentle fun of this power; in terms of ethics, it means doing everything possible to avoid an irreversible situation. Nothing is lost by failing; everything is lost by giving up. Given this fact, the decalogue is not a fantasy, nor even a programme, but a simple necessity. To let it slip away through negligence, sluggishness or duplicity will not leave us with a clear conscience. Each person has to choose. To yield without counter-attack, to counter-attack so as not to yield. In the casino of the future, the chips are almost down. All that remains, aesthetically or lucidly, is to back the least probable option, the about-turn. Europe, this strange continent, is effectively retracing its steps and, pivoting on itself, is once again picking up Ariadne's thread; will the course of history never falter?

Notes

1 See preceding chapters.
2 See preceding chapters.

Index

1992 (*cont.*):
　financial revolution, and　130–3
　fiscal earthquake　154–7
　France, and　103
　free circulation of capital　132, 133
　French socialists, and　104
　German advantages　152–3
　Germany, and　103, 137
　Great Britain, and　103
　instrument of modernization, as　104
　Italy, attitude of　138
　Keynesianism, and　127
　lack of institutions, and　195–6
　liberal economy, and　121
　'liberal Marxists', and　108
　liberalization, effect of　116–17
　macro-economic fairy tale　124–7
　magic formula for growth, as　105
　military approach, and　105–6
　monetary backbone　133–6
　myth of　102–6
　nationalism, and　142–3
　need to reject totalitarianism of　245–6
　non-European banks, and　141
　non-Europeans, and　140
　perspectives on　6–11; action checklist
　　for single market　7–8; age of
　　development　8–10; age of
　　enterprise　6–7; age of reason　7–8;
　　age of transformation　10–11;
　　consciousness revolution　10;
　　enterprise and community　6;
　　evolution and harmony　8–9; freedom
　　and order　7; interactive checklist for
　　diverse market　9–10; transaction
　　checklist for the big time　6–7;
　　transcendent checklist for unified
　　Europe　11
　political abdication, and　111–15
　possible readjustments　151
　potential beneficiaries　136
　protectionist policies, and　125–6
　public opinion, and　143
　public sectors, and　153–4
　reliance on economy, and　107
　risks　115–19
　shortcomings in rules of play　180–5
　Société Générale de Belgique
　　takeover　142–4
　Spain, and　102–3, 138
　state intervention, and　118
　tensions in store　118–19
　value of　101
　will of nation states, and　108
nuclear blackmail　59–61
　idea doomed to failure　59–61
　mutual annihiliation, and　60

　nature of weapons　59–60
　strong by weak, of　59–61

opinion polls　203
Ostpolitik　20, 37, 44–6

Pacificism　20–1, 35–6
perestroika, effect　238–9
Pershing, deployment of　20–1
political organizations　185–8
　'embryonic European government'　187
　network system　186
political parties, organization of　197–8
politics, importance of　251
principle, questions of　230–6
production, effect of 1992 on　149
professions, effect of 1992 on　148–9
public opinion　203–4
　society, and　204

Radio Free Europe　53
reciprocity, principle of　183–4
religious organizations　197

savings, taxes on　156, 158–9
Schmidt plan　77
Second Maginot Line　58–78
Second World War　25
single market
　European industry, and　181
　global visions, and　181–5
　rest of the world, and　181
Société Générale de Belgique
　bureaucratic coup d'etat, possibility
　　of　92–3
　takeover　142–4
Soviet Union
　aims　26
　American medium-range nuclear
　　weapons, and　82–3
　concept of nuclear deterrence　81
　defensive weapons　70
　'détente, entente and cooperation',
　　and　95–6
　different nature from other powers
　　228
　disarmament, and　88
　economic growth, dream of　88–9
　'enlightened despotism'　89–91
　European protectorate, and　89–90
　foreign policy after 1945　81–4
　France, and　60, 73–4
　graphic representation of possible
　　outcomes　97
　guardian of Europe, as　84
　immobility　82
　instability　79–80

Index compiled by Robert Spicer

Developmental Management

The following titles have now been published in this exciting and innovative series:

Ronnie Lessem: *Developmental Management* 0 631 16844 3 ☐
Charles Hampden-Turner: *Charting the Corporate Mind** 0 631 17735 3 ☐
Yoneji Masuda: *Managing in the Information Society* 0 631 17575 X ☐
Ivan Alexander: *Foundations of Business* 0 631 17718 3 ☐
Henry Ford: *Ford on Management** 0 631 17061 8 ☐
Bernard Lievegoed: *Managing the Developing Organization* 0 631 17025 1 ☐
Jerry Rhodes: *Conceptual Toolmaking* 0 631 17489 3 ☐
Jagdish Parikh: *Managing Your Self* 0 631 17764 7 ☐
John Davis: *Greening Business* 0 631 17202 5 ☐
Ronnie Lessem: *Total Quality Learning* 0 631 16828 1 ☐
Pauline Graham: *Integrative Management* 0 631 17391 9 ☐
Alain Minc: *The Great European Illusion* 0 631 17695 0 ☐
Albert Koopman: *Transcultural Management* 0 631 17804 X ☐
Elliott Jaques: *Executive Leadership* 1 55786 257 5 ☐
Koji Kobayashi: *The Rise of NEC* 1 55786 277 X ☐

* Not available in the USA   All titles are £18.95 each

You can order through your local bookseller or, in case of difficulty, direct from the publisher using this order form. Please indicate the quantity of books you require in the boxes above and complete the details form below. NB. The publisher would be willing to negotiate a discount for orders of more than 20 copies of one title.

Payment

Please add £2.50 to payment to cover p&p.

☐ Please charge my Mastercard/Visa/American Express account
 card number ☐☐☐☐☐☐☐☐☐☐☐☐☐☐☐☐

Expiry date ⎽⎽⎽

Signature ⎽⎽⎽
                        (credit card orders must be signed to be valid)

☐ I enclose a cheque for £⎽⎽⎽⎽⎽⎽ made payable to **Marston Book Services Ltd**
 (PLEASE PRINT)

Name ⎽⎽⎽

Address ⎽⎽

⎽⎽⎽

⎽⎽⎽⎽⎽⎽⎽⎽⎽⎽⎽⎽⎽⎽⎽⎽⎽⎽⎽⎽⎽⎽⎽⎽⎽⎽⎽⎽⎽ Postcode ⎽⎽⎽⎽⎽⎽⎽⎽⎽⎽⎽⎽⎽

Tel No ⎽⎽⎽

Signature ⎽⎽⎽⎽⎽⎽⎽⎽⎽⎽⎽⎽⎽⎽⎽⎽⎽⎽⎽⎽⎽⎽⎽⎽⎽⎽⎽⎽ Date ⎽⎽⎽⎽⎽⎽⎽⎽⎽⎽⎽⎽⎽

Please return the completed form with remittance to:
Department DM, Basil Blackwell Ltd
108 Cowley Road, Oxford OX4 1JF, UK
or telephone your credit card order on 0865 791155.

Goods will be despatched within 14 days of receipt of order. Data supplied may be used to inform you about other Basil Blackwell publications in relevant fields.
Registered in England No. 180277 Basil Blackwell Ltd.